D1563784

THE BROTHERS OF ROMULUS

THE BROTHERS OF ROMULUS:

FRATERNAL *PIETAS* IN ROMAN LAW, LITERATURE, AND SOCIETY

Cynthia J. Bannon

PRINCETON UNIVERSITY PRESS

PRINCETON, NEW JERSEY

PUBLISHED BY PRINCETON UNIVERSITY PRESS, 41 WILLIAM STREET,
PRINCETON, NEW JERSEY 08540
IN THE UNITED KINGDOM: PRINCETON UNIVERSITY PRESS, CHICHESTER,
WEST SUSSEX

LIBRARY OF CONGRESS CATALOGING-IN-PUBLICATION DATA

BANNON, CYNTHIA JORDAN. THE BROTHERS OF ROMULUS : FRATERNAL PIETAS IN
ROMAN LAW, LITERATURE, AND SOCIETY / CYNTHIA J. BANNON.
P.   CM.
INCLUDES BIBLIOGRAPHICAL REFERENCES AND INDEX.
ISBN 0-691-01571-6 (ALK. PAPER)
1. ROME—CIVILIZATION. 2. BROTHERS—ROME—CONDUCT OF LIFE. 3.
INTERPERSONAL RELATIONS—ROME. 4. BROTHERS IN LITERATURE. 5. KINSHIP
(ROMAN LAW). 6. ROMULUS,—KING OF ROME—FAMILY.
I. TITLE.
DG231.3.B36   1997   97-7562 CIP
306.85′2′0937—DC21

THIS BOOK HAS BEEN COMPOSED IN SABON
PRINCETON UNIVERSITY PRESS BOOKS ARE PRINTED ON ACID-FREE
PAPER AND MEET THE GUIDELINES FOR PERMANENCE AND DURABILITY
OF THE COMMITTEE ON PRODUCTION GUIDELINES FOR BOOK
LONGEVITY OF THE COUNCIL ON LIBRARY RESOURCES
PRINTED IN THE UNITED STATES OF AMERICA
1 3 5 7 9 10 8 6 4 2

For my parents

omnia cum Bauio communia frater habebat,
unanimi fratres sicut habere solent,
rura domum nummos at⟨que⟩ omnia; denique, ut aiunt,
corporibus geminis spiritus unus erat.
sed postquam alterius mulier ⟨sibi⟩ concubitum ⟨ire⟩
non vult, deposuit alter amicitiam.
[et] omnia tunc ira, tunc omnia lite soluta,
⟨et⟩ nova regna duos accipiunt ⟨dominos.⟩

Bavius' brother used to own everything in common with
him—just as like-minded brothers used to do—land, home,
money, and everything; as a consequence, as they say, there
was one breath in twin bodies. But after one brother's wife
didn't want to go to bed with the other, he abandoned the
alliance; then everything dissolved in anger and lawsuits,
and new domains acquired two masters.

Domitius Marsus, *Cicuta* 1 (Courtney)

CONTENTS

ACKNOWLEDGMENTS

MY WORK ON this book has been supported by two Summer Faculty Fellowships awarded by the Research and University Graduate School at Indiana University and by a semester's release from teaching through the Department of Classical Studies. As a visiting assistant professor at Emory University, I had the opportunity to pursue comparative study of the family in Italy through a seminar at the Folger Shakespeare Library with Diane Owen Hughes; I want to thank both the Department of Classics and Emory University for enabling me to participate in this enriching seminar.

This book began as a doctoral dissertation at the University of Michigan. I have the warmest thanks for Bruce Frier for directing me toward a project that led me to Roman law and the history of the Roman family. I also benefited from the advice of the other members of my committee: Stephen Hinds, David Potter, and Raymond Van Dam. As I revised and expanded my dissertation, Richard Saller offered valuable suggestions and criticisms, which helped me to improve the book. The report of the anonymous reader for the Press allowed me to see the topic from important, new perspectives. I would also like to thank my editor, Brigitta van Rheinberg, for adopting and supporting my project.

I have learned much from friends and colleagues who read and discussed my work with me. Special thanks are due to James Halporn and Dennis Kehoe who generously read the entire manuscript; their comments and corrections have saved me from countless errors; all mistakes are my own. I am grateful also to Sander Goldberg, Thomas McGinn, and Niall Slater, who read earlier drafts of chapters and offered advice and encouragement. Lastly, I would like to express my deepest gratitude to my parents for giving me the first, best lessons about family, and to Michael, who has been like a brother to me.

THE BROTHERS OF ROMULUS

INTRODUCTION

*Romulus aeternae nondum formaverat urbis
moenia, consorti non habitanda Remo*
Romulus had not yet built the walls of the eternal city
where his brother Remus was not to live in partnership.
(Tibullus 2.5.23–24)

LIKE THE STORY of Romulus and Remus, the fraternal relationship held a privileged position in Roman culture. In founding the city, these twin brothers set a pattern both for political partnership and for rivalry, when Romulus killed Remus in a dispute over the new city walls. The Romans, who saw themselves as descendants of Romulus and Remus, considered brothers central to their public and poetic myth making, to their experience of family life, and to their ideas about intimacy among men. This book explores the many dimensions of the fraternal relationship at Rome. Through the analysis of literary and legal representations of brothers, my study attempts to re-create the contexts and contradictions that shaped Roman ideas about brothers. The Augustan poet Tibullus, in denying that Remus was to be Romulus' partner, focuses on an essential dynamic in Roman ideas about brothers—the tension between conflict and cooperation. This book charts the variations on this theme, drawing together Roman expressions of brotherly love and rivalry around an idealized notion of fraternity.

The idea of brotherhood is so pervasive in western culture that it seems almost a cliché, and yet each culture, each generation breathes new life into the experience of fraternity, whether the spiritual brotherhood of the early Christians, the "band of brothers" in Shakespeare's *Henry V*, the *fraternité* of the French Revolution, or the "hey bro'" of Black American English. Although the idea of brotherhood might seem universal—all human (and some animal) societies recognize blood kinship—expressions of kinship vary. To what extent can the relationship between brothers be understood through biological kinship and their roles in the family? Where do our ideas about brothers go beyond kinship, and how do we limit and justify this metaphorical extension of fraternity? We may derive a sense of shared humanity from cross-cultural answers to these questions—our shared humanity is itself often represented metaphorically as brotherhood—but even if our answers differ, we are drawn to the relationship between brothers because fraternity recurs in the moral, political, and emotional discourses that arise in different cultures throughout history. If universal generalizations escape us, we can begin to understand brotherhood by investigating its expression in one society at a moment in history. Even within a single culture, for example, at Rome, the fraternal relationship embraced a range of meanings and experiences from family life to the political world. Calling a Roman "brother" had various implications depending on whether he was a sibling, friend, lover, or fellow soldier; invoking fraternity in the forum stirred different responses than did an appeal to the familial *pietas* of brothers at home. Where do these different meanings of "brother" intersect in the Roman experience? And how did the Romans account for the boundaries, intersections, and contradictions in their ideas about brothers? Starting with the foundation story of Romulus and Remus, the Romans' experience of family, intimacy, politics, and history was shaped by their ideas about brothers.

Roman literature and history is full of brothers, praising them, explaining events as the result of fraternal devotion, justifying or condemning conflicts between brothers. Retellings of the Romulus and Remus story tend to focus on either the twins' rivalry or on the nearly perfect harmony between them when they lived as shepherds before they founded the city and before Romulus killed Remus. If the fraternal relationship can be thought of as a range of behaviors and attitudes, the brothers who founded Rome represent the extremes of this relationship: idealized cooperation and fratricide. For most Romans, the experience of fraternity fell somewhere between these two extremes. Yet, the ideal influenced the choices Roman brothers made and the sentiments they associated with their brothers. Ideals—how Romans thought brothers should behave—often contrast with what brothers were saying and doing. Few brothers resorted to fratricide to resolve their differences. Instead, we find in Roman accounts of brothers a rich variety of reactions, expressions, and options that reveal the flexibility of the fraternal relationship at Rome. As brothers participated in the varied social, political, and familial situations, they conformed, challenged, and redefined their ideals of fraternity.

Romans' perceptions of and reactions to brothers were shaped by their expectations of fraternal devotion or *pietas*. Fraternal *pietas*, the idealized devotion of brothers, was a subset of the traditional Roman virtue *pietas*, the blend of affection and duty that structured kinship.[1] For the Romans, the fraternal relationship was first defined in the family through brothers' roles in managing family property and caring for relatives. Roman law and inheritance practice fostered cooperation among brothers in these familial duties and offered mechanisms that resolved conflicts by balancing the brothers' interdependence and autonomy. Because family

---

[1] R. P. Saller, "*Pietas*, Obligation and Authority in the Roman Family," 393–410.

connections played an important part in Roman politics, a brother could be a valuable asset in a man's public career. Appeals to fraternal *pietas* in political rhetoric found a ready audience among the elite who shared power at Rome. Fraternal ideals were meaningful also to Romans outside the elite social world because they believed that kinship was a natural phenomenon which transcended social and civic status. Although the Romans created legal kinship through adoption, they accorded special status to what they called natural kinship and to the experience of *pietas*. Their ideas about brothers reflect the importance of blood kinship and its power to generate affection and duty. Because brothers were a model of the natural identity among kin, the fraternal relationship became a model also for other relationships among men to which Romans ascribed comparable identification and attachment. Brothers not only served as models for personal relationships, namely between friends, lovers, and soldiers, but fraternal *pietas* also came to symbolize the emotional and moral bonds that were the basis of civic society. Brothers seem to have captured the Roman imagination, perhaps because the surviving literature was written mostly by and for men in a society where political power was vested in men who believed that their city was founded by a pair of brothers.

As Rome expanded its political and cultural horizons during the Republican era, military expansion fostered economic growth and cultural diversity that generated changes in Roman society. Roman writers explored these changes and articulated new perspectives on their political and social relationships through fraternal metaphors. Because the traditional force of fraternal *pietas* within the family remained strong, Roman ideas about brothers formed a stable core of meaning around which new ideas could be oriented and through which new experience could be understood and reconciled with the past. Both poetry and history use fraternal symbolism in figuring the past and responding to social change. The triumviral period, ca. 60–31 B.C.E., during which Cicero, Sallust, Vergil, Horace, and Livy all wrote, produced some of the richest reflections of this social change and the most tender expressions of fraternal sentiments. In the literature of this era, the foundation story of Romulus and Remus became inextricably bound up with Romans' conflicting reactions to civil war. Augustus' establishment of empire brought peace and an end to civil war, and with it new perspectives on fraternal symbolism. Because Romulus and Remus had become emblematic of civic strife, Romans sought new models for their idealization of brothers. The divine twins Castor and Pollux, who shared one lifetime of immortality by living on alternate days, satisfied both traditional expectations of fraternal *pietas* and the new political contexts created by dynastic politics surrounding the emperor and his family.

Despite the pervasiveness of brothers and fraternal symbolism in Roman literature and history, there has been no thorough investigation of the topic. Scholarly interpretations of the Romulus and Remus story are rich and plentiful.[2] Historical analyses of Roman politics have long recognized the importance of kinship in political life at Rome.[3] Recent research in social history has looked inside the Roman family, exploring the workings of kinship in the family at large and in relationships between individual family members.[4] My study of brothers has grown up amidst these scholarly conversations and will, I hope, contribute to them. There is a long tradition of investigating the Roman family through Roman law. Building on this tradition, modern scholars have grafted ideas from such fields as the sociology of law, demography, and economics onto the standard philological methods that have long been the tools for our study of the ancient world. I draw on both old and new methods to re-create the social, political, and familial contexts in which Roman brothers acted, thought, and spoke, using this understanding of the fraternal experience to show how it enriches our appreciation of literary and ideological depictions of brothers.

This study develops through an examination of Roman literary and legal texts that describe, evaluate, and analyze brothers. Legal and literary sources provide complementary evidence for both sentiment and behavior, both ideals and practice in the fraternal relationship. The writings of the Roman jurists compiled in the *Digest of Justinian*, which include legal definitions, hypothetical cases, and controversies about legal interpretation, help us to reconstruct brothers' roles in the family. Cases from the *Digest* offer insight into the economic motives and the inheritance strategies which shaped and were shaped by fraternal *pietas*. These legal sources yield a rich sample of the problems and the range of acceptable solutions that Roman brothers might have devised as they lived and worked together.[5] Roman literature allows us to refine and expand our understanding of the fraternal relationship. This study analyzes anecdotes about brothers in Latin literature written during the classical period, ca. 200 B.C.E.—120 C.E., from various genres: history, biography, rhetoric, epic and lyric poetry, as well as personal letters. Both literary and legal sources present intriguing and sometimes contradictory images

[2] Represented most recently by T. P. Wiseman, *Remus: A Roman Myth*.

[3] At least as early as M. Gelzer, *Die Nobilität der römischen Republik*.

[4] To name only a few notable studies, K. Bradley, *Discovering the Roman Family*; S. Dixon, *The Roman Mother*; J. Hallett, *Fathers and Daughters in Roman Society: Women and the Elite Family*; B. Rawson, ed., *The Family in Ancient Rome: New Perspectives*; R. Saller, *Patriarchy, Property and Death in the Roman Family*; S. Treggiari, *Roman Marriage: Iusti Coniuges from the Time of Cicero to the Time of Ulpian*.

[5] On the nature of hypothetical cases and their relation to social life, B. W. Frier, *The Rise of the Roman Jurists: Studies in Cicero's "pro Caecina,"* 163–71.

of brothers and what Romans thought about them. Brothers may not have always followed legal prescriptions; literary vignettes respond not only to social and historical circumstances but also to literary traditions. Because the sources are diverse and because fraternity had many meanings, I have adopted an interpretive approach that does not so much seek to reconcile differences as to understand the varied and sometimes contradictory expressions of fraternal *pietas*. Roman ideas about brotherhood come to life when we appreciate how patterns and apparent contradictions come together to create the complex, changeable experience of being a brother at Rome.

My approach to the literary and legal sources for Roman brothers combines literary criticism with historical narrative and legal analysis, a collection of interpretive methods that generates fuller readings and reconstructions of the past than each alone can do. I begin with the legal institution of *consortium*, an archaic form of partnership in which brothers jointly own the family property. Over time, Romans generalized the concept of *consortium* to represent an idealized form of fraternal *pietas* through which brothers resolve conflict through cooperation. Analyzing legal rules and the roles of brothers offers insight into the relationship between historical reality—the way brothers really lived—and the laws and norms that shaped their experience. The collection of attitudes, behaviors, and sentiments associated with fraternal *pietas* constitutes what we might call, to borrow a term from Bourdieu, the practice of being a Roman brother. *Consortium* and fraternal *pietas* offer a guide to this practice which explains "what it is right to do or say," but does not and cannot catalogue all possible acts and expressions.[6] Fraternal *pietas* can be understood as a social norm that operates in a least two ways: as an enforceable standard of conduct, what we call "normal behavior," and as a desideratum, an ideal, how one should behave.[7] The representations of brothers in Roman literature and law reflect the duality of reality and ideal.

Fraternal *pietas* embodied the ideal and set limits on what the Romans considered brotherly. Roman reactions to and expectations of brotherly behavior were oriented around the norms inherent in *pietas* and *consortium*. It is the interaction between these ideals and the practice of being a brother that my study explores. Instead of simply describing the norm of fraternal relations, I consider how descriptions and evaluations of brothers' behavior respond to these ideals, challenging, reshaping, and

---

[6] P. Bourdieu, *Outline of a Theory of Practice*, trans. R. Nice, 10–11.

[7] In general, on the flexible interaction of norms and laws, see R. B. Edgerton, *Rules, Exceptions, and Social Order*. For an interesting case study concerning ranchers, suburbanites, and straying cattle in northern California, see R. C. Ellickson, *Order without Law: How Neighbors Settle Disputes*.

reinforcing them.[8] I do not attempt to reconcile all accounts of brotherly behavior under the rubric of *consortium* so much as to explicate disruptions, intensity, and intersections between brotherly behavior and other social relationships.[9] When did Romans perceive intimacy among men to be fraternal rather than filial or erotic? Were there clear distinctions between erotic and fraternal love? Why was fraternal *pietas* such a powerful symbol at Rome?

My study is organized around the places, real and metaphorical, where brothers met and through their interaction established the limits and powers of fraternal *pietas*. The first chapter, "At Home" explores the roles brothers played in managing family property and caring for close relatives. Decisions about family finances tell us how economic circumstances affected the relationship between Roman brothers, and they tell us even more than that, because economic motives are usually balanced against other considerations. For example, in bequeathing property, a Roman might be moved as much by affection as by the desire to assure financial security for his brother or his sons after his own death. Hypothetical cases from the *Digest of Justinian* illustrating the legal rules on inheritance and guardianship offer us insight into some of the strategies that Romans adopted in balancing the diverse needs of family life. Because brothers appear quite often in the legal sources dealing with inheritance, it is fair to say that the fraternal relationship had significant influence on the structure and quality of family life in ancient Rome. The way brothers shared or divided their paternal inheritance, for example, could either secure or threaten their financial security and the future of their children. Because of the demographic shape of Roman society (low population growth and high mortality), partible inheritance, that is, sharing the family property among all children, provided brothers with profitable and flexible solutions that allowed them both to sustain their sense of family community and to benefit from the economic opportunities that Roman expansion offered. While informal cooperation was prized as an expression of fraternal *pietas*, Roman brothers also used formal legal

[8] Compare S. Humphreys' approach to family quarrels in classical Athens: ". . . to recapture the actors' perceptions of the situation and possible strategies open to each of the parties involved as they developed and changed" ("Family Quarrels," *JHS* 109 [1989] 185). Compare also the practices of Florentine families during the Renaissance, see T. Kuehn, *Law, Family & Women*, 131–33.

[9] In drawing distinctions between the fraternal and other male relationships, I have found E. K. Sedgwick's notion of homosociality helpful; the notion is developed in *Between Men: English Literature and Male Homosocial Desire*. Simply put, homosociality is the phenomenon of relationships among people of the same biological sex, a continuum of relationships—erotic, social, familial, political, economic—that are distinct but may also overlap.

arrangements, such as partnership, guardianship, and contracts, to buttress natural devotion and to negotiate conflict.

Fraternal *pietas* influenced brothers' daily and long-term decisions about the family, yet the source of their devotion lies deep in their sense of common kinship. The second chapter explores fraternal intimacy, what goes on "Between Brothers" and why their cooperation was exceptional. Romans believed that kinship was inherently natural, or what we would call biological, something that all humans, even slaves, shared in the same way. Adoption could create legal kinship between fathers and sons, and fathers could release their sons from *patria potestas* and thus end their legal relationship, but the relationship between brothers could not be either replicated or removed. Friends could be like brothers, but no one was as close as a brother, because brothers were thought almost to share a single life by virtue of their shared parentage. Because brothers share the same parents, Romans expected them to be naturally similar and united in affection. In addition, because Romans privileged natural kinship, the relationship between brothers came to be seen as a model for other kinds of relationships especially among men of the same age or generation, not only soldiers but cousins, friends, and lovers. The normative role of fraternal *pietas* in resolving conflict and fostering cooperation provided a model for intimacy in male relationships to which Romans accorded a comparable devotion. When Cicero wanted to express his affection for Atticus, he wrote "*et nos ames et tibi persuadeas te a me fraterne amari*," "love me and believe that I love you as a brother."[10] In a society like Rome's where sexual intimacy between men could be politically charged and was condemned by traditional social morality, fraternal devotion offered a safe, even honored, expression for men's emotional attachments.

The influence of fraternal *pietas* extended from brothers' private life out into the forum, the site of my third chapter, which examines the expression of fraternal *pietas* in politics. Brothers cooperated in pursuing their public careers, much as they worked together within the family. Cicero's relationship with his brother Quintus is the best documented example of how brothers worked together in public life, and a case study of these brothers is included in this chapter. Cicero's letters offer us a unique opportunity to get inside the relationship between Roman brothers, to examine how they adapted social expectations of fraternal *pietas* to their own individual desires and necessities. The case study of the Ciceros also adds a more nuanced view of brothers' home life. Because Romans recognized continuity between public and private life, the

[10] Cic. *Att.* 1.5.8.

way a man treated his brother could make or break his reputation. Elite brothers exploited Roman assumptions about fraternal *pietas* as they competed for political prestige. Appeals to fraternal *pietas* could galvanize public opinion around a man or his policies: Gaius Gracchus exploited the Romans' deeply held sentiments about brothers when he portrayed himself as his brother's successor, garnering support for his political agenda by stirring up sympathy for his brother's death. But Romans were also aware that fraternal *pietas* could be mere pretense, invoked as a cover for ambition or actions dangerous to the state. Cicero's speeches as well as historical accounts of brothers in politics illustrate both sides of this dynamic. The fraternal relationship had practical implications for a public career at Rome as well as ideological value in representing political morality. The Scipiones—Africanus and Asiagenus, and their father and uncle—were idealized, especially in Livy's history, for balancing their devotion to each other against their duty to Rome. Even so, the notorious trials of the Scipiones provided a venue for debate about the extent and nature of fraternal cooperation in politics. Although such debates concerned primarily elite brothers, the issue of fraternal *pietas* appealed to a broader audience, because the idea of brotherhood was extended metaphorically to represent the sense of community among Roman citizens and soldiers.

Both the military expansion of the Republican era and Roman martial traditions created important contexts which shaped the expression of fraternal *pietas*. Chapter 4, "On the Battlefield," traces the political symbolism of fraternal *pietas* in battle narratives and in historical accounts of the civil wars of the late Republic. Roman soldiers who lived and fought together thought of themselves as brothers, suggesting an implicit analogy between brothers' roles in the family and the soldier's role in protecting Rome and his fellow citizens. Elite brothers played up their military service to Rome in crafting a public image, as for example the Scipios discussed in Chapter 3. The image of brothers fighting together for Rome appealed to Romans: Livy and Vergil emphasize this fraternal solidarity among soldiers, especially when their narratives featured real brothers. As this image of the brother-soldier melds with the traditional Roman ideal of the citizen-soldier, fraternal *pietas* is metaphorically extended to the relationship between citizens. The relationship between brothers thus acquires a broad political symbolism representing traditional social and political morality, what the Romans called the *mos maiorum*. Changes or perceived threats to this tradition were associated with neglect or even abuse of fraternal *pietas*, as for example in Sallust's condemnation of Jugurtha's ambitions and of Rome's involvement with him. Fratricide becomes the ultimate metaphor for the public and personal conflicts generated by civil strife. Accounts of the battle of Pharsalus, the decisive battle in the war between Caesar and Pompey, give special attention to fraternal symbolism in their analysis of strategy and in dramatizing the costs of civil war. In the literature of the late Republic, anxieties about civil war gather in retellings of the Romulus and Remus story, as fraternal symbolism is focused on the fratricide in the foundation myth. Literary responses to civil war develop fraternal symbolism to express both the moral chaos and the emotional experience of citizens fighting against each other instead of with each other.

As Augustus' establishment of the principate ended nearly a century of civil wars, imperial government created new challenges for fraternal *pietas*. While the economic and social circumstances of Roman brothers remained fairly constant from the late Republic through the early Imperial era, the establishment of empire changed the political contexts and significance of fraternal *pietas*. Dynastic politics focused attention on the brothers in the imperial household as they vied for power and priority in inheriting not just the family farm but imperial power, and the success of appeals to fraternal *pietas* now depended on the emperor's response. Fraternal *pietas* remained a popular theme in public image-making: Tiberius' rededication of the temple of Castor and Pollux in his own and his brother's name is a salient example. Tacitus and Suetonius chronicle the dynastic intrigues among brothers and rivals for imperial power, their strategies, and the public fascination with this high-stakes sibling rivalry. Statius' *Thebaid* explores these fraternal conflicts through the story of Polynices and Eteocles, Oedipus' ill-starred sons, who fought to the death for the kingdom of Thebes. The Greek myth distanced the theme of fratricide from Rome, past and present, in contrast to the story of Romulus and Remus, which continued to be an all-too-ready paradigm. While the foundation story of the twin brothers developed in the mid to early Republic in response to Rome's emerging political identity, in the charged context of the civil wars of the late Republic, Romulus and Remus became problematic figures: Romulus was the eponymous founder of the city, yet, because he killed his brother, the name Remus evoked the dilemmas of civil war and the troubling costs of power. Myths about brothers, especially Romulus and Remus, represented social and political issues with extraordinary sharpness for the Romans because the fraternal relationship was central to their experience of public and private life. In the chapters that follow, this study explores the familial, legal, and political contexts of which shaped Roman responses to Romulus and Remus and the larger beliefs and practices that made up the everyday reality of being a brother at Rome.

ONE

AT HOME

Quid enim timebam? ne, si rescisset pater, moleste ferret
filium suum hominem avarum non esse, fratrem pium esse?
What was I afraid of? That, if my father found out about
my promise, he would be annoyed that his son was not a
greedy man but a devoted brother?
(Sen. *Con.* 6.1)

WHEN A FATHER disinherits one of his sons, the other cuts a
deal with his brother to share his inheritance fifty-fifty, so
long as the disinherited brother does not protest because he is
disinherited.[1] Their father is outraged, not only because his son has
flouted paternal authority by circumventing his will but even more because he abuses his brother with this financial deal. The brother replies
indignantly that it wasn't greed but brotherly devotion that motivated
him. Both father and son assume that brothers ought to share their inheritance, but they differ about the appropriate manner and occasion for
this sharing. For both father and son, inheritance accomplishes more
than just the transmission of property from one generation to the next.
Inheritance draws the generations of a family together as it bridges their
inevitable separation. The choices a father makes in dividing property
among his children may take into account a variety of factors, including
but not limited to sentiment and economic considerations. How can he
secure financial security for himself in old age and for his children after
his death? How can property arrangements express and mediate his love
for his children and their devotion to him and to each other? The way
brothers react to their father's will is equally telling. Do they accept his
decisions or challenge them selfishly or in the name of a greater good?
Inheritance creates conversations about a family's emotional and economic well being. In Roman terms, this dialogue was about property as
well as *pietas*, the affectionate devotion among family members. In the
father-son relationship, *pietas* played a counterpoint to paternal authority by inspiring in fathers a protective spirit, obedience in sons, and in

---

[1] For a similar scenario in a legal case, see Scaev. [*Quaest. Pub.*] D. 32.103.1. Plutarch,
Mor. 482 D also observes that most writers begin a work on brothers with the division of
their father's goods. (Here and throughout, all translations are my own unless otherwise
noted.)

both a sense of duty and affection.[2] Although there was no legal equivalent to *patria potestas* in the fraternal relationship, *pietas* was a powerful influence on brothers' behavior and attitudes, and both fathers and sons could also be brothers. Ideally, fraternal *pietas* would cohere with paternal and filial *pietas* strengthening the bonds among fathers, sons, and brothers. Tension between fraternal and filial *pietas* did, however, crop up around the issue of inheritance and the terms of a father's will.

Consortium, which arose within the traditional, male-oriented system of inheritance, shaped the ways that fathers, sons, and brothers negotiated about *pietas* and property both before and after their father's death. The archaic practice of *consortium* directed the family heirs to inherit and own the family property jointly as an undivided partnership through the process of intestate succession. Although sisters inherited an equal share with brothers, *consortium* was associated specifically with brothers' role in handing down family property. Later inheritance law changed the contexts in which fraternal *pietas* was expressed. Roman inheritance practice involved a system of partibility in which property was divided equally among the children or closest heirs. In addition, leaving a last will and testament became common, at least among elites. These new legal mechanisms, far from replacing old-fashioned tradition, provided new contexts in which the norms vested in *consortium* and intestate succession continued to operate and to privilege brothers.[3] Romans who did not write wills may have continued to live in accordance with the traditional patterns inscribed in *consortium*. Since wills were most common among the propertied classes (who arguably had the most to worry about because they left the most behind),[4] the literary and legal sources documenting the negotiations around wills tell us most about Roman elite brothers. It may be possible, however, to extend our observations to families from the lower classes by drawing on comparative evidence from other societies.

This chapter attempts to re-create the workings of the fraternal relationship within the *domus* in the contexts of family and familial property. My discussion moves between examples from the *Digest of Justinian* and the social perspectives represented in Latin literature. The controversies surrounding inheritance and disinherison elicited from Romans explana-

---

2 Saller, "*Pietas*."

3 E. Champlin, *Final Judgments: Duty and Emotion in Roman Wills, 200 B.C.–A.D. 250*, 126. Wills could and did fail, leaving the brothers to inherit through intestate succession: when a testator named an heir and also a substitute for the heir, for example, the rules of intestate succession came into play if the substitution failed (Tryph. [21 *Disp.*] D. 34.5.9.*pr.*).

4 Champlin, *Final Judgments*, 42–46, 55. Others may have have left informal wills: the simple expression of one's wishes could suffice, (Paul. [14 *Resp.*] D. 28.1.29.1).

tions, justifications, and protestations about how and why they treated their brothers as they did. Literary and legal texts describing brothers' behavior and choices show us what was possible, acceptable, and scandalous: our sources offer a reality of the possible, what could have happened, what sometimes did happen, and what Romans were likely to think about it. Roman law prescribed partible inheritance; that is, each child received an equal share of the familial property. At first glance such equality might seem to eliminate controversy, but, as in other societies that practiced partible inheritance, at Rome fulfilling legal prescriptions for equality was seldom simple or straightforward. "Equal" didn't always mean "same," and equality could be measured in terms other than economic. Defining these terms in any individual situation engaged Roman brothers in cooperation and conflict. Central to my investigation is the archaic institution of *consortium*, which offered a paradigm for fraternal *pietas* and its expression in brothers' roles in the family. The first section of this chapter analyzes Roman ideas about *consortium* and how these ideas came to represent fraternal *pietas*. The second and third sections explore the interaction between Roman ideas about brothers, fraternal ideology, and family life, first in the process of inheritance and then as brothers negotiated their continuing relationships within the family.

Consortium and Fraternal *Pietas*

Consortium was an institution of archaic Roman law. The jurists treated it as a kind of partnership and as part of the process of inheritance. Roman notions about *consortium* center on brothers' roles in inheritance and the family and can be associated with fraternal *pietas*. Ideas about brothers and *consortium* engage with the laws on inheritance and with economic and personal aims to circumscribe the practice of family life and of being a brother at Rome. Such ideas do not present us with a photographic image of the Roman family, but rather they represent possibilities, choices, and values—a fraternal ideology—that Roman brothers invoked in what they said and in what they did.

Consortium was originally part of the process of intestate succession, one of the ways that family property was handed down to the next generation when the father died leaving no last will and testament. When the *pater familias* died intestate, all those in his *potestas* automatically became his heirs, jointly owning the family property in a kind of partnership that was called *consortium*. The fullest surviving description of *consortium* occurs in a legal textbook, Gaius' *Institutiones*, in his discussion of partnership:

(154a) *Est autem aliud genus societatis proprium civium Romanorum. olim enim mortuo patre familias inter suos heredes quaedam erat legitima simul et naturalis societas, quae appellabatur ercto non cito, id est dominio non diviso: erctum enim dominium est, unde erus dominus dicitur: ciere autem dividere est unde caedere et secare dicimus.*

(154b) *Alii quoque qui volebant eandem habere societatem poterant id consequi apud praetorem certa legis actione. in hac autem societate fratrum ceterorumve qui ad exemplum fratrum suorum societatem coierint, illud proprium erat, quod vel unus ex sociis communem servum manumittendo liberum faciebat, et omnibus libertum adquirebat; item unus rem communem mancipando eius faciebat qui mancipio accipiebat . . .*

There is, however, another kind of partnership available specifically to Roman citizens. For, long ago, at the death of a *pater familias*, there was among the *sui heredes*, a certain kind of partnership, at once legal and natural, which was called *ercto non cito*, that is, with the family estate not divided: for *erctum* means patrimony, whence a property-owner is called *erus*: while *ciere* is to divide, whence we derive *caedere* and *secare*.

Other people, also, who wanted to form the same kind of partnership could do so through the *praetor* in accordance with a specified legal procedure. But, in this partnership of brothers or of others who came together in a partnership on the model of *sui fratres*, the characteristic feature was that if just one of the partners made a jointly owned slave free by manumitting him, he made him a freedman for them all; likewise, one partner who acquired something by *mancipatio* made it common property through his act of *mancipatio*. Gaius *Inst.* 3.154a, b.[5]

According to Gaius, there were two kinds of *consortium*, the original *consortium* created among family members through inheritance and an analogous *consortium* that later developed as a form of partnership. The characteristic feature of both forms of *consortium* was joint ownership: property was not divided into shares but all the *consortes* equally owned the whole or, to put it another way, each *consors* owned the whole property and was empowered to dispose of any or all of it.[6] Instead of providing equal shares for all the heirs, as in later Roman inheritance law and practice, *consortium* granted a kind of totalizing equality in that each heir owned the whole estate.

Gaius' description of *consortium* adds to our understanding of archaic inheritance practices because his information complements the law of

---

[5] V. Arrangio-Ruiz and A. Guarino, *Breviarum iuris Romani*, 135–36 (first published in V. Arrangio-Ruiz, "Frammenti di Gaio," *PSI* 1182 [1935]: 7–10).

[6] M. Kaser, "Neue Literatur zur 'Societas,'" *SDHI* 41 (1975): 282–83; and *Das römische Privatrecht*, 1:99–101; C. W. Westrup, *Introduction to Early Roman Law*, 3:272–73.

inheritance described in the *Twelve Tables*. The archaic practice of *consortium* was consistent with the process of intestate succession set out in the *Twelve Tables*.[7] When a *pater familias* died intestate (without leaving a will), his immediate family, the *sui heredes*, had the first priority in inheritance. The *sui heredes* were the closest relatives of a *pater familias*, his children, his wife (if she was married *cum manu*), and anyone else in his *potestas*.[8] Similarly, Gaius tells us that the *sui heredes* formed a *consortium* when they inherited the property of their *pater familias* undivided—*domino non diviso* or *ercto non cito*.[9] The creation of *consortium* and the process of intestate succession both privilege the immediate family, whether the estate was divided or not. Although the *Twelve Tables* do not specifically mention *consortium*, they do provide the *actio familiae erciscundae*, a legal procedure for splitting up jointly held familial property.[10] The existence of such a procedure tends to confirm the existence of *consortium* or some other form of joint ownership in the archaic family.[11] In addition, the association of *consortium* with brothers in Gaius accords with the emphasis on male kinship in intestate succession: the agnates (those related through men) were next in line to inherit after the *sui heredes*; and thus brothers might figure prominently in both intestate succession and *consortium*. The archaic *consortium* may in fact have arisen as part of the process of intestate succession: the description

[7] *Twelve Tables* 5.4–5.

[8] On archaic law of inheritance, P. Voci, "Diritto ereditario romano I," *ANRW* 2, no. 14 (1982): 394–401 and 554–55 on *consortium* in particular. On *consortium* as an early mechanism of transferring inheritance, see J. Gaudemet, *Étude sur le regime juridique de l'indivision en droit romain*, 65; and G. Diòsdi, *Ownership in Ancient and Preclassical Roman Law*, 44–46.

[9] The *societas* among *sui heredes* can been identified as *consortium* on the basis of the phrase *ercto non cito*. Although this phrase is not preserved in the text but is a conjecture, the immediate context of the phrase, specifically the partially preserved definition of the terms *erctum* and *citum*, makes the restoration secure. The other occurrences of the phrase *ercto non cito* in classical and late antique literature, confirm the identification of *societas ercto non cito* with a partnership of heirs who own their property jointly. See Donatus in Serv. *A.* 8.642; Festus p. 72L; Nonius 405–406L. Further references in the *TLL* s.v. *cieo* col. 1054 and *erciscere* cols. 744–45, cf. A. Ernout and A. Meillet, *Dictionnaire étymologique de la langue latine*, 200.

[10] *Twelve Tables* 5.10.

[11] See R. Saller, "Roman Heirship Strategies: In Principle and in Practice," in *The Family in Italy from Antiquity to the Present*, ed. D. I. Kertzer and R. P. Saller, 31; and A. Watson, *Rome of the XII Tables*, 52ff., 59–60, 68. Similarly, the abundance of lawsuits contesting the division of familial property in classical Athens attests to the practice of joint inheritance: fraternal joint management is at issue in several speeches: Demosthenes 44 *Leoch.* 10, 18; 47 *Euerg.* 34; Aischines 1 *Timarch.* 102; cf. W. K. Lacey, *The Family in Classical Greece*, 125–31, 292; and A. B. Cooper, "The Family Farm in Greece," *CJ* 73 (1977–78): 163–64. On the equal division among heirs, see A.R.W. Harrison, *The Law of Athens*, 1:131–132, 151, 239.

of *consortium* as a *societas legitima*—legitima is used regularly of heirs in intestacy—links this fraternal partnership with the practice of intestate succession. Thus, circumstantial evidence suggests that *consortium* was part of the practice of intestate succession in early Rome.

Gaius treats the legal institution of *consortium* as an outgrowth of "natural" familial relationships, as if the Roman family once long ago had taken the form of a *consortium*—and subsequently law formalized the partnership. In other words, the jurist sees in the legal concept the pattern of actual family life in archaic Rome. Some modern studies of the Roman family in a similar way identify the archaic Roman family with *consortium*, as if Roman ideas about *consortium* could be directly mapped onto an historical family form: the archaic Roman houschold was identified with *consortium* and defined as an extended fraternal family, that is, more than one nuclear family and more than two generations living together in the same household and jointly owning the family property.[12] Alternatively, *consortium* was incorporated into an evolution of family forms as a transitional stage between the archaic extended family and the nuclear family in the later Republican and Imperial eras.[13] Such joint fraternal households are associated in these studies with the primarily agricultural economy of early Rome in which cooperative economic and living arrangements could best insure survival and the distribution of scarce resources.[14] In studies of the family in other societies,

[12] Westrup, *Introduction*, 1:24–27; Kaser, *Privatrecht*, 1:51; R. Sieder and M. Mitterauer, *The European Family: Patriarchy to Partnership from the Middle Ages to the Present*, 24–26; A. Michel, "Fonction et structure de la famille. La famille agnatique ou *consortium*," *Cahiers internationale de sociologie* 29 (1960): 113–35; P.G.F. Le Play, *L'organisation de la famille selon le vrai modèle signalé par l'histoire de toutes les races et de tous les temps*, with D. Herlihy, *Medieval Households*, 136–37. On type of households in general, see. J. R. Goody, "The Evolution of the Family," in *Household and Family in Past Time*, ed. P. Laslett, 104, and R. Wheaton, "Family and Kinship in Western Europe: The Problem of the Joint Family Household," *Journal of Interdisciplinary History* 5 (1975): 621.

[13] This model is assumed in Westrup, *Introduction*; Le Play, *L'organisation*; P. Lacombe, *La famille dans la société romaine: étude de moralité comparée*. See also Gaudemet, *Étude*, 61; C. C. Zimmerman, *Family and Civilization*, 128–32; R. Paribeni, *La famiglia Romana*, 11–20.

[14] Westrup, *Introduction*, 2:14, 24, 38, 41–42, 136 and 3:290; Kaser, *Privatrecht*, 1:51 and "Neue Literatur," 283–84; Michel, "Fonction et structure," 114–116; Bretone, "'*Consortium*' e '*communio*,'" *Labeo* 6 (1960): 200–201. This argument is not inconsistent with anthropological explanations of the advantages of corporate communities. See, for example, E. R. Wolf, "Kinship, Friendship and Patron Client Relations in Complex Societies," in *The Social Anthropology of Complex Societies*, ed. M. Banton , 4–5, and E. B. Leacock, Introduction to *The Origin of the Family, Private Property and the State*, by F. Engels Compare also inheritance practices in Classical Athens: the continuity of family property was motivated, at least in part, by economic concerns—financial security for the family and for agricultural production—similar to those which may have conditioned the

fraternal joint families have been associated with low population growth and with the practice of impartible inheritance, handing down the family property undivided, as in *consortium*.[15] When a family had several children, selecting only one child as heir to the undivided estate prevented the property from being divided into shares that were too small to support each child. This strategy protected the family property and at the same time imposed conditions on relations between the children: either they would have to cooperate with the heir or find some other way to make a living. Such situations may have arisen in Rome when there was more than one child to inherit, as suggested by some of the cases from the *Digest of Justinian* discussed in the next two sections of this chapter. In general, however, at Rome, because the population was growing only slowly or not at all,[16] joint inheritance would not often threaten the economic survival of the family, because each generation would merely replace its predecessor.[17] In those families where more than one brother survived to inherit the family property, *consortium* offered an alternative to selecting a single heir.

The traditional interpretation of *consortium* as an archaic family form does not adequately respond to either methodological or historical issues. First, this interpretation ignores the nature of our sources and their historical contexts. Mapping *consortium* onto a specific form of the Roman family forces an equation between ideology and practice: Roman ideas about *consortium* become the reality of family life. But the relationship between our sources for *consortium* and its role in shaping family life is more complex. Because our sources are removed in time from the archaic family, *consortium* is visible through filters of historical writing, nostalgia, and the experiences of Romans living in later eras. In some ways, archaic Rome was as inaccessible to Romans in the late Republic as it is to us.[18] Therefore, while it is possible that the archaic family took the shape of *consortium*, the extent and nature of the practice cannot be

institution of *consortium* in archaic Roman society. See D. Asheri, "Laws of Inheritance, Distribution of Land and Political Constitutions in Ancient Greece," *Historia* 12 (1963): 20; A. B. Cooper, "The Family Farm in Greece," 163–65. For a comparison of the Roman *familia* to the Greek οἶκος, see W. K. Lacey, *The Family in Classical Greece*, 15, 237 at note 3.

[15] L. K. Berkner, F. F. Mendels, "Inheritance Systems, Family Structure, and Demographic Patterns in Western Europe, 1700–1900," in *Historical Studies of Changing Fertility*, ed. C. Tilly, 209–213.

[16] Recent demographic work on Republican and Imperial Rome is based on a stationary population, and it seems likely that similar assumptions would work for the archaic era. See Saller, *Patriarchy*, 41–42; T. G. Parkin, *Demography and Roman Society*, 66, 92.

[17] Compare, for example, early twentieth century China, as analyzed by W. Lavely and R. Bin Wong, "Family Division and Mobility in North China," *Comparative Studies in Society and History* 34 (1992): 453.

[18] Consider for example Livy's consternation about records for the early years of the Republic, 2.21.4.

assessed. When we turn to the late Republican and early Imperial eras, however, the influence of *consortium* on brothers and the family can be discerned in contemporary literary and legal sources, where it appears as part of the *mos maiorum*, an old-fashioned but still relevant guide to the present. Shifting our focus to the late Republic and early Empire in turn introduces new historical contexts that affect our understanding of *consortium*. Changes in inheritance law and in economic conditions during the Republic created new situations in which *consortium* in its original form did not offer appropriate or practical solutions to questions about family property and brothers' rights and duties. Economically, *consortium* might be a disadvantageous practice in a market economy. If all their property were tied up in an indivisible familial estate, Romans would not have been able to profit so successfully, as we know they did,[19] from the diverse and growing economy built through military expansion. Legal developments also left *consortium* behind. The prominence of brothers in *consortium* is consistent with the inheritance practices suggested by the laws of the *Twelve Tables*, practices that privilege agnates (or those related through men). Since intestate succession persisted alongside wills, families may have continued to form *consortia* in its original form or in a less formal way when they inherited without a will. But, as the practice of leaving a last will and testament became more common in the late Republic and early Empire, *consortium* may not have been used as a legal institution; by the mid-second century C.E. it could be considered archaic. Yet, despite changes in practice, ideas about *consortium* persisted. What relevance, then, did these ideas have for Roman elites in the early Empire and late Republic?

Romans retained a memory of *consortium* and vested new ideas in what they considered an old-fashioned family institution. *Consortium* retained symbolic value representing fraternal *pietas* in Roman literature and law. Varro's etymologies of *sors* and *consors* suggest the continuity in Roman ideas about *consortium* and its connection with inheritance. The radical notion of *consors* is to be found in *sors*:

> *Hinc etiam, a quo ipsi consortes, sors; hinc etiam sortes, quod in his iuncta tempora cum hominibus ac rebus.*
> From this also comes destiny [*sors*], from which they themselves are called *consortes*; and also from this lots [*sortes*], because in lots times are joined with men and events. Varro, *LL* 6.65

---

[19] See H. W. Pleket, "Agriculture in Comparative Perspective," in *De Agricultura. In Memoriam Pieter Willem De Neeve (1945–1990)*, 317–42, and in general, J. H. D'Arms, *Commerce and Social Standing in Ancient Rome*; I. Shatzman, *Senatorial Wealth and Roman Politics*; R. A. Nisbet, "Kinship and Political Power in First Century Rome," in *Sociology and History: Theory and Research*, ed. W. J. Chanman and A. Boskoff, 258–61.

Consortes are those who have a common *sors*, that is portion or lot in life: "fate is what is yours by chance," *sors quod suum fit sorte*.[20] Another ancient etymology ties *sors* and *consors* directly to inheritance: *sors et patrimonium significat, unde consortes dicimus*, 'lot' also means inheritance; from which we call them partners in inheritance."[21] This lot in life was understood both literally and metaphorically in the usage of *consors* and *consortium*. From a legal perspective, *consortium* could be a literal sharing of one's lot in life, which amounts to an individual's inheritance, his interest in the family collective. Metaphorically, *consortium* represents sharing of interest among brothers.

A similar community of interest motivates partnership or *societas* in Roman law. Gaius identifies *consortium* with two kinds of partnership (both known as *consortium*, one for brothers, one for others), and legal scholars have associated it with yet a third, the *societas omnium bonorum*. The association of *consortium* and *societas* raises many questions about the nature of partnership and about how the different forms of partnership were related to *consortium*. Answers tend to follow two schools of thought. W. Kunkel posits an evolutionary relationship among the various forms of *societas*. *Consortium* among *sui heredes* was the oldest form of *societas* and it first served as a model for artificial *consortium* among the extended family. The artificial *consortium* in turn was the model for *societas omnium bonorum* among non-kin, which finally evolved into consensual *societas*.[22] Alternatively, M. Kaser and A. Guarino do not distinguish *consortium* among *sui heredes* from *consortium* among the extended family, but rather see them as forms of succession, rather than consensual partnership.[23] Kaser's interpretation, his distinction between *consortium* as a form of succession and consensual *societas*, coheres with the later extralegal significance of *consortium* as a norm of fraternal *pietas*.

These three forms of partnership offer differing degrees of autonomy in managing the partners' property: the original *consortium* is the most restrictive; the later consensual partnerships and *societas omnium*

---

[20] Varro, *LL* 5.183; Isid. *Orig.* 10.51.

[21] Festus p. 380–381L.

[22] W. Kunkel, "Ein unbeachtetes Zeugnis über das römische *consortium*," *Annales. Faculté de Droit d'Istanbul* 4 (1954): 56–78.

[23] Kaser, "Neue Literatur," 288–300, and A. Guarino, "*Societas consensu contracta*," *Atti dell'accademia di scienze morali e politiche di Napoli* 3 (1972): 261–359, cf. M. Talamanca, *Istituzioni di diritto Romano*, 407–409; and S. Tondo, "Ancora sul consortio domestico nella Roma antica," *SDHI* 60 (1994): 601–12. For this distinction between *consortium* and other partnerships, see [Quint.] *Decl.* 320.4. A similar modeling of legal partnership on the fraternal joint family has been observed in later European periods when, because of changes in population, more distant relatives took the place of brothers and close kin in forming a family unit, see R. Wheaton, "Family and Kinship," 621.

bonorum are more flexible. Different forms of partnership allowing more flexibility developed in response to changes in the Roman economy that demanded legal autonomy.[24] As the legal terms of partnership were adapted to fit changes in society, the legal force of *consortium* fell by the wayside and the Romans' ideas about it became fossilized. Yet, even when *consortium* had been freed from the strict bounds of legal partnership, its connotations recalled the terms of the original fraternal partnership. For example, a passing reference to *fratres consortes* in Cicero's *pro Flacco* concerns a certain Asclepiades and his brothers from Acmona in Asia. This Asclepiades accused Flaccus of extorting from him some two hundred and six thousand drachmas and claimed to have made the payment through his own brothers and one A. Sextilius.[25] Cicero ironically describes Asclepiades and his brothers as *consortes mendicitatis*, "partners in begging," as if to imply that these brothers were exploiting, for illicit gain, Flaccus' all too Roman expectations that brothers would cooperate financially. Cicero assumes that his audience will understand the brothers' scheme in terms of *consortium*, just as, in one of his *Verrine* orations, he uses the same notion to describe the legitimate farming interests of three Sicilian brothers. Characterized as *consortes*, these brothers epitomize the Roman virtue of fraternal *pietas*, which ought to elicit sympathy from his audience.[26] In the same speech, Cicero flips the coin, portraying a pair of schemers as *consortes* because they are identical in their vices.[27] The metaphor of *consortium* could apply not only to men who shared economic interests but also to the similarity in character that might draw them together. In Cicero's usage, the metaphorical significance of *consortium* moves between practices that recall *consortium* and abstract notions of unity and similarity. This flexibility in connotations of

[24] Kaser, "Neue Literatur" 286–287, and 297 on use of the terms *societas* and *communio* outside legal contexts.

[25] Cic. *Flac.* 34–35. On Sextilius' enterprises at Acmona see J. Hatzfeld, *Les trafiquants italiens dans l'orient hellenique*, 123, and "Les Italiens résidant à Délos mentionnés dans les inscriptions de l'ile," *BCH* 36 (1912): 78.

[26] Cic. *Ver.* 2.3.57. Whether or not the brothers participated in a legal partnership, their situation is consistent with *societas*. Cicero seems to imply that all three brothers shared all profits and losses equally as partners would, for example, in a *societas omnium bonorum*, Paul. [3 *ad Ed.*] *D.* 17.2.3.1, cf. Paul [6 *ad Sab.*] *D.* 17.2.30, Ulp. [1 *Resp.*] *D.* 17.2.73.

[27] Cic. *Ver.* 2.3.155. This passage describes the partnership between Apronius and Timarchides, colleagues of one of Rome's most infamous villains, C. Verres. As part of the evidence against Apronius, Cicero cites excerpts from a letter found in Apronius' house in Syracuse. This letter was sent to him by Timarchides, urging Apronius to trust him: *volo, mi frater, fraterculo tuo credas*, "my brother, I want you to trust your brother dearest." Cicero comments on this advice: *consorti quidem in lucris atque furtis, gemino et simillimo nequitia, improbitate, audacia*, "truly he was your partner in money-making schemes and in larceny, your twin and most like in baseness, immorality and outrageousness."

consortium reveals its symbolic or ideological force as a paradigm for social relations that is rooted in the relationship between brothers.

When *consortium* is removed from the immediate context of brothers, Roman assumptions about kinship are metaphorically applied in the new contexts. As kinship underlies the fraternal relationship, other natural affinities, like shared intellectual and spiritual qualities, can provide the basis for friendship.[28] When Ovid describes his fellow poets as *consortes studii*,[29] or Cicero praises Hortensius as a *consors*, we can glimpse the dynamics of fraternal *pietas*. Although, early in his career, Cicero was Hortensius' political adversary and oratorical rival, the two came to be political allies as well as friends in later years.[30] Cicero pays tribute to Hortensius' friendship at the opening of the Brutus:

> . . . *dolebamque quod non, ut plerique putabant, adversarium aut obtrectatorem laudum mearum sed socium potius et consortem gloriosi laboris amiseram. (3) Etenim si in leviorum artium studio memoriae proditum est poetas nobilis poetarum aequalium morte doluisse, quo tandem animo eius interitum ferre debui, cum quo certare erat gloriosius quam omnino adversarium non habere? Cum praesertim non modo numquam sit aut illius a me cursus impeditus aut ab illo meus, sed contra semper alter ab altero adiutus et communicando et monendo et favendo.*
>
> I was grieving because I had lost not a rival and malignant critic of my renown—as most people think—but rather an ally and partner in a glorious undertaking. For indeed if, in the pursuit of less serious arts, we remember that poets grieve at the death of their peers, with what spirit, then, should I bear the death of this man, with whom it was more glorious to compete than to have no rival at all? Especially since not only was his career never blocked by me, nor mine by him, but on the contrary one of us was always helped by the other through conversation, advice, and exchanging favors. Cic. *Brut.* 2–3

---

[28] For instance, when Quintillian, *Inst.* 12.1.4, prescribes the moral purity necessary for the orator, he says *primum quod si in eodem pectore nullum est honestorum turpiumque consortium,* "that there can be no partnership of vice and virtue in the same heart."

[29] Ovid *Tr.* 5.3.47; cf. H. B. Evans, *Publica Carmina: Ovid's Books from Exile,* 141.

[30] When the two came head to head in the prosecution of Verres in 70, Cicero won the day and a reputation to rival Hortensius'. In arguing for the Manilian law, Cicero also sided against Hortensius. The change in their relationship seems to have come with Cicero's consulship in 63; from then on, they were often aligned on political issues, and both had considerable power and status, so that when Hortensius advised Cicero to go into exile in 58, Cicero interpreted this advice as betrayal, Cic. *Att.* 3.7.2, with D. R. Shackleton Bailey, *Cicero's Letters to Atticus,* 2:142. Yet, Hortensius' death brought Cicero pain, Cic. *Att.* 6.6.2, cf. Shackleton Bailey, *Cicero: A Political Biography,* 30, 35, 40, 43–44, 61–62, 98, and A. E. Douglas, ed., *M. Tulli Ciceronis Brutus,* 1.

The description of Hortensius as a *socius* and *consors* characterizes their cooperation and affection as a positive kind of rivalry and antagonism, which is contrasted with the negative relationship expressed in *adversarius* and *obtrectator*. The comparison implicit in this rhetorical antithesis suggests the qualities associated with *consors*. A *consors* is neither an opponent nor a malicious critic; his role is complementary to a *socius*.[31] A *consors* is not merely a "yes-man," acquiescing in all that his partner decides and selflessly promoting him; instead, the partners share the same experience and, in the case of Cicero and Hortensius, they also share the same profession. Through the metaphor of *consortium* we can see fraternal *pietas* as a model for the give and take that resolves rivalry between friends and colleagues.

A passage from Aulus Gellius' *Noctes Atticae* brings together the traditional, familial context of *consortium* with its metaphorical extensions. Gellius describes the communal lifestyle of the Pythagoreans as follows:

> *Sed id quoque non praetereundum est, quod omnes, simul atque a Pythagora in cohortem illam disciplinarum recepti erant, quod quisque familiae, pecuniae habebat in medium dabat et coibatur societas inseparabilis, tamquam illud fuit anticum consortium, quod iure atque verbo Romano appellabatur 'ercto non cito.'*
>
> It also should not be overlooked that all the Pythagoreans, as soon as they were received by Pythagoras into that company of principles, each one contributed to the common fund whatever money or property he had, and an indivisible partnership was formed, just like that archaic partnership which is called in Roman legal terminology "*ercto non cito.*" Gellius, *NA* 1.9.12

The Pythagoreans pooled their resources and formed a partnership which Gellius equates with *consortium* and *societas ercto non cito*. Gellius' description of this cooperative as a *societas inseparabilis* is consonant with the kind of joint ownership described in Gaius' definition of *consortium*: property is inseparable in that it is owned collectively by its members.[32] As the family partnership of *consortium* provides a model for other forms of partnership in legal definitions, similarly, the term *consortium* provides a metaphor for economic cooperation and the sharing of a philosophical lifestyle. At a further remove, *consortium* could carry an even more general concept of shared ownership. In Pliny's *Naturalis Historia*, animals who live on land share the earth with humans in a partner-

---

[31] Compare the compatibility and rivalry of the *socii*, Mamurra and Caesar, in Catullus 57.

[32] On the concept of total community of property, see M. Kaser, "Neue Literatur," 282–83, and Westrup, *Introduction*, 2:61–62.

ship, *consortio*, analogous to the fraternal *consortium*.[33] Thus, through at least the first century of the common era, *consortium* represented for the Romans ideas of joint ownership and community of interest originally vested in the familial relationship among brothers.

Roman writers applied legal terms of partnership to other relationships, and conversely Roman jurists drew analogies from society and the family, as Gaius does in his explanation of the two kinds of *consortium*. Beyond *consortium* itself, Roman legal discussions of partnership retain an imprint of the fraternal relationship. The relationship between brothers became a model for legal reciprocity. For example, when two people shared a legacy, they were joined by a partnership in the property, not a consensual partnership.[34] In other words, partnership could arise simply from joint ownership regardless of the intent of the owners, much as a *consortium* among *sui heredes*. The very fact of ownership was enough, much as the very fact of kinship sufficed to ground *consortium*. The jurist Ulpian, in a case about partners' shared liability, explains the relationship between partners specifically by analogy with brothers. He conceives of the central force that motivates and governs partnership as a *ius fraternitatis*, "law or rights of brotherhood":

> *verum est quod Sabino videtur, etiamsi non universorum bonorum socii sunt, sed unius rei, attamen in id quod facere possunt quodve dolo malo fecerint quo minus possint, condemnari oportere. hoc enim summam rationem habet, cum societas ius quodammodo fraternitatis in se habeat.*
>
> What seems right to Sabinus is true that even if it is not a total partnership but a partnership in one undertaking, the partners still ought to be held liable for what they can pay or for what they fraudulently avoid paying. This principle has the strongest justification because partnership involves in some degree what we think of as the right of brotherhood. Ulp. [31 *ad Ed.*] D. 17.2.63.*pr.*

Quodammodo suggests the jurist's self-conscious extension of fraternal relations to other social and legal relationships. The phrase *ius fraternitatis* seems more than a rhetorical flourish. *Ius*, with its connotations of law, code of behavior, moral rectitude, implies a recognizable pattern of appropriate brotherly behavior that operated even outside the semantic field of *consortium*. This concept, then, could be detached from actual brothers and applied analogously to other relationships of reciprocal responsibility, even beyond the family. Whereas partnership was redefined and kept alive as a legal institution, *consortium* was transformed from legal institution into a social code that shaped the ethical and economic practices of Roman brothers.

[33] Pliny, *NH* 9.1.1.
[34] Paul. [23 *ad Ed.*] D. 10.2.25.16.

Consortium certainly had historical significance for the Romans, who thought it was an archaic legal institution, part of their heritage at least. Although *consortium* had long since become obsolete as a legal institution, it retained a strong influence on the organization of the Roman family and on the roles of brothers. According to Gaius' description, the original *consortium* came into existence without legal procedure among *sui heredes* possibly through the process of intestate succession. Whereas in the archaic period laws relevant to *consortium* may have developed from family practices, in the later periods practice was more flexible and varied. New legal mechanisms such as wills with specific allocation of property through legacy and trusts existed side by side with more traditional patterns such as joint inheritance. Yet traditional ideals embodied in *consortium* continued to shape the process of inheritance and brothers' roles in it even when families had a wide range of legal and social possibilities for managing their property. Instead of a decline in the fraternal relationship, as presumed in the evolutionary theory, persistent attention to the norms implicit in *consortium* both sustained ethical standards and reinforced the traditional roles of brothers in the family.[35] The institution of *patria potestas* is an instructive parallel. *Patria potestas* is generally recognized as an important influence in the Roman family throughout the Republic, even though changes in Roman society made it less useful and new legal institutions circumvented its powers (e.g., *emancipatio, peculium*).[36] Nevertheless, the Roman father retained considerable power within the family and the figure of the powerful father persists.[37] It is perhaps because the literary sources for *consortium* are less rich than for *patria potestas* that the importance of *consortium* has been overlooked. *Consortium* complements *patria potestas* not just conceptually for us as outside observers, but more importantly in the Roman experience of male kinship. Similar combinations of old and new have been observed in families of later eras; for example, in Portugal and

[35] The force of *consortium* as a social norm could also counter the divisive effects of serial divorce described by K. R. Bradley, "Dislocation in the Roman Family," in *Discovering the Roman Family*, 125–55. On the persistent duty to leave children as heirs, see C. Paulus, *Die Idee der postmortalen Persönlichkeit im römischen Testamentsrecht: zur gesellschaftlichen und rechtlichen Bedeutung einzelner Testamentsklauseln*, 50–58.

[36] On the development of *peculium* as a flexible economic and legal relationship for fathers and sons, see A. Kirschenbaum, *Sons, Slaves and Freedmen in Roman Commerce*.

[37] See R. P. Saller, "*Pietas*," 393–410, and "*Patria Potestas* and the Stereotype of the Roman Family." *Continuity and Change* 1 (1986): 7–22; W. K. Lacey, "Patria Potestas," in *The Family in Ancient Rome: New Perspectives*, ed. B. Rawson, 121–44; A. Watson, *Society and Legal Change*, 23–30. This uneven pattern of social change, in which new social influences cause changes in some institutions such as law but not in others, in particular the family, has been discussed from a theoretical perspective by T. K. Harevan, "The Family as Process: The Historical Study of the Family Cycle," *Journal of Social History* 7 (1973–74): 322–29.

France during the nineteenth century after the introduction of the Civil Code, which mandated equal inheritance among children, traditional practices persisted, evading the legal requirements Athens and giving some children preference.[38] At Rome, what was once a legal rule of inheritance became a tradition or a social norm that shaped the brothers' rights and responsibilities within the family.

The Romans' ideas about *consortium*—however historically imprecise they may have been—had symbolic or ideological value as an ideal around which were oriented brothers' behavior and emotions as well as broader social judgments about brothers. The next two sections of this chapter explore the ways that the ideals rooted in *consortium* influenced inheritance practice and specifically attitudes toward brothers' roles in the family.

Inheritance Practices: Brothers and Sons

Although Roman law and society changed remarkably from the time when archaic inheritance practices like *consortium* might have been common, there is a striking continuity in Roman ideas about inheritance. This continuity links old practices and new: intestate succession and the practice of writing wills; joint inheritance and dividing the family estate into shares; the traditional privilege of agnates, which was gradually extended to cognate kin or those related through women.[39] These new ways to hand down family property did not replace old practices; rather tradition and innovation interacted with each other as Romans in the late Republic and early Empire worked out the best ways to insure their family's future. *Consortium* is one of those traditional ideas, and its influence is evident especially in the priority given to brothers above other family members in inheritance and also in the importance of equality in dividing up property among brothers.

Like *consortium*, the priority of brothers arose within the system of intestate succession, which privileged both sons and daughters over more

[38] Berkner and Mendels, "Inheritance Systems," 220–23; C. B. Brettell, "Kinship and Contract: Property Transmission and Family Relations in Northwestern Portugal," *Comparative Studies in Society and History* 33 (1991): 443–65; H. Smith, "Family and Class: The Household Economy of Languedoc Wine Growers, 1830–1870," *Journal of Family History* 9 (1984): 64–87.

[39] A comparable tension has been observed in Classical Athens between the power of the testator to dispose of his property and the tradition of transfering property to the family. Although Athenians were prohibited from disposing of their property by will if they had legitimate sons, there were attempts to use wills to do this and there were court cases challenging the innovation, for example, Isaeus 2.7; see S. Humphreys, *The Family, Women and Death*, 5–9, and Harrison, *Law of Athens*, 1:131, 151.

distant relatives. In intestate succession, the *sui heredes* or household heirs were first to inherit when a *pater familias* left no will. Those same relatives who were included in the nuclear family while the father was alive were given priority as *sui heredes* after his death: they were first in line to inherit through intestate succession and privileged in wills.[40] The *sui heredes* bore additional responsibilities for the family cult and graves, for patronage and protection of family members, duties that reflect their importance in sustaining the family over the generations.[41] Burial practices also emphasized the unity and importance of this family grouping. Family graves, *familiaria sepulchra*, were distinguished from hereditary graves, *hereditaria sepulchra*, the one for family members and the other more generally for all heirs.[42] The children of the deceased got special treatment, which may reflect their traditional role as *sui heredes*; whether heirs or not, they had the right to be buried in either kind of tomb, unless the testator expressly forbade it.[43] The physical solidarity of the family tomb and the indivisibility of the land on which it was built symbolized the community of property among *sui heredes*.[44] *Consortium* was another way of expressing this continuity. As *consortium* arose without formal, legal procedures, so the *sui heredes* inherited automatically in the absence of a will. The *sui heredes* were nearly owners, *quodammodo domini*, even while the *pater familias* was still alive; they inherited not so much as heirs but as owners.[45] In intestate succession, inheritance mediated a change primarily in control, not ownership, of familial property.[46] When brothers inherited jointly, Romans conceptualized this continuity in ownership as *consortium*. Thus the position of *sui heredes* was analo-

[40] Champlin, *Final Judgments*, 15, 107, 113, 142.

[41] On the extrapatrimonial rights attendant on intestate succession and *consortium* see Kaser, *Privatrecht*, 1:98–99. For a connection between *pietas* and the duty to maintain the family cult, M. Manson, "La *Pietas* et le sentiment de l'enfance à Rome d'après les monnaies," *Revue belge de numismatique et de sigillographie* 121 (1975): 24. On the heirs' responsibility for funeral rights, D. P. Harmon, "The Family Festivals of Rome," *ANRW* 16, no. 2 (1978): 1601–1603. Harmon assumes a connection between the heir and the family that may not always apply; see E. A. Meyer, "Explaining the Epigraphic Habit in the Roman Empire: The Evidence of Epitaphs," *JRS* 80 (1990): 74–78.

[42] Gaius [9 *ad Prov. Ed.*] D. 11.7.5. On the distinction between these kinds of graves, see S. Lazzarini, *Sepulcra familiaria: Un' indagine epigrafico-giuridica*.

[43] Ulp. [25 *ad Ed.*] D. 11.7.6.*pr.*

[44] The land on which family graves were placed was indivisible, Mod. [6 *Resp.*] D. 10.2.30, and see M. De Dominicis, "Il 'ius sepulchri' nel Diritto Successorio Romano," *RIDA* 13 (1966): 180, 199, 203.

[45] Gaius, *Inst.* 2.157, Paul [2 *ad Sab.*] D. 28.2.11.

[46] A similar ambiguity characterized inheritance practices in Roman Egypt: D. J. Thompson, *Memphis under the Ptolemies*, 174. Compare also the Chinese practice of *fenjia* which, instead of inheritance transfering ownership from father to son, creates joint ownership between them: Lavely and Wong, "Family Division and Mobility in North China." See also, in general, Diósdi, *Ownership*.

gous to that of brothers in *consortium*. As in *consortium*, the legal category of *sui heredes* implies correspondence between a relative's role in the living family and his or her right to inherit. The reality of family life, then, corresponded to legal rights and concepts, but, was not necessarily limited by it.

Although *consortium* was associated in general with the traditional role of the agnates in succession, its lasting influence singled out brothers from this larger group of relatives related through male kinship. While the *sui heredes* included all family members under the father's *potestas* at the time of his death, brothers were central in Roman approaches to sustaining the family over the generations. Sisters and brothers alike were *sui heredes*, yet sisters were not so closely associated with *consortium* because of the practice of dowry and because of the traditional priority of male relatives in intestate succesion. While a sister had the right to an equal share as heir, her marriage affected the way she participated in inheritance and how her participation was understood. A daughter might take all or part of her share in the inheritance as dowry when she married.[47] Her dowry could be separated from her brothers' portions of their paternal inheritance and transferred to her husband from the paternal estate, which was associated with the fraternal *consortium*. If she were married *cum manu*, she would no longer be in her father's *potestas* and thus no longer a *suus heres* with an equal right to inherit with her brothers. If married without *manus*, however, a daughter would inherit equally with her brothers, and her dowry might or might not factor into the division. Because the practice of dowry complicated the process of inheritance for sisters, they were not identified so closely as brothers with continuity in family property over the generations. The rules of intestate succession further emphasize the role of brothers in handing down family property: a brother, as closest agnate, was given the next priority after the nuclear family in intestate succession.[48] The privileged position of brothers in intestate succession was carried over into Roman wills both in spirit and in actual arrangements. Because the law required a father either to name his son as heir or to disinherit him by name,[49] it appears

[47] Treggiari, *Roman Marriage*, 362–63, and Saller, *Patriarchy*, 204–24, esp. 207–10, 217–20. For an assessment of women's disadvantages in Roman inheritance, Champlin, *Final Judgments*, 114–20. Cf. the etymology of *soror* in Gellius, *NA* 13.10.3: '*soror*' inquit appellata est quod quasi seorsum nascitur separaturque ab ea domo, in qua nata est, et in aliam familiam transgreditur, "she is called 'soror,' he says, because it is as if she is born separately, and she is separated from the household in which she was born and crosses over into another family." D. Konstan observes a tension between succession and marriage, "a daughter was the locus of crossed loyalties," in his interpretation of Livy's depiction of Tullia and of Horatia ("Narrative and Ideology in Livy: Book 1," *Cl. Ant.* 5 [1986]: 212).

[48] *Twelve Tables* 5.4–5.

[49] On *nominatim exheredare* for sons, see Gaius, *Inst.* 2.123, 127; Ulp. [1 ad Sab.] D.

that sons had a prior, perhaps original, claim to the property.[50] If there were more than one son, they would jointly share this priority with their father's brothers (i.e., the paternal uncles), thus extending the fraternal privilege over two generations.[51] A man who did not name his brother his heir could be thought guilty of the most grievous iniquity.[52] The priority shared by brothers mimics the fraternal joint ownership in *consortium*, and this perhaps explains Gaius' description of *consortium* as *societas fratrum suorum*. The different treatment of sons and daughters in Roman inheritance expressed both the equality of partible inheritance and the symbolic force of *consortium* as a metaphor for fraternal *pietas*. Even when cognate kinship—kinship through women—was recognized in Roman law and society, brothers remained central to the ideology of equality in inheritance expressed in fraternal *pietas*.

The increasing role of women was only one of the changing contexts in which ideas about *consortium* persisted. The practice of leaving a last will and testament also provided new situations in which old ideas about fraternal *pietas* could be adapted. During the Republican period, Romans began to write wills directing the disposition of their property instead of relying on the system of intestate succession set out in the *Twelve Tables*. The surviving texts of this archaic law do not specify whether the heirs should inherit in shares or jointly, as prescribed in *consortium*. Later legal texts, however, assume that the family estate was divided into shares, whether or not the father left a will. These divisions varied in complexity, but when the estate was divided among the children of the deceased, siblings' shares tended to be equal.[53] Thus, the characteristic equality of *consortium* was consistent both with the system of intestate

---

28.2.1; Ulp. [6 *Reg.*] D. 28.2.2; Ulp. [1 *ad Sab.*] D. 28.2.3.*pr.*; Flor. [*Inst.* 10] D. 28.2.17. For sons and daughters as a class, see Paul. [12 *Resp.*] D. 28.2.25.*pr.*; cf. Kaser, *Privatrecht*, 1:705–707.

[50] Brothers or sons were central to inheritance even if they had yet to be born, Ulp. [14 *ad Sab.*] D. 38.16.3.9; cf. Gaius, *Inst.* 2.130. The essentially masculine identity of the family may be reflected in its *genius* or reproductive force, possibly related to the Etruscan *genius*, which was represented by the phallus, D. G. Orr, "Roman Domestic Religion," *ANRW* 16, no. 2 (1978): 1569–70. On the role of the heir in sustaining the family name and property, Champlin, *Final Judgments*, 25–26.

[51] Ulp. [13 *ad Sab.*] D. 38.16.2.2.

[52] Val. Max. 7.8.4.

[53] For a case assuming that brothers deserve an equal share of their paternal estate, Gaius [2 *Leg. Praet. Ed.*] D. 35.1.17.2–3, cf. Scaev. [4 *Resp.*] D. 31.89.4. For a father who gives equal shares to his sons and a smaller share to his nephew, Papin. [6 *Resp.*] D. 28.5.79.2. Though often sons receive a larger share than daughters (inheritance plus dowry), some brothers and sisters take equal shares, Ulp. [6 *Opin.*] D. 5.4.6, and Scaev. [3 *Resp.*] D. 32.93.3. Compare the practices of Roman Egypt, on which see A. K. Bowman, *Egypt after the Pharaohs*, 131, cf. 98, 101, and D. W. Hobson, "House and Household in Roman Egypt," *YCS* 28 (1985): 211–229.

succession and with partible inheritance. The division into shares preserves the spirit of *consortium* while at the same time providing the flexibility that Romans needed as they expanded and diversified their economic activities. Legal mechanisms for dividing jointly owned property acknowledge this need. As early as the *Twelve Tables*, brothers could use the *actio familiae erciscundae* to divide an estate that they had inherited together.[54] While legal remedies were available, cooperation was preferable to litigation and had a moral value that preceded the legal solutions. The jurist Papinian recognized a moral motivation for brothers to divide the family property by consensus: when they do so, he writes, they are fulfilling the duty of *pietas*.[55] A case from outside the legal sources, included in Quintilian's *Institutio Oratoria*, sets these presumptions in a context of filial *pietas*.[56] A father had two sons, one a clever speaker who defended his father in court; the other, though he refused to appear in court, heroically restored his brother and father from exile. When the father died without a will, the brothers were left to share the estate. Even Quintilian's less perceptive observers would see that both sons ought to have a share: if the clever speaker claimed the whole estate, he would be judged greedy and immoral because his brother's heroic devotion had earned his right to a share.

Traditional ideas about fraternal *pietas* and equality provided a source of moral strength that helped both brothers and fathers resolve disputes about property.[57] The next few paragraphs examine hypothetical cases from the *Digest of Justinian* which illustrate the tenacity of traditional ideas about *consortium*. This analysis reveals points of contact between what we might call fraternal ideology and the practice of being a brother. In the legal cases, ideas about fraternal *pietas* interact with what could be actual situations that arose as brothers and fathers negotiated the transmission of property from one generation to another. My discussion addresses several different legal procedures: wills, the *querela de inofficioso testamento*, and *possessio bonorum contra tabulas* with the related procedure of *collatio*. Neither the legal rules of inheritance nor the norms associated with *consortium* tell the whole story; rather they offer a guide to understanding the choices Romans made and the potential power of fraternal *pietas* in their lives.

Romans could and did use wills to reinforce the priority accorded to brothers and sons in intestate succession.[58] Brothers were the most fre-

---

[54] Ulp. [19 *ad Ed.*] *D.* 10.2.1.*pr.*

[55] Papin. [2 *Resp.*] *D.* 10.2.57.

[56] Quint. *Inst.* 7.1.42–45.

[57] Cf. Plut. *Mor.* 484B–C.

[58] On the consonance between wills and intestate succession, Champlin, *Final Judg-*

quently named relatives in Roman wills,[59] and they were preferred when the testator named a substitute heir.[60] A father's will could even direct his sons to share their inheritance in ways reminiscent of *consortium*. Fathers often instructed sons to restore their share of his estate to their brothers, if they died childless.[61] A father's decision, *iudicium* or *voluntas*, could confirm a division of property among his sons.[62] One father left some of his property individually to each of his four sons, and the rest he left undivided to them and their sister.[63] Alternatively, a father's division of his property could protect his sons from each other's financial losses.[64] The explicit involvement of fathers in their sons' division of property suggests both the potential for conflict between brothers and, just as important, the value Romans placed on resolving these conflicts. Preserving fraternal harmony was one goal of paternal authority, at least as expressed in wills.[65] A father's involvement could be important if, after his death, one son sought to change his portion of the property. Two cases from the *Digest* illustrate the problem. In the first, a father gave one son a piece of property to secure a loan and subsequently bequeathed the same property to him. After the father's death, the son paid the interest on the loan; if his creditor then seized the property, this son could not

---

ments, 127. Compare similar practices at Athens: R. Lane Fox, "Inheritance in the Greek World," in *Crux: Essays in Greek History Presented to G.E.M. de Ste. Croix on his 75th Birthday*, ed. P. A. Cartledge and F. D. Harvey, 208–24.

[59] Champlin, *Final Judgments*, 127.

[60] Scaev. [2 *Resp.*] *D.* 28.5.86. Compare the practice of reciprocal substitution of brothers in their father's will, Mod. [*Heur.*] *D.* 28.6.4.2, Jul. [24 *Dig.*] *D.* 28.6.25. When a father instituted a legitimate and a "natural" son reciprocally, a claim of cognate kinship by the legitimate son's mother could overrule such a substitution, Paul. [12 *Resp.*] *D.* 28.6.45. *pr.*

[61] E.g. Marc. [1. *Resp.*] *D.* 30.123.*pr.*, Ulp. [3 *Fid. Com.*] *D.* 36.1.3.4, Ulp. [2 *Fid. Com.*] *D.* 36.1.18.5, Papin. [8 *Resp.*] *D.* 36.1.59; cases involving this condition and brothers and sisters, Iul. [39 *Dig.*] *D.* 36.1.26.2, Scaev. [4 *Resp.*] *D.* 36.1.64, Scaev. [20 *Dig.*] *D.* 36.1.79.*pr.* Similarly, a father who instructed his daughter not to make a will until she had children affirmed her brother's right to inherit as closest agnate, Paul. [2 *Decret.*] *D.* 36.1.76.*pr.*

[62] Even an oral declaration dividing the property was valid and had the legal force of a will, (Ulp. [19 *ad Ed.*] *D.* 10.2.20.3), and a father could confirm such a division in his will.

[63] Papin. [7 *Resp.*] *D.* 34.4.23. Chance might create a similar if limited situation when two sons receive legacies from their father before his death, and one of them receives a slave who has a *peculium*; the brothers share this *peculium* in the event of the slave's death, (Scaev. [1 *Resp.*] *D.* 10.2.39.4).

[64] Compare brothers' (sons') responses, pp. 51–54.

[65] We might compare the role of Roman fathers, with a father from early modern Chile who, in his will, encouraged his sons to a "harmonious division of his estate," asking them to "divide their patrimony in a brotherly fashion and without engaging in litigation"; M. Lamar, " 'Choosing' Partible Inheritance: Chilean Merchant Families, 1795–1825," *Journal of Social History* 28 (1994): 125.

recover its value from his brother, because the property was his share under their father's division.[66] Such a paternal division could, however, in other circumstances, help a son to obtain his rights against his brothers. In the second case, a father left one of his sons a piece of land that the father thought he owned. If, in fact, the property was not his and his son was evicted, the son had no action against his brothers and co-heirs, unless their father had made a division among his sons. This division, the father's last wishes, should guide an arbiter dividing the estate among these brothers.[67] The father's division established not just a pro-portional distribution of property among his sons but each son's right to a share. If one brother received less than his share, through eviction in this case, his brothers should compensate him so that their holdings con-form to their father's will.[68] Equal shares did not always mean that chil-dren received exactly the same kind or amount of property. Instead, at Rome, as in other societies that practiced partible inheritance, a father defined equality among his children based on their individual needs and capacities and in response to social or economic circumstances.[69]

While a father's will could mediate property arrangements among his sons, a flaw would make his will an ineffective agent of fraternal cooper-ation. Questions about brothers' shares arose more often in complicated situations where children did not simply inherit in accordance with their father's will, for example in cases involving challenges to wills or the division of a jointly inherited estate. The *querela de inofficioso testa-mento* provided a legal channel for protesting a will that wrongly passed over or disinherited a close relative.[70] All relatives more distant than the immediate family would do better to save their trouble, wrote Ulpian, and not file suit, because they have little chance of success.[71] And even brothers might have done better to work with or around their father's will, as the many legal cases addressing such accommodations suggest. Here again, the preference for cooperation over conflict asserts itself in fraternal relations.

When a father failed either to name a son heir or to disinherit him

[66] Scaev. [1 *Resp.*] D. 10.2.39.5.

[67] Papin. [8 *Resp.*] D. 31.77.8.

[68] Compare also the cases where a father directed his sons to manumit a slave that was part of his estate: if some of the brothers manumit the slave, they owe their brothers and co-heirs compensation for the slave, Ulp. [5 *Fid. Comm.*] D. 40.5.30.6.

[69] Brettell, "Kinship and Contract," 458–62, and Lamar, "'Choosing' Partible Inheri-tance," 125–26.

[70] Marc. [3 *Dig.*] D. 5.2.5. An inheritance of one-fourth of the estate was, however, enough to remove grounds for the *querela*, Ulp. [14 *ad Ed.*] D. 5.2.8.8.

[71] Ulp. [14 *ad Ed.*] D. 5.2.1. On the natural basis of this right, see for example Cic. *S. Rosc.* 53 with E. Renier, *Étude sur l'histoire de la querela inofficiosi en droit romain*, 82–83.

properly, the son and his brothers could claim the inheritance by appealing to the praetor for possession contrary to the will. Through *bonorum possessio contra tabulas*, the praetor allowed *sui heredes*, children and spouses, to apply for the right to inherit even when a will existed (provided that they had been neither instituted heir nor disinherited by name).[72] In effect, *bonorum possessio contra tabulas* reestablished and expanded the rules of intestate succession alongside and in response to testamentary succession.

> *Praetori enim propositum est, cum contra tabulas bonorum possessionem dat, eas partes unicuique liberorum tribuere, quas intestato patre mortuo in hereditate habiturus esset, si in potestate mansisset: et ideo sive emancipatus sive is qui in potestate mansit sive in adoptionem datus ex minima parte heres scriptus sit, non redigitur ad eam portionem, ex qua institutus est, sed virilem accipit.*

The praetor's objective, when he awards *bonorum possessio contra tabulas*, is to give each of the children the share in the inheritance which he would have had if his father had died intestate and if the child had remained *in potestate*; and in the same way, whether he did remain *in potestate* or was emancipated or adopted or if he was made heir to the smallest share, he is not limited to the portion to which he was heir, but he receives an equal share. Ulp. [40 *ad Ed.*] D. 37.4.8.14

Bonorum possessio contra tabulas gave the children the share each would have taken as *suus heres* through intestate succession, thus recreating circumstances that could give rise to a fraternal *consortium*. The Latin describing each share in *bonorum possessio contra tabulas* is the adjective *virilis*, which means first "a man's" in distinction to "a woman's," and then "due to each person" or "equal"; this term reflects subtly the presumption that the heir would be a man, and possibly a brother rather than a sister.[73] While in practice *bonorum possessio* accorded daughters and sons equal shares, the implicit ideology tends to focus on male heirs and brothers. *Bonorum possessio* seems to have preserved a brother's right to inherit as closest agnate, as suggested by a brief but complicated case involving a failed will and two brothers, each of whom had a son.[74] One brother had named his son heir in his will and

[72] Ulp. [39 *ad Ed.*] D. 37.4.1.pr.-2, cf. Paul [41 *ad Ed.*] D. 37.1.6.1; Afr. [4 *Quaest.*] D. 37.4.14.pr.; Marc. [9 *Dig.*] D. 37.8.3, with Kaser, *Privatrecht*, 1: 719.

[73] For the presumption of equal sharing in *bonorum possessio* and *collatio*, Scaev. [*Quaest. Publ.*] D. 32.103.2–3, and Ulp. [40 *ad Ed.*] D. 37.8.1.11. Cf. *OLD s.v. virilis*.

[74] Papin. [6 *Resp.*] D. 29.4.27.1. A paternal uncle had a similar right when the testator's heir and brother died before accepting the inheritance, Iul. [27 *Dig.*] D. 38.7.4.

substituted his nephew (the other brother's son); that is, if his son were to be incapable of becoming heir, his brother's son would be his heir if he were an adult and free from his father's *potestas*. As it happened, the one brother died before his son had become an adult capable of inheriting, and the surviving brother did not emancipate his son. As a result, the will failed, and the surviving brother inherited by intestate succession as closest agnate. According to the jurist Papinian, this brother's right to inherit in the case was in accord with the spirit of the praetor's edict on *bonorum possessio*, and presumably the deceased's son would not succeed if he sued for possession. There is a practical advantage in allowing the brother to inherit, because as an adult he would be a more capable steward of the family property than either of the young sons. The rules of intestate succession that come into play through *bonorum possessio* and when wills fail serve the family's economic security and rely on brothers to take responsibility for each other and for the relatives and property they share.

When brothers took their paternal inheritance through *bonorum possessio contra tabulas*, a simple division of inheritance might not result in equal shares. To remedy this potential inequality among brothers, emancipated sons were required to pool their assets with their brothers who remained *in potesate* through a procedure known as *collatio*.[75] Each brother's contribution to the *collatio* was calculated in proportion to his share as a *sui heres* in intestate succession, so that each brother had an equal share. If two brothers were heirs to their father, each would take half his estate, so the emancipated son contributed half of his property to his brother.[76] In this example, each brother ended up with the same amount of property, but *collatio* could also create a different kind of equality, as illustrated in another, more complicated case, involving four brothers.[77] In this family, two brothers were emancipated and two remained *in potestate*. They took *bonorum possessio contra tabulas* of their father's estate, which is valued at HS 400 for the purposes of this hypothetical case.[78] One emancipated brother (A) had property worth HS 100, the other's (B) was worth HS 60, the brothers *in potestate* have nothing.

[75] Ulp. [40 *ad Ed.*] D. 37.6.1.*pr.* and 1.

[76] Paul [41 *ad Ed.*] D. 37.6.2.6; cf. Ulp. [40 *ad Ed.*] D. 37.6.1.3, 4, 12, 24; Iul. [23 *Dig.*] D. 37.6.3.6; Scaev. [5 *Quaest.*] D. 37.6.10. Paternal uncles took an equal share with brothers, Paul. [41 *ad Ed.*] D. 37.6.2.7, and Ulp. [40 *ad Ed.*] D. 37.8.1.16, 17. If one brother did not apply for *bonorum possessio*, his share accrued to his brothers, Gaius [14 *Prov. Ed.*] D. 37.4.12.*pr.* *Collatio* applied also to daughters' property and their dowries in certain circumstances.

[77] Jul. [23 *Dig.*] D. 37.6.3.2.

[78] The value of HS 400 probably reflects a stylization of numbers rather than an accurate assessment of a particular estate, see W. Scheidel, "Finances, Figures and Fiction," *CQ* 46 (1996): 222–38.

after *collatio*

A: 33 ⅓ (from his own   + 100 (from the paternal estate)   = 133 ⅓
     property)

B: 20 (from his own property)   + 100 (from the paternal estate)   = 120

C: 33 ⅓ (from brother A)   + 100 (from the paternal estate)   = 153 ⅓
     + 20 (from brother B)

D: 33 ⅓ (from brother A)   + 100 (from the paternal estate)   = 153 ⅓
     + 20 (from brother B)

Although each brother takes an equal share of the paternal estate, HS 100, the brothers *in potestate*, taking 153 ⅓ a piece, come out ahead of their independent brothers in *collatio*. "Equal" in this instance does not mean "same." What does it mean? Or, rather, what other goals or motives need to be factored into the calculation of *collatio*? The advantage to brothers *in potestate* may serve to compensate them for economic opportunities lost because they remained part of their father's household while the others were free to pursue solely their own interests. In this way, *collatio* protects both fathers and sons. Because it defers compensation to sons who stay with their father, *collatio* guarantees financial security for the father's old age. Financial incentive shores up *pietas*. In turn, the sons' devotion to their father is rewarded with a financial edge in inheritance against brothers who did not take up the responsibility for caring for their father. Comparative evidence reveals that in other societies that practiced partible inheritance, differences in "equal" shares were also used to secure care for old and infirm relatives.[79] Both *bonorum possessio contra tabulas* and *collatio* show how the kind of fraternal cooperation that characterized *consortium* was extended to achieve other familial goals like care for elderly parents. The reversibility of *collatio*—if brothers begin but do not complete the process, each can recover what he contributed—contrasts with the apparent permanence of *consortium*.[80] These procedures offer greater flexibility while at the same time also requiring a sense of equality among brothers that expresses the spirit if not the letter of *consortium*.

The process of inheritance, contested or otherwise, created a dialogue between fathers and sons through which they expressed their devotion and also their desire to control the terms of their relationships. The legal cases illustrating *possessio bonorum*, for example, present rather realistic scenarios that offer us insight into the interaction between law and sentiment, finance and *pietas*, ideology and practice in the process of inheritance. Several of Seneca's *Controversiae* explore these same dynamics

[79] Brettell, "Kinship and Contract," 461, and Lamar, " 'Choosing' Partible Inheritance," 134–36.
[80] Marc. [13 *Reg.*] D. 12.4.13, cf. Kaser, *Privatrecht*, 1:730–31.

among fathers, sons, and brothers, offering perspectives that complement the legal cases.[81] Because these rhetorical exercises dance around a question, offering arguments from every angle, we are invited to see brothers from a variety of perspectives, which reveal both patterns and contradictions in Roman ideas about male kinship, and to understand brothers in relation to other male kin, especially fathers and sons, as they would have interacted in Roman society. The ideals associated with *consortium* are a subtext to these perspectives. In each *controversia*, brothers are expected to share the family estate, and fraternal *pietas* works in concert with filial devotion. Despite the sometimes fierce struggles between fathers and sons, these rhetorical debates reinforce an idealized balance between duty to a brother and duty to a father.

The opposition between filial and fraternal duty is sketched most sharply in *Controversia* 6.1 with which this chapter opened. In this short set of arguments, a father and son debate the son's promise to share his inheritance with his brother, whom the father has disinherited. The heir gives his brother a written undertaking for half their inheritance, on the condition that he not protest his disinherison. The father's argument interprets this fraternal agreement as a betrayal of filial *pietas*: it is a parricide's pledge anticipating evil:

> *Tantum aeris alieni habet quantum vivo patre non possit solvere. Vis scire cuius fidei sis? ne frater quidem tibi sine chirographo credidit. Alterius spem moror, alterius fidem. Vivo, et iam patrimonium meum divisum est. Nisi succurritis, vincet me et ille qui tacuit. Non dissimulo me hodie duos abdicare. Chirographum prode, parricidarum foedus et nefariae spei pactum, chirographum danti impium, accipienti turpe, patri periculosum.*

> He has so great a debt that he cannot pay it off while his father is alive. Do you know what your credit is like? Not even your brother trusted you without a written undertaking. I am delaying the hope of one son and testing the loyalty of the other. I am alive, and my estate is already divided up. Unless you come to my aid, he will defeat me, even the son who keeps quiet. I do not hide the fact that I am disinheriting two sons today. Bring out that written undertaking, that parricides' pledge, an agreement of evil expectation, a written undertaking unholy for the one who gives it and base for the one who receives it, dangerous to the father. Sen. *Con.* 6.1

The sons are encroaching on their father's authority by acting as if his estate is already theirs to dispose of, even though he is still alive; in essence, they are acting *ut quodammodo domini*, "as if owners," just as we would expect the *sui heredes*, or brothers, to act taking responsibility for their inheritance even without legal ownership. The father's interpreta-

---

[81] See also L. A. Sussman, "Sons and Father in the Major Declamations Ascribed to Quintilian," *Rhetorica* 13 (1995): 179–92.

tion of the situation reflects the precarious balance inherent in the role of the *sui heredes*: the *quodammodo* is crucial to understanding brothers' roles in the family while their father is alive. The adverb marks a boundary between paternal authority and fraternal responsibility. Brothers ought to respect their father's power even while anticipating their own active administration. In this *controversia*, the brothers' agreement to circumvent their father's will goes beyond respectful expectation because the brothers behave as if they really were already masters of the estate. But, the father's argument finds fault not only with his son's filial *pietas* but also with their own fraternal relationship. The father implies that he is now disinheriting his second son because he is financially irresponsible: only a deadbeat would have to give a written document to his own brother.[82] The underlying assumption of fraternal cooperation activates disapproval of the brothers' failure to trust each other. The father accuses his second son of betraying himself, his brother, and his father by making this deal with his brother. We cannot see a fraternal *consortium* in this situation, because the father specifically describes their agreement as dividing the estate. Nevertheless, expectations of fraternal cooperation persist. The son's answer offers an alternative interpretation of the brothers' deal, an interpretation that reintegrates fraternal and filial *pietas*.

The son who was not disinherited begins with a pledge of devotion to his brother, devotion that will endure hardship. He explains that the deal with his brother actually serves filial *pietas* because it allows the brothers to stand together without interfering in the father's power to dispose of the familial estate. He encourages his brother to treat their father just the same as if he had not been disinherited, a plea that recalls the possibility of *bonorum possessio contra tabulas*. He portrays himself as equally devoted to his brother as to his father, and he expects their father to share his belief that fraternal and filial *pietas* are not just compatible but complementary. In an alternative question to his father, the son imputes absurdity to his father's objections:

> *Quid enim timebam? ne, si rescisset pater, moleste ferret filium suum hominem avarum non esse, fratrem pium esse?*
> What was I afraid of? That, if my father found out about my promise, he would be annoyed that his son was not a greedy man but a devoted brother?
> Sen. *Con.* 6.1

Why should the brother be afraid of his father finding out that he has helped his brother? The son suggests two reasons for his father's anger. The first reason implies ironically that a father should not be annoyed with his son for *not* being greedy, although a father could be angry with

[82] Cf. Cic. *Rosc. Com.* 23.

his son for being *too* greedy. The second reason returns the focus to fraternal *pietas*: surely a father would not chastise his son for taking care of his brother! In other words, by promising to share his inheritance with his brother, the second son proves not only that he is not greedy but also that he is a devoted brother. His father should praise him on both counts: *ita mihi contingat patrem utrique nostrum placare*, "in this way I may make our father pleased with the both of us." The brothers' devotion is integral to their reconciliation with their father. Both the father's and the son's arguments depend on the belief that fraternal and filial *pietas* deserve equal care and that the two kinds of relationships—father/son and fraternal—thrive together.

The interdependence of brothers and fathers motivates both sides of the question in *Controversia* 3.3, where a father has disinherited one son because he is profligate. When the other, good, i.e., fiscally responsible, son is captured by pirates, his disinherited brother ransoms him. Upon their return, the good son adopts his profligate brother, bringing him back into the family. In response, their father disinherits the good son. The good son argues that both he and his brother acted out of fraternal *pietas*: the one in rescuing, the other in adopting. The father ought to thank them both because their devotion to each other restored them to him and re-created their family.[83] The father, however, sees their action not as fraternal devotion but as a challenge to his legal power as father. Although the legal arguments imply a strict application of *patria potestas*, they are intertwined with *pietas*. Even if the sons pursued their fraternal devotion in compliance with the law, their obligation to their father transcends legal restrictions. Their father argues:

> *Lex te ad ministerium patrimonii admisit, non in dominium. Est aliqua aetas a qua aliquis filius esse desinat?*
> The law charged you to manage your father's property, not to own it. Is there any age after which someone ceases to be a son? Sen. *Con.* 3.3

Again, the legal situation recalls the ambiguous position of the *sui heredes*, who share responsibility but not ownership before the death of the *pater familias*. Legal questions aside, kinship endures: filial *pietas* remains in force even without legal sanction. While the law may be at issue in this *controversia*, the more pressing question concerns the proper balance between filial and fraternal *pietas*. Which relationship should have more influence in a man's decisions? The son's argument suggests that both kinds of devotion should be reconciled in the common goal of

---

[83] Plutarch expects parents to be sustained in their old age by their sons' fraternal devotion and condemns those who attack their brothers rather than defend them to their parents, *Mor.* 480B–C and 482E–483C.

keeping the family together, a goal that is very much at the center of the fraternal *consortium.*

The last *controversia* that we will discuss is in fact the first in the collection. Unlike 3.3 and 6.2, it is preserved in full. Twelve different voices speak on each side of the question and comment on rhetorical strategy. Because the arguments are expressed in more detail, this *controversia* offers a more complex picture of the tensions between fathers and brothers in questions of inheritance and family property. Although the principle issue in *Controversia* 1.1 is a child's responsibility to support his parents, the dilemma turns on the tension between filial and fraternal *pietas.*

> *Duo fratres inter se dissidebant; alteri filius erat. Patruus in egestatem incidit; patre vetante adulescens illum aluit; ob hoc abdicatus tacuit. Adoptatus a patruo est. Patruus accepta hereditate locuples factus est. Egere coepit pater: vetante patruo alit illum. Abdicatur.*
>
> Two brothers were feuding; one had a son. His paternal uncle fell on hard times, and even though his father forbade him, the young man supported his uncle. For this reason he was disinherited but did not protest. The young man was adopted by his uncle. The uncle then became rich when an inheritance came his way. The young man's natural father then begins to be in need: even though his uncle forbids him, the young man supports his father. He is being disinherited [by his uncle]. Sen. *Con.* 1.1.*pr.*

Whereas in the other two *controversiae* fraternal *pietas* was supposed to supplement filial *pietas*, in *Controversia* 1.1 the son's argument inverts the equation: his filial duty both to his paternal uncle/adoptive father and to his natural father should reconcile his two parents, the two brothers.[84] It is unjust, he claims, to be disinherited because he was only doing what a brother ought to do himself. The son bridges dissensions between his uncle and his father, between the two brothers, by acting *in loco fratris.* Alternatively, he can reunite the brothers by being a good son. The father-son relationship has the potential to repair the brothers' relationship: if the son cannot restore fraternal *pietas*, perhaps he can at least stop them from being bad fathers.[85] Loving their son, they will discover themselves brothers. While the son's arguments rely on the integration of filial and fraternal *pietas*, the arguments for the father focus on complicating conflicts of interest.

The son portrayed his intervention as reconciliation, but to the brothers it is divisive. When the son thought he was being kind, only doing what a brother would do, he was in fact overstepping his bounds. By standing in for his father's brother, he seemed to rebuke his uncle for

[84] Sen. *Con.* 1.1.1–3.
[85] Sen. *Con.* 1.1.7.

neglecting his brother, denying him a chance to show his fraternal *pietas*.[86] Other arguments for the father deny the potential for fraternal devotion. No matter what the son did, the brothers would hate each other. The situation enacts the proverbial depth of fraternal hate: *vos iudices, audite quam valde eguerim: fratrem rogavi*, "men of the jury, hear how badly I was in need: I begged my brother."[87] Mythical *exempla* put this pair of brothers in perspective: Thyestes fed his brother's children to him; this brother is only returning his brother's son by disinheriting him. Whatever the degree of hostility between these brothers, their animosity is expressed in their relationship with their son through their power over property, their right to bequeath and to disinherit. The control over familial property is a potent field for conflict, especially at the moment of transition between one generation and the next. A father's power to affect the future of his property depends on his sons' cooperation with each other as much as on their filial devotion. In matters of inheritance, Romans perceived fraternal *pietas* as an extension of paternal care-taking: for example, Horace acknowledged a certain Proculeius who divided his own wealth in equal portions and shared it with his brothers after their own property had been lost in the civil wars: *vivet extento Proculeius aevo / notus in fratres animi paterni*, "Proculeius, who is known for his paternal spirit toward his brothers, will live to a ripe old age."[88] *Patria potestas* expires with the father: only fraternal *pietas* continues after his death, sustaining his influence and reconciling brothers to the new family arrangements.[89]

Because inheritance practices aim at more than a simple transfer of property from father to son, legal rules of inheritance only begin to tell the story of what is at stake. Inheritance created occasions for conflict and cooperation for fathers, sons, and brothers. So long as their father was alive, providing a locus of undivided authority, brothers' disputes could be invisible, eclipsed or precluded by *patria potestas* and filial *pietas*. A father's last will and testament could attempt to forestall disputes

[86] Sen. *Con.* 1.1.18, 19.

[87] Sen. *Con.* 1.1.21, and 23 for Thyestes.

[88] Hor. *Carm.* 2.2.5–6. For the biographical sketch, see Porphyrion *ad* Hor. *Carm.* 2.2.6. Compare also the behavior of Scipio Aemilianus and Fabius Maximus, the natural sons of Aemilius Paullus, see below Chapter 3 and 4, pp. 65 and 124.

[89] Cross-cultural analysis of the European family suggests that the continuing cooperation among Roman brothers, who might or might not share a household, fits into a broader pattern: "Joint fraternal households are most frequent in societies with strongly patrilineal kinship systems; where land and sometimes most property is inherited through male consanguines, and where marriage is usually virilocal . . . where cohesiveness of the household rests primarily on the ties between the father and his sons, it will tend to divide at his death. The frequency with which a joint household continues on as a frérèche underlines the strength of ties between male siblings" (Wheaton, "Family and Kinship," 619–20).

among his sons, or it could raise as many questions as it answered: should brothers compensate for or adjust their father's distribution of the family property if he disinherits or neglects one of them? If so, how? What if dividing the family estate left each brother with such a small inheritance that he was unable to support himself?

As early as Plato, keen observers of society were concerned about the effects of partible inheritance on the wealth of individual families and on the distribution of wealth among rich and poor.[90] Population growth can lead to fragmentation of family property: the more children born to each family, the smaller the share each inherits. Extreme fragmentation in turn endangers the economic survival of individual families and can change their social status. Romans were aware of the dangers of partibility.[91] Martial (5.38) jokes about a pair of brothers whose paternal inheritance meets the census requirements for the equestrian class, but for just one *eques*: how can two brothers ride on one horse? Because the brothers must share their inheritance, only one can maintain the equestrian status of their father, unless they do a Castor and Pollux routine, taking turns riding their inheritance.

Even if dividing an inheritance caused hardship in some cases, the practice of partible inheritance was not always self-defeating for societies or for families. Demographic and economic circumstances affect the strategies that families adopt in negotiating between *pietas* and inheritance law as well as the success of those strategies. At Rome, high mortality rates and slow or little population growth limited the number of children competing for a share. According to Saller's population simulation, roughly three-quarters of Romans would have had one or two siblings at age thirty-five but by age fifty, when about half of them would have lost a parent, it was more likely that only one sibling would still survive to share the paternal estate.[92] Taking into account sex distribution, only about one-quarter of these families would have to divide the estate between two sons. Sometimes, an estate divided in one generation could be recombined in the next, as apparently happened in the case of Sp. Ligustinus, who was married to the daughter of his father's brother.[93] Although Martial's epigram suggests that even some brothers near the top of the socioeconomic heap may have felt constrained by partible inheritance, for these classes, dividing the estate probably did not cause poverty as it might for the lower classes.

The enthusiasm for equality that is evident in both legal and literary

[90] For example, Plato *Laws* 922C, and Aristotle *Pol.* 1265A–B.

[91] See M. Corbier, "Les comportements familiaux de l'aristocratie romaine," in *Parenté et stratégies familiales dans l'antiquité romaine*, ed. J. Andreau and H. Bruhns, 225–249.

[92] Based on Saller's population simulation and analysis (*Patriarchy*, 48–65).

[93] Livy 42.34.3.

sources may document an elite perspective on partible inheritance. Comparative evidence suggests, however, that partible practices could have worked well for families with smaller holdings. For example, in early modern France, while wealthy families passed their estates to a single heir, in working-class families children took equal shares and, building from this small inheritance, they pursued a variety of economic activities so that each generation rebuilt its resources enough to pass on the same inheritance to its children.[94] Differences in fertility between rich and poor may also account for successful partible inheritance among the lower classes, as for example, in early twentieth-century China, where the rich had more property, but they also had more children: poor families seldom had more than one heir.[95] In fact, for these Chinese families, partible practices combined with a growing economy to foster social mobility for the lower classes, which would change the social hierarchy. To the contrary, however, at Rome, the difference in fertility between elites and the lower classes[96] does not seem great enough to make partible inheritance significantly less satisfactory an inheritance strategy for wealthy families. Furthermore, in the thriving economy generated by Rome's military expansion in the late Republic, sons who inherited a small share would have had many opportunities to enrich themselves, as we know they did from anecdotes reflecting different attitudes toward acquired and inherited wealth.[97] Whereas partible practices tended to diminish wealth and facilitate social mobility in societies where fertility varied by class, at Rome, partible inheritance benefited both rich and poor. These economic and social conditions allowed both elites and Romans from the lower classes to share the ideology of equality associated with *consortium* as they pursued similar strategies in negotiating partible inheritance.

This section has considered the influence of *consortium* on the law and

[94] H. Smith, "Family and Class," 64–87.

[95] Usually only once in every three or four generations, see Lavely and Wong, "Family Division," 439–63. For an analysis of the dynamics of inheritance, fertility, and economics, see Wheaton, "Family and Kinship," 601–28, and Berkner and Mendels, "Inheritance Systems," 209–23.

[96] Saller, *Patriarchy*, 22–25, considers two patterns of mortality, but the more optimistic pattern that he associates with senatorial families is still far behind the fertility of twentieth-century developed countries. In the less optimistic pattern, just less than half of all ten-year-olds survive to fifty, as against 57 percent in the more optimistic view; more than 75 percent of today's ten-year-olds survive to seventy. S. Hodkinson, "Land Tenure and Inheritance in Classical Sparta," CQ 36 (1986): 378–406, argues for a similar relationship between fertility and inheritance at Sparta. The problem in the ancient world was having a family heir at all.

[97] Corbier, "Comportements familiaux," 243. See also Shatzman, *Senatorial Wealth*, 1–83, and, for the real-estate dealings of the Roman elite, see E. Rawson, "The Ciceronean Aristocracy and Its Properties," in *Studies in Roman Property*, ed. M. I. Finley, 85–102.

practice of inheritance. The discussion focused on strategies adopted by fathers not just to secure the family's financial security but also to foster fraternal *pietas* among their sons. In the next section, we chart how brothers negotiated law, sentiment, and economic circumstances in managing family life.

Consortium and Brothers' Roles in the Family

After their father's death, brothers were on their own, legally independent but still bound to each other and to the family by sentiment, duty, financial circumstance, or some combination of factors. Through their father's death, brothers became legally independent, *sui iuris*, each the head of his own family. Even emancipated sons, who were already *sui iuris* before their father's death, could be drawn into the family orbit when their father died. Inheritance created new roles and challenges for brothers as they took over their father's authority and his responsibility for the family and its property. This transition was thrust on at least half of all Roman brothers by age fourteen and on most of them by thirty-five.[98] Roman brothers would not only have to negotiate the shoals of inheriting their father's property but might also have had to live with their settlement for a good many years, since about half of the adult men who survived to age forty would have had a brother who lived at least as long.[99] It fair to say, then, that a brother, if he had one, was the closest male relative a Roman man would know through his adult years, that a brother really was a partner in life. These social and demographic circumstances focused Roman attention on fraternal *pietas* in the process of inheritance and in the familial organization that developed out of this transition.

As we saw in the preceding section, a father's will could help brothers to navigate family life, defining the terms of their equality in inheritance and encouraging cooperation rather than dispute. Not all fathers left wills; not all wills were effective; and a will could not always foresee the various situations that might face brothers after their father's death. Changing economic circumstances could make his division less profitable, or the brothers might simply have different ideas about the best strategies for handling the challenges of partible inheritance. Brothers also made choices about how to care for each other and other close rel-

---

[98] Saller, *Patriarchy*, 59, 63.

[99] K. Hopkins, *Death and Renewal*, 100–107. While Hopkins's statistical projections for the number of brothers vary, as many as 43 percent in the Republic to as few as 0 percent in the families of suffect consuls 70–235 C.E., his models suggest that there were many more brothers than the sources document.

atives. If a father's death left one or more young sons, these brothers were likely to be involved in *tutela* or guardianship, an institution of Roman law designed to protect children and their inheritance until they reached the age of legal adulthood.[100] Adult brothers could also employ a variety of legal procedures—for example, partnerships, contracts, and wills—to structure their relationships with each other. Hypothetical cases from the *Digest of Justinian* dealing with these legal institutions allow us to reconstruct some of the options available to Roman brothers for maintaining their own well-being and that of their families. In the legal cases, economic motives are interwoven with sentiment and duty or, in Roman terms, with fraternal *pietas*. Literary anecdotes about brothers' family life reveal similar patterns. Throughout the sources, the interworkings of *pietas* and economic interests are oriented around the idealized fraternal relationship associated with *consortium*. Whether brothers owned property jointly or in shares, this traditional ideal shaped the ways they resolved conflict, charting a sometimes fragile balance between autonomy and interdependence, *pietas* and financial opportunity.

This section picks up the story of brothers' family life where the last left off, just after their father's death when the brothers took charge of their own lives and whatever paternal property they inherited. Inheritance was only the beginning of brothers' responsibilities in the family, but it was a significant beginning both because it could happen when the brothers were still young and because the patterns embedded in inheritance influenced the continuing practice of fraternal *pietas*. This section first examines the institution of *tutela* or guardianship and its role in the transition between generations, from paternal authority to legal independence. Then the discussion broadens to consider the interactions of adult brothers and Roman attitudes toward fraternal family life. In both phases of brothers' lives, as children and as men, there is evidence of tension and potential conflict. Perhaps more importantly, however, our sources consistently emphasize reconciliation, cooperation, and affection—in other words, fraternal *pietas*. This pervasive emphasis on resolving conflict through cooperation rather than division recalls the original fraternal *consortium* but in a symbolic way, representing an ideal or a norm against which the behavior and attitudes of brothers could be assessed. The continuity in ideals and practice is evident, as before, in the transition between generations and the institutions that facilitate this change in family life.

The legal institution of *tutela* mediated the transition from paternal to fraternal responsibility for family property when one or more of the chil-

---

[100] Paul. [38 *ad Ed.*] D. 26.1.*pr.*, 1.

dren was still a minor at the time of the father's death. A legal guardian or *tutor* was responsible for the care of minor children and their property.[101] The rules governing *tutela*, which are traced in their earliest outline to the *Twelve Tables*,[102] combine the principles of intestate succession with wills and praetorian innovation. Guardians could be appointed in three ways: by will, through intestate succession, or by the praetor in the absence of a will or if there were no appropriate relatives. In intestate succession, the duty to act as *tutor* followed the inheritance because both heir and guardian were responsible for the family property: whoever wanted the benefit of the property also had to bear responsibility for protecting it.[103] Thus, the closest agnate or male relative, often a brother, became *tutor legitimus*, guardian, to his younger siblings automatically through intestate succession (unless of course the closest agnate was a woman, because a woman could not serve as *tutor*).[104] If the children's mother was alive, she did not assume the role of guardian, but rather she was supposed to have a *tutor* appointed and keep an eye on his activities.[105] In fact, if a relative was available, the guardian named in the will could avoid taking the job.[106] The legal position of *tutor legitimus* corresponds to the role of brothers in *consortium*, who automatically acquired responsibility for the family property.

As brothers had priority among agnates in intestate succession, so, too, they were preferred as guardians. The preference for a brother could include not only the brothers of the child in *tutela* but also his father's brothers or his paternal uncles. For example, when a brother or uncle was in enemy hands, *tutela* was not transferred to the next closest agnate; instead, the praetor appointed an interim *tutor* to serve until the fraternal relative came home to take up his responsibilities.[107] If no guardian was appointed by will and a paternal uncle was available, no one else should

101 Saller, *Patriarchy*, 181–203.

102 Ulp. [35 *ad Ed.*] D. 26.4.5.*pr.*

103 Ulp. [14 *ad Sab.*] D. 26.4.1.*pr.*

104 Ulp. [14 *ad Sab.*] D. 26.4.1.1, cf. Ulp. [14 *ad Sab.*] D. 26.4.1.3, and Hermog. [2 *Epit.*] D. 26.4.10. Gaius, *Inst.* 1.156, lists the closest agnates: first is a brother born of the same father, followed by the brother's son, grandson, and then by the paternal uncle and his son and grandson. See also Voci, *Istituzioni di diritto*, 93, 563.

105 J.-U. Krause, *Witwen und Waisen im Römischen Reich III. Rechtliche und soziale Stellung von Waisen*, 88–89, cf. 111–12.

106 Scaev. [2 *Resp.*] D. 27.1.37.*pr.*

107 Ulp. [14 *ad Sab.*] D. 26.4.1.2. For a sample will appointing a paternal uncle and another *tutor*, see Scaev. [2 *Resp.*] D. 26.7.47.*pr.* Acting *in loco patris*, a paternal uncle could appoint a *tutor* in his will for his nieces and nephews, Papin. [11 *Quaest.*] D. 26.3.5. Of course, if a dispute arose between uncle and nephew, the praetor could and should appoint another guardian. For instance, if the uncle claimed that the nephew was an imposter, Tryph. [14 *Disp.*] D. 26.2.27.1, or if the uncle claimed that he himself was heir and that the *pupillus* had been disinherited, Iul. [20 *Dig.*] D. 27.1.20.

be appointed by the praetor.[108] Although fraternal priority reached beyond the nuclear family in some situations, the law recognized a closer tie or imposed a greater duty on the brothers of the child in *tutela*. A brother could replace even a guardian appointed by will: if all the brothers were children when their father died, obviously none could serve as *tutor*, but as soon as one of the brothers became an adult, he would replace the current guardian.[109] In other words, a brother was the first and natural choice as guardian, because he had a special relationship both with the ward, his brother, and with their father. The special status of a fraternal *tutor* is evident in the legal provision concerning the remuneration of guardians. If money had been set aside from an inheritance to remunerate guardians, and they were subsequently exempted, the heirs (not the *tutors*) could keep that money, except when the *tutor* was the testator's son and co-heir with his brother. In such a case the *tutor* could keep the money set aside for him because, the jurists argue, the father's decision to give him the money arises not from his role as *tutor* but from his status as son.[110] This legal provision recognizes the close relationship among brothers and grounds their legal rights in this kinship: because brothers are so closely related, they have greater discretion over familial property than other guardians do. Fraternal privilege, however, was not always unlimited.

Although Romans expected brothers to take the lead in managing family property during the transition between generations, brothers were not given free rein with the family's future well-being. The very notion of guardianship heightened a brother's duty to care for his siblings. A passage from Cicero's *De Oratore* suggests how strong this fraternal obligation was thought to be. Cicero cites a speech from Pacuvius attributed to Telemon in which he blames his son Teucer for the deaths of his brother and his brother's son, who was entrusted to his care, *qui tibi in tutelam est traditus*.[111] To emphasize Teucer's failure, the poet describes his responsibility for his brother's son as *tutela*, borrowing a legal term to convey the moral force of fraternal *pietas*. In fact, both the law of guardianship and a father's will could enforce a brother's responsibility as *tutor* through circumscribing his rights over their shared and separate property. Just as a father could use his will to divide his property among his

---

[108] Tryph. [14 *Disp.*] D. 26.2.27.pr. If there were more than one agnate of the same degree of kinship, all would serve as *tutores*, Paul [38 *ad Ed.*] D. 26.4.8. An uncle's status as *tutor legitimus* could be buttressed by a testamentary appointment, which held good even if he were away from Rome, (Papin. [5 *Resp.*] D. 26.7.39.8), but a paternal uncle might serve along with other testamentary *tutores*, as M. Iunius did for his nephew, Cic. *Verr.* 2.1.139.
[109] Ulp. [25 *ad Ed.*] D. 27.3.9.1.
[110] Papin. [5 *Resp.*] D. 27.1.28.1.
[111] Cic. *De Orat.* 2.193.

sons, he could use the same legal document to give them instructions about how to organize and manage their own resources. These instructions could be particularly important if one or more of the brothers was a child when he died, because these children depended for support on older brothers who might be more or less inclined to cooperate. The provisions of one father's will, as represented in a hypothetical case from the *Digest*, suggests one way to secure fraternal cooperation.[112] This father instituted his two sons heirs to equal shares; since one son was of legal age and the other a minor, he used a *fideicommissum* or trust to create a *de facto* guardianship. The father directed his elder son to give certain property to his brother when he turned fourteen, and in the meantime to pay the taxes on this property and to keep the revenues from it. He also instructed him to pay for his brother's eduction after he turned twelve. Through the use of a trust this father's will created almost an informal *consortium* for his sons. His instructions reveal the potential fragility of such a situation. The father offers a financial incentive to his elder son, allowing him to enrich himself from his brother's share of the inheritance while he held it in trust. This reward seems designed to benefit both brothers: the financial incentive should motivate the elder to manage his brother's property at a profit, thus at the same time insuring that the younger, when he is old enough, will receive his rightful share of their father's estate. The father's provisions attempt to engineer a balance between his sons' individual and common interests in such a way that both are served. Financial arrangements thus realized in practical terms the ideal of fraternal *pietas*.

Where either *pietas* or economic motive was lacking, the Roman law of guardianship provided sanctions for brothers who failed to balance their duty to each other with their desires for independence in managing family property. A brother who served as *tutor* had to live up to the same standards as other guardians, since the right to sue a *tutor* for mismanagement applied just the same even if the guardian was a brother.[113] In this provision, the legal system anticipated the possibility that a brother might act irresponsibly toward his younger siblings. The right to sue protects even minor brothers' shares in the paternal estate and their future financial security. But what constituted irresponsible administration of *tutela*? After he grew out of *tutela*, the ward could sue if, for example, his *tutor* failed to make an inventory of his property or if he diverted the money of the ward for his own purposes without paying interest.[114] These same actions, viewed through the lens of *consortium*, look more like fraternal cooperation than fraud. Within the confines of

112 Scaev. [22 *Dig.*] D. 33.1.21.5.
113 Papin. [5 *Resp.*] D. 26.7.39.17.
114 Ulp. [35 *ad Ed.*] D. 26.7.7.*pr.*, 10.

guardianship, the law restricted what might be traditional patterns of share-and-share-alike among brothers, in order to insure the financial well-being of younger brothers. Though a *tutor* and his brothers might manage their property jointly, the law recognized each brother's potential independence, for example, in the provisions that the elder brother and *tutor* was responsible for his own expenses and could not compel his brother to share them when they later divided the property (unless they were necessary expenses).[115] A brother's right to manage family property as guardian was thus balanced by legal checks that defined his responsibilities for the well-being of his siblings. The expectation that a brother would be guardian echoes the roles of brothers in *consortium* while the legal rules for *tutela* limit those roles, redefining them to recognize the potentially divergent interests that might divide brothers.

If brothers needed threats or incentives to perform adequately the duties of guardian, they were no different from other Romans for whom guardianship could be a burden, and it was an unavoidable burden unless the prospective *tutor* could show that he was already administering three other *tutelae*. The legal rules for determining what counted as three guardianships offer insight into how the Romans conceptualized the family. The assumptions about family organization embedded in these rules reflect traditional ideas about intestate succession, *consortium*, and the fraternal relationship. The rules address both the tutor's household and the household of the wards. First, the *tutor* was not necessarily counted as an individual; to put it another way, guardianships administered by a father or son or brother who shared a household were counted together.[116] Similarly, a household counted as a single *tutela* even if there were several children. For example, the guardianship of three brothers whose estate was undivided counted not as three separate *tutelae* but as one.[117] Or, if one *tutela* was especially troublesome to administer, the *tutor* could be exempted from other guardianships, unless the troublesome *tutela* involved *fratres consortes* who shared a patrimony.[118]

The collective reckoning of guardianships suggests a notion of the family as a group of male relatives, especially brothers, who shared a household. This conception of the family not only reflects the traditional agnatic family but it bears a striking likeness to *consortium*. In the cases from the *Digest* illustrating the adaptations of fraternal guardianship there is again the combination of old and new ideas, of independence and interdependence of brothers in family life. A literary anecdote about the Clau-

---

[115] Mod. [2 *Resp.*] D. 3.5.26.
[116] Ulp. [1 *Off. Praet. Tutel.*] D. 27.1.5.
[117] Ulp. [1 *Off. Praet. Tutel.*] D. 27.1.3.
[118] Paul. [6 *Quaest.*] D. 27.1.31.4.

dii, Cicero's contemporaries, attests to a similar flexibility in fraternal practices. The Claudii may have participated in an informal *consortium* when their father died leaving his eldest son, Appius (cos. 54), responsible for two younger sisters and two younger brothers (Gaius [pr. 56], Publius Clodius [tr.pl. 58]).[119] The evidence for the early life of these Claudii is an anything but straightforward passage from Varro's *De Re Rustica*, which introduces the discussion of bee-keeping near the beginning of Book 3. Appius explains that he began to have honey with his wine after he came into a legacy relinquished to him by Lucullus: *a quo hereditate me cessa primum et primus mulsum domi meae bibere coepi ipse*.[120] He claims that he could not afford to have honey with his wine because the family was so poor, *propter parsimoniam*, and that he even gave one of his sisters in marriage without a dowry. Giving a sister in marriage without a dowry implies real poverty—an implication that is hard to tally with the Claudian reputation for wealth and with their status in the senatorial class. Instead, the poverty Appius describes is better interpreted as a cash flow problem resulting from delays in the settlement of his father's will.[121] Appius' drinking habits, then, result from his frugal management style, which may well have been forced on him because he was responsible for his younger siblings, possibly as legal *tutor*. The Claudii seem to have pooled their resources—we do not know whether or not they inherited jointly—and during a difficult transition period, their family adopted the form of a *consortium* because sharing the family's resources was a successful strategy for surviving financial troubles. The example of the Claudii suggests that Roman families were able to adapt traditional practices like *consortium* to the changing economic circumstances that arose as the family made the transition from one generation to the next.

After brothers had settled their paternal inheritance and were legally independent, their choices and priorities were still shaped to some extent by traditional patterns of family life associated with *consortium*. In the Republican era, the right to an equal share of the paternal estate no longer entailed a total community of property; nor did it exclude a brother's right to own separate property. Yet some brothers still chose to maintain the kind of joint household associated with *consortium*, as the Q. Aelius Tubero who married the daughter of L. Aemilius Paullus (cos. 182) seems to have done. He was poor, Plutarch explains, because he

---

[119] Large families seem to have been a Claudian tradition: E. Rawson, "The Eastern Clientelae of Clodius and the Claudii," *Historia* 22 (1973): 234.

[120] Varro, *RR* 3.16.2.

[121] W. J. Tatum, "The Poverty of the Claudii Pulchri: Varro, *De Re Rustica* 3.16.1–2," *CQ* 42 (1992): 194–195. On the expectation of dowry and possible difficulty raising it, Treggiari, *Roman Marriage*, 323, 347, and Saller, *Patriarchy*, 217.

lived with sixteen of his relatives in a little house on the small piece of family property:

ἦσαν γὰρ ἑκκαίδεκα συγγενεῖς, Αἴλιοι πάντες, οἰκίδιον δὲ πάνυ μικρὸν ἦν αὐτοις, καὶ χωρίδιον ἕν ἤρκει πᾶσι, μίαν ἑστίαν νέμουσι μετὰ παίδων πολλῶν καὶ γυναικῶν.

For there were sixteen relatives, all Aelii, and the house was rather small for them, and one farm was enough for them all; they maintained one hearth with many wives and children. Plut. *Aem.* 5.7[122]

Although no ancient source names the family members or reveals how or why they lived this way, the total of sixteen implies more than one conjugal family and possibly more than one generation. While such a Kennedyesque compound might have been unusual, the sources seem more interested in the moral implications of these living arrangements.[123] It is not the communal household itself that occasions interest. What is so amazing, to Valerius Maximus and Plutarch alike, is that the Aelii brothers get along with each other. Their ability to live together sharing their paternal estate not only correlates with but accounts for their integrity and political success.[124] For the Romans, lifestyle informs morality, and living according to the norms of *consortium* wins laurels both in both political and moral arenas, as Varro's characterization of Appius Claudius also recognizes. Even if poverty induced the Aelii to pool their resources,[125] they were to be commended for making it work. Fraternal devotion was seen as complementary and necessary to other virtues, and it possessed as much moral force as economic value. The philosopher Musonius Rufus even argued that a wealth of brothers was more valuable than the economic advantage of being the only son and heir.[126]

From a late Republican perspective, the second century Aelii might be considered old-fashioned, except that the same ideas about fraternal *pietas* and family management persist in the later legal and literary sources, albeit with modifications that respond to changing social and economic

[122] Cf. Val. Max. 4.4.8, and compare Cato's household, Plut. *Cat. Ma.* 24.1.

[123] The structure and importance of kinship relations do not depend on the composition of the household, although living arrangements may affect behavior patterns. See Goody, "Evolution of the Family," 119. See also Herlihy, *Medieval Households*, 4; R. Wall, J. R. Laslett, and P. Laslett, *Family Forms in Historic Europe*, 79; M. Anderson, "The Sentiments Approach," in *Approaches to the History of the Western Family 1500–1914*, 39–64; C. Levi-Strauss, "The Family," in *Man, Culture and Society*, ed. H. L. Shapiro, 261–85.

[124] Plut. *Aem.* 5.4–5, 28.7, and Val. Max. 4.4.9; cf. Pliny, *NH* 33.142. On the moral purpose of Plutarch's *Lives*, see A. Wardman, *Plutarch's Lives*, 37, and C. P. Jones, *Plutarch and Rome*, 103.

[125] The use of the diminutive *domuncula* in Valerius Maximus' description may reflect the smallness of the family's resources. Poverty is not the only issue, as J. A. Crook, "Patria Potestas," *CQ* 17 (1967): 117, argues.

[126] Musonius, *Ep.* 15B.

circumstances. Where the archaic *consortium* prescribed a total community of property, brothers in later eras inherited their paternal estate in shares and had only a limited legal responsibility toward one another. Legal limitations on fraternal interdependence might make a generous brother like Scipio Aemilianus appear even more praiseworthy,[127] but they did not erase the social and moral traditions of fraternal cooperation. Although the Roman jurists certainly recognized the potential for dispute among brothers, they privileged cooperation. A brother who was at first unwilling to participate in *collatio*, if he later changed his mind, should be given a hearing "especially when dispute arises among brothers about their parent's property," *maxime cum de bonis parentis inter fratres disputetur*.[128] Solidarity expressed in inheritance remained central to the fraternal relationship in its various workings. But, instead of a total community of property, brothers negotiated their interdependence and autonomy drawing on both law and traditional morality. The notion of fraternal *pietas* represents this dynamic relationship and its responses to individual needs and desires. Where sentiment and social pressure did not suffice, however, law could reinforce at least a limited kind of fraternal *pietas*. The process of negotiation is visible in the many hypothetical cases from the *Digest* that focus on the intersection between cooperation and independence in the fraternal relationship. Throughout the sources, traditional Roman ideas about *consortium* shape the choices and strategies that brothers employ as they work toward cooperation.

Although it was legally possible for brothers to be completely independent, both literary and legal evidence suggests that most brothers charted a middle course balancing shared and self-interest. Even when brothers inherited jointly, their accounts could be kept separate, as a hypothetical case involving a trust or *fideicommissum* illustrates. A father named his four sons heirs to equal shares and he also bequeathed a farm to each of them individually, presumably by *fideicommissum*. When the brothers inherited, all the father's property was encumbered, and so they borrowed against it from a second creditor to pay the first creditor. The second creditor then sold all the property to one of the brothers. The legal issue in this case is whether or not the other brothers could sue for their property under the *fideicommissum*. They could not unless they paid their share of the debt to the brother who purchased the property.[129] One brother, by buying the property, kept the family property together, but separated himself from his brothers. In this case, the law acknowledged both the brothers' financial independence and the potential for their continuing cooperation. Similarly, even if a man was his

---

[127] Cf. below page 124.
[128] Papin. [3 *Quaest.*] D. 37.6.8.
[129] Scaev. [4 *Resp.*] D. 31.89.4.

brother's heir, he was not automatically responsible for all his brother's debts: his liability was limited to his share of the inheritance.[130] In at least one case, a brother used his will to mimic the continuity of *consortium*. He named his brother heir on the condition that he not alienate the family property and that he bequeath it within the family, *ne domus alienaretur, sed ut in familia relinqueretur*, otherwise the rest of the family could claim a share.[131] This incentive and the very need for it implies that holding the family property together had become less desirable, possibly less profitable than other strategies. Maintaining the values embedded in *consortium* had thus attained a symbolic value representing fraternal *pietas* and its importance in the survival of the family. The triumvir M. Crassus may have been inspired by such symbolism. He not only shared a household with his two married brothers, but he also married his brother's widow.[132] By marrying his brother's widow, Crassus effectively merged himself with his brother's family, extending the communality implicit in *consortium* to family members as well as property.[133] Crassus' solution to the family problems created by his brother's death are comparable to the practices of other societies that use partible inheritance. When dividing the family property would create shares too small to support each brother and his family independently, one brother would marry and raise a family while the others would *fa a zio* or play the role of uncle, as bachelors living in the same household, supported by

[130] Marcell. [1 *Resp.*] D. 46.1.24. This case is concerned with what to do if the brother who promises security dies and the creditor wants to sue his estate to recover the loan. If he names his brothers heir to one-third of his estate, his creditor can only recover up to the brother's share in the inheritance.

[131] Papin. [19 *Quaest.*] D. 31.69.3, and on prohibitions on alienation in general, see D. Johnston, "Prohibitions and Perpetuities: Family Settlements in Roman Law," *ZRG* 102 (1985): 220–90. Conversely, a man who does not want to be his brother's heir on intestacy must only use his share of their joint property, Pomp. [35 *ad Quintum Mucium*] D. 29.2.78.

[132] Plut. *Crassus* 1.1. Brothers' financial independence could extend to the responsiblity for the children of a deceased brother (as in Crassus' family), but didn't always. A paternal uncle was not liable to pay his niece's dowry from his own property, unless he knowingly promised more than she owned, and in such a case his promise constituted either a gift or fraud, and he is liable, Paul. [7 *Quaest.*] D. 26.7.43.1.

[133] Two of Seneca's *Controversiae* mention the expectation that a man would marry his brother's widow and care for his children after his death. In both *Controversiae*, extraordinary circumstances interfere with the norm. In *Con.* 2.4, a brother refuses to marry his brother's widow because she was a prostitute while the other shows his baseness by abandoning his brother's son. In *Con.* 8.3, a man refuses to marry a wife who was implicated in his brother's death. These cases recall the epigram about Bavius and his brother whose fraternal estate was divided by their relationships with women. Like Bavius, a certain Gallus, in Catullus 78 takes a misguided approach to caring for his brothers' families: he facilitates an adulterous affair between one brother's son and his other brother's wife.

and contributing to the family's resources.[134] In some such families, brothers practiced what is known as temporary marriages, where several brothers would marry a single wife, who would bear heirs to all of them in turn.[135] While the Roman ideology of the *univira*, a woman's devotion to one husband, seems at odds with the practice of temporary marriage, the way Crassus stepped into his brother's marriage suggests that his family may have opted to allow only two sons to marry in order to secure the family's future.[136] When his brother died, Crassus took the opportunity to move from uncle to husband, a move that may have served his own interests as well as fraternal *pietas*.

Although many brothers probably cooperated informally, as Crassus and his brothers seem to have done, the law provided formal relationships with which they could structure their joint and separate responsibilities. Like the father whose will shored up his son's duty as guardian, brothers also used legal instruments to give teeth to *pietas*, as for example, the pair who stipulated a penalty for acting contrary to their division of property.[137] A brother could use his will to recombine his property with his brother's: in one case from the *Digest*, a man directed his heir to keep only 100 *aurea* and to return the rest of the inheritance to his brother, replicating through his will the brother's right to inherit as nearest agnate.[138] Some brothers seem to have formalized their relationship in partnership, and unless they did so, they could not be held responsible for each other's debts.[139] Even brothers who formed a voluntary partnership, *voluntarium consortium*, could keep their military salary separate.[140] Though legal rules encouraged fraternal *pietas*, only a legal relationship could compel cooperation, because sentiment and morality could be unreliable, as the following case implies. Two brothers started out owning their property jointly; one of them pledged a portion of the

---

[134] This pattern occurs in both ancient and modern societies, for example, in Classical Athens, Lane Fox, "Aspects of Inheritance," 217, and in nineteenth- and twentieth-century Corsica, L. E. Cool, "Continuity and Crisis: Inheritance and Family Structure on Corsica," *Journal of Social History* 21 (1987): 741–46. For a theoretical perspective, Berkner and Mendels, "Inheritance Systems," 212–14.

[135] Lane Fox, "Aspects of Inheritance," 222–23, interprets Polyb. 12.6B.8 as implying the existence of this practice in classical Sparta. When temporary marriages produced both male and female children, marriages between cousins consolidated the family's holdings, much as brother-sister marriage did in Ptolemaic Egypt; see K. Hopkins, "Brother-Sister Marriage in Roman Egypt," *CSSH* 22 (1980): 303–54.

[136] Plutarch tells us that Crassus started his career with moderate resources, *Crassus*. 2.1.

[137] Scaev. [28 *Dig.*] D. 45.1.122.6.

[138] Papin. [19 *Quaest.*] D. 31.69.*pr.*

[139] Scaev. [1 *Resp.*] D. 10.2.39.3; the brothers are *in omnibus socii*.

[140] Ulp. [31 *ad Ed.*] D. 17.2.52.8. A man's military salary could also be kept separate from *collatio*, Papin. [9 *Resp.*] D. 40.5.23.2.

undivided property as security on a loan. When they subsequently divided their property, they did not divide the debt. The brothers agreed that if the borrower did not free the land from his creditor, his brother could take property worth half of the pledge from the borrower's share of the division. In other words, the brothers agreed not to share the loss if the land was forfeited; the borrower would compensate his brother for his interest in the undivided property. If a question arose over which pledge should be paid first—the one to the brother or the one to the creditor—the jurist Papinian gave priority to the brother; the borrower could not have made the pledge to the creditor without his brother's consent, because he was pledging property that the brothers owned jointly: *quoniam secundum pignus ad eam partem directum videbatur, quam ultra partem suam frater non consentiente socio non potuit obligare*.[141] The jurist's description of the brother as *socius*, partner, may indicate that the brothers had owned property jointly in a formal partnership, which could account for the brother's priority. Alternatively, the term *socius* may indicate that joint ownership had created an obligation like partnership.[142] If the brothers did not have a formal, legal partnership, the term *socius* implies that the jurist conceptualized fraternal cooperation in terms of partnership. In any case, the division created separate rights and ownership for the brothers that coexisted with their joint ownership of the pledge, so that each brother owned his own share independently and both brothers continued to own the pledged property jointly. Sorting out brothers' joint and separate assets may have occupied the jurists and courts, but less legally minded Romans could profit from ambiguities in brothers' legal and financial relationships.

In a private letter to Paetus, Cicero wrote about the real-estate dealings of one M. Fabius and his brother. It appears that Fabius' brother had sold their jointly held estate at Herculaneum—*qui fundus cum eo communis esset*—and Cicero suspected foul play.[143] Fabius' enemies must have bamboozled his brother into selling the farm. His brother would never have sold the farm without consulting him unless he was subjected to nefarious influences. Cicero's suspicion betrays an assumption about fraternal cooperation: whether or not the brothers had any kind of legal arrangement, Cicero expects them to cooperate as if they were partners. These same assumptions drive the rhetoric of the *pro Quinctio*, in which Cicero describes the relationship between his client, P. Quinctius, and his

141 Papin. [11 *Resp.*] D. 20.4.3.2.

142 Cf. Scaev. [25 *Dig.*] D. 41.4.14. In the absence of his brother, a man acts in his behalf, selling a farm that the two inherited from their sister. The buyer may take ownership over time so long as he believes that the sale took place with the consent of the absent brother.

143 Cic. *Fam.* 9.25.3. Cicero's description of the farm as *communis* could suggest a variety of different legal relationships, or none at all.

deceased brother's partner, Naevius. After his brother Gaius died, P. Quinctius became his heir and stepped into his partnership with Naevius. Quinctius wanted to sell some of the property owned by the partnership to pay his brother's debts, but Naevius dissuaded him and promised to pay them himself, saying, as Cicero tells it, what's yours is mine "on behalf of your former fraternal relationship and my own kinship with you through marriage," *pro fraterna illa necessitudine et pro ipsius affinitate*.[144] (P. Quinctius was married to Naevius' cousin.) Naevius implies that he and P. Quinctius had a preexisting relationship because Quinctius' brother had been Naevius' partner. Kinship, even by marriage, and sense of brotherhood ought to have strengthened the legal relationship between partners. But Cicero claims that Naevius was insincere when he said this; he was only pretending to be a good man, all the while laying a trap for Quinctius. In presenting Naevius' promise as the words of a good man, Cicero draws on assumptions about fraternal *pietas* that he expects his audience to share. The audience will agree that Naevius invoked fraternal *pietas* in order to dupe Quinctius and will sympathize with the victim because he believed, as they themselves do, that he should have been in a special position with his brother's partner. The argument is persuasive only if Cicero's audience recognized the affinity between brothers and partners, and wasn't too fussy about the legal categories. While legal texts distinguish between brothers who were partners and those who weren't, these distinctions might not matter so much in defining socially and morally acceptable behavior. What Cicero's contemporaries seem to have cared about was the cooperation between brothers, the belief that brothers would seek each other's consent in their business dealings. Since the legal sources may be as much as five centuries removed from the late Republic, it is possible to say that Cicero's contemporaries may not even have been aware of the legal distinctions.[145] In any case, his presentation demonstrates that social norms and practice were more fluid than the hypothetical cases from the *Digest* might suggest. In fact, Romans seem to have taken pleasure in exploiting the flexibility of fraternal relationships in legal and social contexts. Bending, extending, embroidering fraternal *pietas* was a successful strategy not only in legal cases, but in social practice and literature.

The symbolic moral force of fraternal *pietas* is cast into relief when conflicts over family responsibilities turn violent.[146] Cicero's denunciation of Oppianicus in the *pro Cluentio* is representative. In 66, Cluentius was charged with poisoning his stepfather, Statius Albius Oppianicus,

---

[144] Cic. *Quinct.* 16; cf. 14–15.

[145] See, for example, Cicero's treatment of the orator's use of legal "research" in *De Orat.* 1.234–245.

[146] Hor. *Serm.* 2.5.16 includes a fratricide in a list of nefarious types.

whom he had prosecuted successfully eight years earlier. During the inter-
vening years, public opinion turned against Cluentius. Accounts of judi-
cial bribery undermined the condemnation of Oppianicus (though without reversing the conviction) and cast suspicions on Cluentius. In his
defense, Cicero strove not so much to demonstrate Cluentius' innocence
as to prove Oppianicus' guilt, cataloguing his many and varied crimes in
lurid rhetoric. Paramount among these crimes was Oppianicus' attack on
his brother and his brother's family.[147] He was not content with simply
murdering his own wife, but he killed his brother and his sister-in-law
and their unborn child as well. In response, Oppianicus' brother, it is
alleged, disinherited him with his dying words, using his last legal powers
to exclude Oppianicus from the fraternal status his behavior has already
undermined. Apparently, Oppianicus had been his brother's heir, recalling the pattern of *consortium*. But Oppianicus had not behaved like a
consors frater. Instead of caring for his brother's family, he first made his
sister-in-law a widow and then killed her and his brother's unborn child
for the sake of money. Unlike the brother in Seneca's *Controversia* 6.1,
Oppianicus was greedy. His desire to inherit everything overwhelmed any
sense of fraternal *pietas*; he forsook all bonds of common interest represented in the *consortium fratrum*. Cicero appealed to the moral sentiments of his audience as if he expected them to condemn Oppianicus for
his offense against fraternal *pietas*. Calling Oppianicus' crime a *frater-
num parricidium* emphasizes its danger by linking fraternal and filial *pietas*; *parricidium* had separate legal status from homicide because of its
implications for the power structure of the Roman family and the
state.[148]

Oppianicus' crime may have been extreme, but it expresses a persistent theme in the lives of Roman brothers. Dispute and difference generated dialogues about what brothers should and could do. The link between fraternal *pietas* and *consortium* was sustained both in the
practice of family life and in Roman moralizing about brothers. Literary
representations of two notorious brothers, Domitius Tullus and Domitius Lucanus, contemporaries of Pliny and Martial, depict the relationship between ideology and practice in the lives of Roman brothers. In a
letter to Fadius Rufus, Pliny lauds Domitius Tullus for the exemplary
use of his will to right a wrong that he and his brother, Domitius Lucanus, perpetrated a number of years earlier when they bilked Lucanus'
daughter out of an inheritance. In his will, Tullus restored to the woman
her rightful property.[149] While Pliny is quick to praise Tullus' will, he

[147] Cic. *Clu.* 31.

[148] Y. Thomas, "Parricidium I. Le père, la famille et la cité," *MEFRA* 93 (1981): 643–
715.

[149] Treggiari, *Roman Marriage*, 395–96.

seems fascinated by brothers' legal maneuvering.[150] Lucanus' daughter, Lucilla, had been made heir to his father-in-law's estate on the condition that her father emancipate her. This Lucanus did. His brother Tullus promptly adopted her.

> *Nam Curtilius Mancia perosus generum suum Domitium Lucanum (frater is Tulli) sub ea condicione filiam eius neptem suam instituerat heredem, si esset manu patris emissa. Emiserat pater, adoptaverat patruus, atque ita circum-scripto testamento consors frater in fratris potestatem emancipatam filiam adoptionis fraude revocaverat et quidem cum opibus amplissimis.*
>
> Because Curtilius Mancia hated his son-in-law Domitius Lucanus (the brother of Tullus), he made his granddaughter his heir on the condition that she would be free from her father's *manus*. Her father released her, her pater-nal uncle adopted her, and, so dodging the will, the partner-brother called his emancipated daughter back into the *potestas* of his brother by the cheat of adoption and indeed with the richest fortune. Pliny, *Ep.* 8.18.4

Ambiguity abounds in this description, and it relies on the inter-changeability of the brothers. It is not entirely clear which brother is which, and each is, in one way or another, also her father. The situation is reminiscent of Seneca *Controversia* 1.1, where a pair of brothers take turns adopting and disinheriting the son of one of them. Whereas the *controversia* debates the possibility of fraternal unity in shared parenting, in Pliny's letter, sharing a daughter does in fact cement the fraternal bond between the Domitii. Pliny marks the fraternal relationship, which is the basis of their shared role as father, with the term *consors*. This passage has been much discussed in the legal scholarship by those seeking to prove or refute the claim that *consortium* involved shared *patria po-testas*.[151] Without rehearsing the legal debate, suffice it to say that the Roman law of adoption precluded the possibility of two fathers sharing *potestas* while *consortium* makes no explicit provision for joint po-testas.[152] Moreover, if the brothers had shared *potestas*, Mancia's condi-

---

[150] The law acknowledged the possibility that uncles might not be benign or prudent: a paternal uncle was required to give security when, as *legitimus heres*, he reallocated the funds in his niece's estate, Scaev. [21 *Dig.*] D. 35.2.95.1.

[151] A textual variant in the passage seems to reflect the confusion over the interpretation of *potestas* relationships among the brothers and Lucilla. Some editions read *patris* for *fratris* in the phrase *in fratris potestatem*. This variant does not remove any of the ambi-guity, because the *pater* could be either the adoptive father or the natural father. All modern texts read *fratris*. See D. Kehoe, "Private and Imperial Management of Roman Estates in North Africa," *Law and History Review* 2, no. 2 (1984): 253 and n. 62; J. W. Tellegen, *The Roman Law of Succession in the Letters of Pliny the Younger*, 1:157, and "Was There a *Consortium* in Pliny's Letter VIII.18?" *RIDA* 23 (1980): 302–304, 310–11; Bretone, " 'Consortium' e 'communio,' " 212–13; Kunkel, "Ein unbeachtetes Zeugnis über das rö-mische *consortium*," 63–68; Talamanca, *Istituzioni di diritto Romano*, 127–29.

[152] Temporary adoptions were frowned upon, Paul. [11 *Quaest.*] D. 1.7.31–32.

tion would have been toothless. Unless he had stipulated that Lucilla be emancipated from both brothers, she would have remained in their joint *potestas*, and his odious son-in-law would have come into his fortune all the same.[153]

While it is possible that the brothers had formed a legal partnership joining their property, as Kehoe suggests,[154] such a hypothesis is not necessary. Pliny's usage of the term *consors* need not imply any legal status at all. It is, rather, metaphorical: the fraternal identification encoded in the term *consors* transcends the legal categories of *pater* and *potestas*.[155] *Consortium* represented a familiar social norm for brothers' roles in the family which, as we saw above, included shared responsibility for family members and shared economic interests. Pliny's choice of the term *consortium* to describe their machinations indicates just how broadly the notion of *consortium* was construed in Roman ideas about brothers' roles in the family. The Domitii are exceptional, if at all, for their adroit manipulation of the law to make a profit from fraternal *pietas*. The brothers grew rich from their holdings in Italy and North Africa, and from the marketing and manufacture of bricks.[156] All of these businesses seem to have been joint ventures.[157] Their public careers were as cooperative as their financial deals: they served together in the Batavian war of 70 C.E., they were praetorian legates in Africa ca. 71–72, consuls in the mid-seventies, and proconsuls in Africa by the late eighties.[158] Similar fraternal cooperation has been observed in classical Athens, where partible inheritance was also the rule and brothers worked the system to their advantage adopting several different strategies to make the most of their shared inheritance,[159] for example, sometimes when Athenian brothers

---

[153] Adoption: Gaius, *Inst.* 1.99, 2.137; Gellius, *NA* 5.19.9; see below pp. 65–66.

[154] Kehoe, "Roman Estates in North Africa," 253 and n. 62.

[155] For a similar rhetorical use of *consors*, see [Quint.] *Decl.* 320.4 with M. Winterbottom, ed., *The Minor Declamations Ascribed to Quintilian*, 481–82. Tellegen, *Law of Succession,* 1:158, writes that the term *consors frater* refers to the close bond between the brothers.

[156] Kehoe, "Roman Estates in North Africa," 252 and n. 55, 254–58, 260. For the Domitii's Italian property, see Martial 3.20.17.

[157] Pliny, *Ep.* 8.18.7 describes how they were adopted together by Domitius Afer, subsequently inherited his estate together, and then took the necessary legal steps to unite their property, the inheritances from Afer and Mancia, as well as their own acquisitions. The brothers' business interests probably also involved other relatives, friends, and slaves, in the kind of open and flexible system described by J. Andreau, "Activité financière et les liens de parenté en Italie romaine," in *Parenté et stratégies familiales dans l'antiquité romaine*, ed. J. Andreau and H. Bruhns, 501–526.

[158] Kehoe, "Roman Estates in North Africa," 254–57.

[159] For the following example, see Lane Fox, "Inheritance in the Greek World." On partible inheritance, see Harrison, *Law of Athens*, 1:131–32, 151. Cf. the law of Gortyn where children are the first heirs (4.31–43), then the brothers of the deceased (5.13–17); for

divided their property, they maintained a common household. When it came time to pay taxes, however, these coresident brothers could assert that they had divided their estate, thus obtaining a lower assessment. For these brothers, a division of the family property did not entail splitting up their shared household; it was a division on paper, but in practice the family stayed together.[160] The legal rules prescribing an equal division, then, might serve for formal legal purposes like tax assessment, but they did not determine the shape of families nor did they rule out strategies that define equality in different ways.[161] Just as Athenian brothers could use division or a joint household to their advantage, so the Domitii and other Roman brothers were not bound by legal categories but freely constructed their own interpretations of fraternal *pietas*. At Rome, a brother was not likely to be considered a rival for wealth and status. Having a brother presented Romans with an opportunity to experiment with a variety of inheritance and economic strategies under the umbrella of partible inheritance. The fraternal ingenuity of the Domitii was not lost on the Dorothy Parkers of the first century: these brothers so successfully exploited fraternal *pietas* that they are celebrated not only by Pliny but also in several epigrams by Martial, one of which offers insights into the psychology of such a fraternal *consortium*.

Martial compares the Domitii to Castor and Pollux. Castor and Pollux offer an apt model for the resolution of fraternal *pietas* and sibling rivalry. The fact that they are twins emphasizes the reciprocity between the brothers, and their perfect, eternal shared life enacts the essential principle of *consortium* as the financial cooperation of the Domitii expresses fraternal *pietas*.[162] But, if the Domitii were offered the same deal as the Castores—to share one eternal life—each would be so considerate of the

---

the text of the law of Gortyn, see R. Meiggs and D. Lewis, *A Selection of Greek Historical Inscriptions*, 94–95. See also Lacey, *Family in Classical Greece*, 125–31, 292, and Cooper, "The Family Farm," 163–64.

[160] Joint ownership need not imply a common household any more than division of property indicates a lack of solidarity among the brothers. See Harrison, *Law of Athens*, 1:239, 240, and Humphreys, *Family, Women and Death*, 2. In addition, brothers could have participated in legal joint ownership, which resembled *consortium*, in that all members owned all property *in toto*, not in shares, and each co-owner had control over all the property, for example, Demosthenes 36 *Phorm.* 8. It was also possible to have joint-ownership of some property while maintaining separate ownership of individual property, Lysias 32 *Diogeit.* 4.

[161] C. A. Cox, "Sibling Relationships in Classical Athens: Brother-Sister Ties," *Journal of Family History* 13 (1988): 391, somewhat overstates the importance of inheritance law in shaping fraternal relations; for similar assumptions about rivalry between Roman brothers, see Hallett, *Fathers and Daughters*, 195–97.

[162] Plutarch, *Mor.* 486B, cites them for their compatibility, which depended on their different talents: Castor excelled in running, Pollux in boxing.

other that they wouldn't be able to decide who would live first—it would
be an "after you . . ." kind of affair:

> Si, Lucane, tibi vel si tibi, Tulle, darentur
>   qualia Ledaei fata Lacones habent,
> nobilis haec esset pietatis rixa duobus,
>   quod pro fratre mori vellet uterque prior,
> diceret infernas et qui prior isset ad umbras:
>   'vive tuo, frater, tempore, vive meo.'

Lucanus, if the same fate was granted to you, or to you, Tullus, as the Laco-
nian sons of Leda had, you two would get into a fine wrangle about devotion and which of you would die for his brother first, and the one who went
to the infernal shades first would say: "live your own life, brother, and live
mine, too." Martial 1.36

The brothers' very determination to act on fraternal *pietas*, to share their
inheritance of immortality, reveals that their fraternal devotion is recur-
sive and paradoxical. Each brother's offer to sacrifice himself is mirrored
by his brother's equal and opposite offer, as the chiastic arrangement of
their names in the first line and of their words in the last line bracket the
poem with their reflection: *si, Lucane, tibi vel si tibi, Tulle, darentur . . .
vive tuo, frater, tempore, vive meo.* Yet this zealous devotion leads to
sibling rivalry, a brawl of pietas, *pietatis rixa*, as Martial puts it, in a
suitably oxymoronic phrase. Each rivals the other to be first at being last,
to assert himself as a devoted brother through his sacrifice of himself in
death. Because only one brother can be first to die, the rivalry necessarily
implies that the other brother has somehow failed in his devotion. Thus
the devotion is self-defeating, because it sets the brothers against each
other and because it leads them to compete selfishly for the privilege of
self-denial. And yet the rivalry also unites them in a shared ambition, that
is, to be the most devoted brother. Martial's play with the psychology of
fraternal devotion problematizes the fraternal *consortium*, finding in its
very equality and identity the potential for conflict. Roman brothers were
not, presumably, immune to sibling rivalry. The norms inherent in *consortium* both attest to the existence of fraternal rivalry and assert the
value of fraternal *pietas* in overcoming that rivalry.

While *consortium* pertained in its original, archaic form to the joint
ownership of inherited property, the concept was generalized to describe
the idealized cooperation of fraternal *pietas*. The practice of dividing
property among brothers, common in the Republican and early Imperial
eras, did not diminish the importance of *consortium* in the transmission
of property between generations. Inheritance was only the beginning of
brothers' responsibilities in the family, but it was a significant beginning
both because it could happen when the brothers were still young and

because the patterns embedded in inheritance influenced the continuing practice of fraternal *pietas*. After their father's death and once the brothers were independent adults, they could and did diversify the workings of their family life and finances. Fraternal *pietas* and the continuing influence of *consortium* inspired the various arrangements and motives, legal and otherwise, that characterized brothers' roles in the family. A brother, far from a competitor for wealth and status, was for the Romans a rare opportunity to exploit inheritance law and other legal institutions in order to advance their family's fortune. Legal rules provided one framework that structured the choices and priorities of Roman brothers, and the hypothetical cases from the *Digest* offer us insight into the interaction of ideals and reality in the practice of being a brother. Dispute was inevitable, but shared assumptions about fraternal *pietas* emphasized cooperation. The archaic *consortium* represented an idealizing image of fraternal *pietas* which guided brothers in navigating their financial and personal responsibilities within the family. Calling a brother *consors* was shorthand for ideas and expectations that informed the practice of being a brother at Rome. *Consortium* provided a basis for fraternal *pietas*, a standard against which to measure their cooperation or antagonism, and a means of mending their disputes. Fraternal cooperation should extend from familial matters outward to brothers' public life, as the careers of the Domitii illustrate, and inward to a reciprocal definition of self. The next two chapters will follow the implications of *consortium* in these two directions: Chapter 3 charts the exploitation of fraternal *pietas* in Roman politics, while Chapter 2 examines the intimate logic of fraternal *pietas*.

TWO

BETWEEN BROTHERS

Nunc tu germanu's pariter animo et corpore.
Now you are my brother equally in body and soul.
(Terence, *Adelphoe* 957)

IN THE denouement of Terence's *Adelphoe*, when the older pair of brothers have reconciled their differences, one says to the other, "now you are my brother equally in body and soul." Throughout the play, one brother, Demea, represents hardy, rustic values, while the other, Micio, enjoys a fancy-free bachelor's life of urbane conversation and fine wine. At the end, their differences are erased when Demea adopts his brother's lifestyle. If brothers could differ, Romans measured their differences against a belief that brothers were innately similar, identical in a way even when they weren't twins. Romans located the source of this identity in nature or what we would call their biological relationship. This is not to say that Romans had solved the nature-versus-nurture conundrum: they had not answered the question whether biology or culture played the more important role in kinship. But, Romans believed that biology mattered, that natural relationships grounded cultural and social expressions of kinship. The inborn similarity between brothers not only motivated fraternal *pietas* but it also served as a model for other close relationships among Roman men.

From a Roman perspective, brothers' biological kinship set their relationship apart; mortality rates, which made full, natural brothers somewhat uncommon, may also have contributed to the special status accorded the fraternal relationship.[1] The political advantage of having a brother may also have intensified the feeling among elite Romans that a brother was a valued asset. As a result, Romans ascribed fraternal qualities to other relationships, for example between friends or lovers, in which they recognized a comparable sense of identity: when a Roman wanted to single out a friend for special praise, he was likely to call him a brother, as Cicero did Atticus.[2] Roman men also called their male lovers

---

[1] Around half of Roman men would have lost their fathers by age twenty-five, three-quarters by thirty-two, see Saller, *Patriarchy*, 39.

[2] This radical notion of fraternity probably motivates the identification of citizens as brothers, descendants of a founding father so to speak, a notion that underlies my discus-

brothers, and Boswell has interpreted this expression of fraternity as an analogue for heterosexual marriage,[3] though there seems to be a crucial difference between Roman views of marriage and fraternity: being brothers was an indestructible, natural relationship, whereas marriage depended on the will of the partners. There were also fraternal social relationships: Varro recognized an etymological link between *frater* and a Greek cognate, *fratria*, a word used in his own time in Naples of brother-hoods, clubs, and fraternities.[4] Why was the fraternal relationship the preferred metaphor and model for close relationships among Roman men? This chapter suggests answers to this question through an investigation of the nature and symbolism of fraternal identity. The first section analyzes evidence for the Roman belief that kinship was rooted in biology and the consequences of this belief: how did Romans expect natural similarity to influence brothers' emotions and actions? Or, to reframe the nature / nurture issue, how did Roman ideas about natural kinship shape the concept of fraternal *pietas*? The devotion between brothers depended on the quintessential Roman family value *pietas*, that blend of sentiment and duty that Romans believed held their families together. Because fraternal *pietas* had natural priority for the Romans, brothers became a powerful symbol of unity, affection, and devotion among men. The fraternal relationship had important implications for Roman expressions of affection and their construction of male relationships. The second part of the chapter pursues these implications through an examination of literary representations of friends, lovers, and brothers. Often, when a Roman writer likens one relationship to another, he stops, as if becoming conscious of the conceptual leap, to remark on the similarities, giving a rationale for the comparison. Other times, the points of comparison and the overlaps are implicit, and are revealed only through an examination of historical and literary contexts. Through the Romans' own comparisons of brothers, friends, and lovers, we can identify the special place of brothers among male relationships in ancient Rome.

---

sion of brothers on the battlefield in Chapter 4. Cf. Plut. *Mor.* 479 B–C, where friendship is an imitation of natural fraternity.

[3] J. Boswell, *Same-Sex Unions in Early Modern Europe,* 53–107, with B. D. Shaw's review of Boswell, "A Groom of One's Own," *The New Republic,* Issue 4, no. 148 and 4, no. 149 (July 18 & 25, 1994): 33–41.

[4] Varro, *LL* 5.85, cf. Strabo 5.4.7 (246): πλεῖστα δ' ἴξνη τῆς Ἑλληνικῆς ἀγωγῆς ἐν- ταῦθα σώζεται, γυμνάσιά τε καὶ ἐφηβεῖα καὶ φρατρίαι καὶ ὀνόματα Ἑλληνικά, καίπερ ὄντων Ῥωμαίων, "the greatest number of traces of Greek culture are preserved there, gymnasia and ephebic training and fraternal organizations and Greek names, even if the people are Romans." See also J. Collart, *De Lingua Latina Livre V,* 134.

Biology and Identity

Roman expectations of fraternal *pietas* were grounded in the belief that natural kinship motivated brothers' behavior and attitudes. Their ideas about brothers are representative of broader assumptions about the nature of kinship. Marriage and adoption, which created legal kinship, existed alongside what we would call biological kinship. Although both law and practice accorded nearly the same rights and responsibilities to legal as to natural kin, Romans distinguished those who were related by blood and ascribed to them a deep sense of identity, and brothers were singled out as representatives of this natural similarity. Roman scholars like Nigidius Figulus, who wrote a *Commentarii Grammatici* in the mid-first century B.C.E. (probably earlier than Varro's *De Lingua Latina*),[5] explained fraternal identity through etymology:

> *'fratris' autem vocabulum P. Nigidius, homo inpense doctus, non minus arguto subtilique ἐτύμῳ interpretatur: "frater," inquit, "est dictus quasi 'fere alter.'"*
>
> P. Nigidius, an exceedingly learned man, clearly explains the word "brother" with a no less clever and precise etymology: a "frater" is nearly a second self. Gellius, *NA* 13.10.4[6]

This grammatical definition, glib as it may seem, captures the defining feature of the relationship between Roman brothers, namely, a similarity that for all intents and purposes constituted identity. The evidence for Roman notions of kinship arises from a variety of sources—theoretical discussions of kinship, comedy, rhetorical exercises, cases from the *Digest of Justinian*. A consistent pattern emerges from these diverse sources, a pattern that privileges the biological bond between brothers.

Terence's *Adelphoe* offers an apt starting point for considering Roman ideas about the natural basis of fraternal *pietas*. The play involves two sets of brothers, an older pair—Demea and Micio—and a younger pair, Demea's sons, Aeschines and Ctesipho. Throughout the play, Demea and Micio represent contrasting philosophies—thrift and indulgence—and the contrasts in their characters also come to life as they wrestle with the duties of fatherhood. Micio had adopted one of Demea's sons, Aschines, and was raising him indulgently, while Demea was bringing up Ctesipho with the discipline of poverty. In the second scene of the play, Demea and

---

[5] On Nigidius Figulus and his etymologies, see E. Rawson, *Intellectual Life in the Late Roman Republic*, 9, 122–24.

[6] This etymology is also reported in Festus p. 80L: *a Graeco dictus est* φρήτρη, *vel quod sit fere alter*, cf. *gram.* 171.

Micio go head to head on the methods of fathering. Demea keeps butting into his brother's relationship with his adopted son, aggressively and with much emotion. Why should he be so bent out of shape? We might explain his behavior as typical of the harsh paternal uncle, if Richard Saller hadn't argued so convincingly against this stereotype.[7] Moreover, why does his brother, Micio, and presumably also the audience, accept his emotional outburst as par for the course? To calm his brother, Micio reminds him that he gave his son Aeschines away in adoption; he says, *natura ut illi pater es, consiliis ego,* "you are his father by nature, I am his father by design."[8] Micio, Aeschines' legal father, bears the rights and responsibilities for his well-being. All the same, Micio accepts and almost expects Demea's continuing concern for his son, and he understands this concern as a consequence of the natural, or biological, relationship between father and son. This biological relationship endures despite changes in their legal relationship and despite the fact that they do not live together as a family. Natural ties similarly unite the younger pair of brothers, Aeschines and Ctesipho, even after Aeschines has been adopted out of Ctesipho's immediate family. The knotting and unraveling of the comic plot depends on their fraternal *pietas.*[9] Whatever the cultural translation from Terence's Greek models, his brothers played to Roman sentiments and expectations about kinship.[10] The original performance context also draws attention to the importance of natural kinship: the *Adelphoe* was staged at the funeral games of L. Aemilius Paullus, games sponsored by his sons, Q. Fabius Maximus and Scipio Aemilianus, who were renowned for their fraternal relationship even after each was adopted by a different father.

Adoption could create contexts in which the distinction between natural and legal kinship came to the fore. According to the legal sources, "nature" should regulate adoption: only those who are in the natural position of fathers and sons, that is, of an age to be father and son to each other, should forge an adoptive relationship.[11] The one apparent exception to this natural model is the provision that allows eunuchs to adopt, but it is in fact no exception, because adoption was designed for those who were unable to father their own sons. The legal sources advise those who already have children not to adopt more: to do so would endanger the financial security of both natural and adoptive children, because there

[7] R. Saller, "Roman Kinship," forthcoming in *The Roman Family in Italy,* ed. P. Weaver.

[8] Ter. *Ad.* 126.

[9] See, for example, Ter. *Ad.* 254–83.

[10] S. M. Goldberg, *Understanding Terence,* 23–29.

[11] Jav. [6 *ex Cassio*] *D.* 1.7.16. Age limits were even prescribed, Ulp. [26 *ad Sab.*] *D.* 1.7.15.2.

would be more children sharing the family property both during the father's lifetime and after his death as heirs.[12] Although adoptive and biological children had equal economic rights in the family, legal adoption created only a limited kind of kinship, not blood ties, *non ius sanguinis sed ius adgnationis*.[13] Adoption created a relationship between adoptive father and child, a relationship underwritten by the father's legal power, *potestas*. An adoptive child was temporarily related to the family of his adoptive father: relationships created by adoption lasted only so long as the adoptive father was alive,[14] quite in contrast to the lasting devotion between natural brothers who were adopted separately. The younger brothers in the *Adelphoe* are a case in point—their devotion drives the comic plot—as are Fabius and Scipio, who sponsored the staging of this play.[15]

Even more compelling evidence for the priority of biological fraternity can be found in legal discussions of slave brothers. The simple fact that Roman law used the same names for slave as for free brothers implies that kinship transcended civic status. In other words, being a brother was something essentially human or natural rather than a social or political right like citizenship. Several legal provisions regarding slave brothers not only recognized their kinship but even based certain rules on it. First, a slave could share financial resources with his free brother.[16] Second, in

---

[12] Eunuchs, Gaius [1 *Inst.*] D. 1.7.2.1–2, and advice against adopting more children, Ulp. [26 *ad Sab.*] D. 1.7.17.3.

[13] Paul. [35 *ad Ed.*] D. 1.7.23: the adopter's wife does not become his mother, though an adoptive son becomes brother to a natural daughter.

[14] Paul. [2 *ad Sab.*] D. 1.7.10. The jurists could draw fine distinctions: an emancipated son and adoptive son are not *fratres*, but an adoptive son is brother to a deceased son, Paul. [6 *Plaut.*] D. 38.10.5. Adoption created *filios familias* in an agnatic relationship with their adoptive father, Mod. [12 *Encycl.*] D. 38.10.4.10, Mod. [2 *Reg.*] D. 1.7.1. Similarly, the relationship between step-children was distinguished from that between natural siblings; for example, a text distinguishing possible, i.e. not incestual, marriage partners, says that step-children could marry, even if they shared a common brother from a new marriage between their parents, Papin. [4 *Resp.*] D. 23.2.34.2, cf. Gaius [11 *Prov. Ed.*] D. 23.2.17. While the child of the new marriage was brother to both his step-siblings, they remain unrelated. An adoptive child became a *suus heres* of his adoptive father through intestate succession with equal right to inherit just as any other *suus*, Ulp. [12 *ad Sab.*] D. 38.16.1.2. Cf. Gellius, *NA* 5.19.9, Ulp. [13 *ad Sab.*] D. 38.16.2.3. Adoptive children also shared the right to *bonorum possessio contra tabulas*, Ulp. [44 *ad Ed.*] D. 38.6.1.6, and Ulp. [40 *ad Ed.*] D. 37.4.8.13. See also Kaser, *Privatrecht*, 1:65–68, and S. Dixon, *The Roman Family*, 112.

[15] On the continuing relationship between Fabius and Scipio, see below Chap. 3, pp. 123–24.

[16] If a slave bought his freedom with money put up by his brother or father, it should be treated as his own money, Papin. [30 *Quaest.*] D. 40.1.19. On using the same terminology for slave and free brothers, Paul. [de grad.] D. 38.10.10.5. See also L. Betzig, "Roman Polygyny," *Ethnology and Sociobiology* 13 (1992): 326–39.

a discussion of agreements to manumit slaves, the jurist Papinian acknowledges that "thoughtful people recognize the natural affection between fathers and sons and among brothers as a basis for good faith in legal dealings," *placuit enim prudentioribus affectus rationem in bonae fidei iudiciis habendam.*[17] Third, slaves were exempted from testifying under torture against their brothers. And finally, consider the rules about selling groups of slaves, in particular, the rule that specifies why a group of slaves should not be separated. The Aedile's Edict gives two reasons, one economic, the other surprisingly sentimental. Slaves should be sold together when separating them would cause either great inconvenience, because they work together—for instance a troop of actors—or when separating them would cause an offense against familial sentiment, because they were close kin: parents, children, brothers, and married couples: *si separari non possint sine magno incommodo vel ad pietatis rationem offensam.*[18] The use of the term *pietas* implies that Romans thought that slaves experienced kinship with the same sentiment and duty that Romans idealized in their own relatives. The experience of kinship was thus not dependent on legal status or legal relationships: *pietas* was independent of the father's *potestas* over his family. Although slaves were treated as property in many legal transactions, Romans did recognize natural kinship among slaves and their potential for *pietas*. Kinship was not reduced to biology, but rather Romans saw natural relationships at the heart of kinship practices. Thus the legal sources show that kinship was considered a preexisting condition, if you will, and it transcended legal categories. From the legal sources, we move on to a more philosophical type of evidence, the theoretical discussions of kinship and friendship in Cicero's *De Amicitia* and in Book Nine of Valerius Maximus' *Factorum ac Dictorum Memorabilium.*

Both Cicero and Valerius compare the merits of kinship and friendship, both to the detriment of kinship. For Cicero, friendship and kinship were distinguished by *benevolentia*: *benevolentia* is the *sine qua non* of *amicitia*, whereas kinship could exist without it.[19] Similarly, in Valerius Maximus' discussion, friendship depended on constant devotion, whereas kinship could exist without emotional attachment.[20] Both au-

---

[17] Papin. [27 *Quaest.*] D. 17.1.54.*pr.*

[18] Ulp. [1 *Cur. Aed.*] D. 21.1.35, cf. Ulp. [2 *Cur. Aed.*] D. 21.1.38.14 and Paul [1 *Cur. Ed.*] D. 21.1.39. Similarly, one of the few circumstances in which a person under twenty-five years old could manumit a slave was if he wanted to manumit a natural daughter or son or brother or sister, Ulp. [6 *de Off. Procon.*] D. 40.2.11. For the exemption on testifying under torture, Ulp. [8 *de Off. Procons.*] D. 48.18.1.10.

[19] Cic. *Amic.* 19; cf. Catullus, Poem 76 with the comments of D. O. Ross, *Backgrounds to Augustan Poetry*, 9–12.

[20] Val. Max. 4.7. *praef.* For an anthropological discussion of the contrast between voluntary reciprocity of friendship and the mandatory reciprocity of kinship see Pitt-Rivers, "The

thors recognized the inevitability of kinship: as the old adage says, "you can't choose your relatives." And they both seem to be saying that the inevitable duty of kinship isn't necessarily motivated by affection. In other words, it appears that the two elements of *pietas*, sentiment and duty, can be separated, and as if kinship could be reduced to a skeleton of rights and responsibilities created by legal institutions such as adoption. The seemingly clear distinction between voluntary friendship and coercive kinship is complicated by the examples cited by each author. Cicero cites Fabius and Scipio as exemplary friends,[21] and Valerius invokes the metaphor of *consortium*, with its fraternal resonance, to describe the fair-weather friends of the tyrant Sardanapalus: they share "in a partnership of delights and pleasure," *in consortione deliciarum et luxuriae*. These friends stand in contrast to Orestes and Pylades, whose friendship, *sodalicium*, is tested by hardship.[22] *Consortio* is associated with the easy, potentially transient, aspect of friendship, the sharing of pleasure, whereas *sodalicium* represents enduring devotion. The allusion to kinship in *consortium*[23] chips away at the sugar coating of delights and pleasure that may conceal coercion imposed in an unequal friendship, such as, in this example, between a king and his subjects. The fraternal implications of the *consortium* metaphor reveal a paradox. On the one hand, kinship supplants *benevolentia*: like false friends, brothers stick together only because they must. Yet brothers could be the best of friends. In fact, the rhetorical opposition of friendship and kinship in both Cicero's and in Valerius' treatments leads to an incomplete appreciation of kinship. Friendship and kinship appear to be incompatible, because they are presented as alternatives. This opposition obscures the role of kinship in motivating both duty and affection. Cicero's explanation of moral sentiment in the *De Officiis* presents a fuller, more consistent view of *pietas* and its roots in natural kinship.[24] In the *De Officiis*, affection and personal relationships motivate *officium* not only within the family but also by analogy in the larger political community. The nuclear family at the heart of this system comprises several distinct relationships, those between husband and wife, parent and child, and sib-

Kith and the Kin," in *The Character of Kinship*, ed. J. R. Goody, 96–97, and, in general, M. Mauss, *The Gift Forms and Functions of Exchange in Archaic Societies*, trans. I. Cunnison.

[21] Cic. *Amic.* 69; also the Gracchi, *Amic.* 38–39, a somewhat more problemmatic example; see below Chapter 3, pp. 127–35.

[22] For the *topos* of adversity as the test of true friendship, see B. R. Nagle, *The Poetics of Exile*, 75–76, and H. B. Evans, *Publica Carmina*, 39–40.

[23] *Sodalicium* could also imply kinship, although Roman etymologies of *sodalis* do not recognize its connection with *suus*, for example, Festus, p. 383L. See E. Benveniste, *Le vocabulaire des institutions indo-européennes*, 1:328–32. On *sodalitates* H. S. Versnel, "Suodales," in *Lapis Satricanus*, ed. C. M. Stibbe, et al., 108–21.

[24] Cic. *Off.* 1.55–58.

lings; these relationships, though they can be isolated, all derive from the natural desire to procreate, which is, in Cicero's analysis, the first cause of these relationships.[25] Kinship generates goodwill and affection, which bind people together; a family's shared history, represented in graves and family cult, reinforces these emotional ties:

> *Sanguinis autem coniunctio et benevolentia devincit homines ⟨et⟩ caritate. Magnum est enim eadem habere monumenta maiorum, isdem uti sacris, sepulcra habere communia.*
> A blood tie binds men through goodwill and affection. For having the same monuments of your ancestors is important, and performing the same rituals and having shared tombs. Cic. *Off.* 1.54–55

Thus, kinship among married couples, parents and children, and among siblings attains special status by virtue of its position in the moral system.[26] Relationships among these people are not mere biological necessity, but are the basis for the affection and obligations that unite them.[27] Rather than a simple disjunction of nature and nurture, for the Romans, nature was implicated in nurture.

The implications of biological kinship between brothers can be explored through a brief examination of the usage of the adjective *germanus*. *Germanus* could be used to designate what we might call full brothers,[28] but more generally it simply emphasized biological kinship,

[25] *Prima societas in ipso coniugio est, proxima in liberis, deinde una domus, communia omnia; id autem est principium urbis et quasi seminarium rei publicae*, "the first partnership is in marriage itself, next among children, third within a single household where everything is shared; it is the foundation of the city, the seedbed of the state" (1.54). After the nuclear family, the next category, "fraternal relationships," are qualified as those among *consobrini* and *sobrini*, thus cousins. For *fratres patrueles* as *consobrini*, see Gaius, *Inst.* 3.10. Cf. Val. Max. 5.5.*praef.*, and Cic. *Inv.* 2.65 and 160–61, with E. Renier, *Étude sur l'histoire de la querela inofficiosi en droit romain*, 58–65.

[26] Val. Max. 5.6.*praef.*, ascribes to relationships between fathers and sons and brothers *artissimis sanguinis vinculis pietas*, "devotion with the tightest bonds of blood [kinship]." Cf. Val. Max. 5.5.*praef.*, where fraternal devotion corresponds to the father-son relationship: *Hanc caritatem proximus fraternae benivolentiae gradus excipit*, "the next degree of fraternal goodwill carries on this affection (i.e., that of father and son)." Law also recognized the special status of the nuclear family in its exemptions from testimony: relatives of the closest degree of kinship could not be compelled to testify against each other, Paul. [2 *ad Leg. Iul. et Pap.*] *D.* 22.5.4. The assumption that members of the nuclear family were in close contact could be exploited for other purposes, as for example the possibility raised in one of Martial's epigrams that an adulterous wife might claim she was visiting her mother, father, or brother when she was actually going to a tryst, e.g. *Ep.* 11.7.

[27] On numismatic evidence for *pietas* in the nuclear family, see M. Manson, "La *Pietas* et le Sentiment de L'enfance à Rome d'après les Monnaies," *Revue belge de Numismatique et de Sigillographie* 121 (1975): 26.

[28] *Germanus* is comparable to Greek ἀδελφός or κασίγνητος, which also designate blood brothers. On the relationship between ἀδελφός and φράτηρ see Benveniste, *Vocab-*

as in this late grammatical definition: *frater aut ex alia matre aut ex alio patre potest esse, germanus ex isdem parentibus sit necesse est,* "a *frater* can be born from a different mother or father, but a *germanus* must be of the same parents."[29] Real brothers were characterized by identity in birth or natural origins. For instance, Livy used *germanus* to contrast the relationship between T. Quinctius Flamininus and his brother with the more distant cousin relationship between Scipio Africanus and Nasica.[30] Cicero chastised Clodius for having greater allegiance to his brother-in-law than to his brother: *se fratrem uxoris tuae fratri tuo germano antelatum videbat,* "he [the brother-in-law] saw that your wife's brother was preferred to your own brother."[31] Word order and the repetition of the possessive adjective seem designed to draw attention to fraternal kinship. Even after a man's natural brother was adopted into another family, Romans continued to emphasize the biological link between brothers, as when Cicero identified Cn. Fannius as *frater germanus* of Q. Titinius.[32] The adjective *germanus* expressed not only natural identity but also, metaphorically, a similarity that depends on natural identity.[33] Things that are identical in physical form or in emotional or ethical qualities were thought to share a kind of kinship. For example, mountains with similar topography were considered brothers, as in Pliny's description of the ter-

---

ulaire Indo-européennes, 1:212–14, 221, 236, and Kretschmer, "Die griechische Benennung des Bruders," *Glotta* 2 (1910): 201–13.

[29] G. L. 7:521.1. Ancient definitions of *germanus* associate the word with natural growth and reproduction. Festus, p. 84L, derives *germani* from *germen,* giving a concrete image of the family tree: *germani, quasi eadem stirpe geniti,* "siblings, as if they were born from the same shoot." Where *stirps* suggests paternal descent, Servius, *A.* 5.412 (citing Varro) understands *germani* as children of the same mother, *de eadem genetrice.* On the semantic relationship between the *gigno/gens/germanus* words and the *nascor/natus/natura* group, see A. Ernout and A. Meillet, *Dictionnaire étymologique de la langue latine,* 272. *Germanus* could, all the same, be used of a half-sibling, for example, Enn. *Annales* Book 1, frag. 29.40 Skutsch, where Ilia addresses her sister Eurydice as *germana soror*; cf. Catullus 64.150, Verg. *A.* 5.412.

[30] For the Flaminini, Livy 35.10.8, cf. Vell. 2.8.2, and see below, Chapter 3, pp. 117–18.

[31] Cic. *Dom.* 118; Cicero implies that Clodius supported his brother-in-law, L. Pinarius Natta, over his brother Gaius to fill a vacancy among the Pontiffs, see D. R. Shackleton Bailey, *Back from Exile,* 88.

[32] Cic. *Ver.* 2.1.128. The relationship between Fannius and Titinius was obscured by the change of name resulting from adoption or because they were sons of the same mother but different fathers, see F. Münzer, *PWRE s.v.* "Titinius" 17. There is similar ambiguity in Cic. *Cluent.* 21. Cf. also Polybius' description of Q. Fabius Maximus Aemilianus as ἀδελφός to P. Cornelius Scipio Aemilianus (Polyb. 31.28.3), and see below Chapter 3, pp. 123–24.

[33] Pliny uses *germanitas* to convey the notion of similarity: wine from the same vat and vintage shares *germanitas* based on common origin, *NH* 14.59, and apples that grow in pairs are likewise united, *germanitatis cohaerentia et gemella, NH* 15.51, and cf. *NH* 6.2 where Pliny says that there is *germanitas concors* between the two Bosporoi, because they have the same physical features.

rain of Algeria: *quos Septem Fratres a simili altitudine appellant.*[34] In a further refinement, *germanus* came to mean genuine, as in "the real thing." Cicero describes Q. Caecilius Metellus Numidicus as *verum ac germanum Metellum,* suggesting that Numidicus was both related to the Metelli and was a real Metellus by his character, literally by his nature, that is both by birth and by character.[35] The quality of being genuine depended on and complemented natural kinship.

The various connotations of *germanus* circle around the biological identity that characterized the fraternal relationship for the Romans. Nigidius' etymology of *frater*, cited above, explicitly links brothers with the principle of identity, which is essential to *germanus*: despite its linguistic improbability, this etymology is, perhaps, so intuitively appealing because it identifies the essence of what it meant to be a *frater*, that is, an alter ego. Such fraternal identity could be most clearly represented by twins, as for example in the plot of Plautus' *Menaechmi*, where identical twin brothers, separated in their youth, overcome time, distance, and personality differences to restore their fraternal relationship.[36] One brother spends six years and all his money searching for his brother and cherishes affection for him, even when he is still unknown to him: *ego illum scio quam cordi sit carus meo,* "I know him, how dear he is to me."[37] These efforts link the brother's natural kinship with their emotional attachment to each other. Their reunion turns, ironically, on a case of mistaken identity. The twins must be able to recognize themselves, and each other, before they can be reunited.[38] Just before the twins discover each other, one brother's slave catches sight of the other and describes him to his master:

[Mes.]   *Speculum tuum . . . tuast imago. tam consimilest quam potest.*
[S. Men.] *Pol, profecto haud est dissimilis, meam quom formam noscito.*
[Mes.]   He's a mirror image of you, . . . he's so much like you.
[S. Men.] What do you know! The spit and image! I see my face in his!
Pl. *Men.* 1063–64

[34] Pliny, *NH* 5.18. Pomponius Mela, *Chorog.* 1.28–29, gives a similar explanation of why these mountains are called *fratres montes: quasi de industria in ordinem expositi ob numerum septem, ob similitudinem fratres nuncupantur.*

[35] Cic. *Verr.* 2.4.147. In Cicero, imitators of Thucydides boast that they are *germani, Orat.* 32; a paragon of Stoicism is *germanissimus Stoicus, Luc.* 132; Cicero confesses to Atticus that his own folly has made him *asinum germanum, Att.* 4.5.3.

[36] On ancient attitudes toward twins, see E. Stärk, *Die Menaechmi des Plautus und kein griechisches Original,* 147–53. Francesca Mencacci, *I fratelli amici,* came out too late for me to include.

[37] Plaut. *Men.* 246; the search, 232–49, 253–65; their happy reunion, 1113ff.

[38] E. W. Leach, "*Meam Quom Formam Noscito,*" *Arethusa* 2 (1969): 30–45.

Only when each Menaechmus recognizes his brother can he know himself; conversely, he knows himself only through identification with his brother. Finding each other, they re-create their fraternal identity. The physical likeness of the Menachemi and their reunion represent the natural identity that Romans expected to see, if not in brothers' faces then in their words and deeds.

One of the minor declamations attributed to Quintilian, *Declamatio* 321, dramatizes the biological source of this fraternal identity and its power to affect brothers.[39] The story begins with a familiar situation: two *fratres consortes* have divided their property because of some dispute, and one of them names as heir a friend, who happened to be a doctor. Subsequently, the brothers were reconciled. After dining at his brother's house, one brother suspected that he had been poisoned and sought a remedy from his friend the doctor. This brother then died. The surviving brother and the doctor each charged the other with murder. *Declamatio* 321 represents the brother's arguments in his own defense and in accusation of the doctor. He argues that greed motivated the doctor and claims that the circumstantial evidence points toward the doctor, not himself, making only a short rebuttal of the doctor's arguments.[40] The brother also explains why the prior dispute between himself and his brother does not constitute a motive for fratricide. Just because the brothers have once been at odds and have separated their estates, there is no reason to presume continued animosity. On the contrary, fraternal love is strong enough to renew affection and to foster reconciliation: *amabamus etiam in praeteritum, nec caritas fuit illa sed invicem satisfactio*, "we loved also in the past, and that was not just [renewed] esteem but mutual apologies."[41] The bulk of the brother's argument, however, relies on the assumption that a brother is less likely to commit fratricide than a friend is to murder, because the fraternal relationship is stronger and more ineradicable than friendship. "No one," he claims, "could fail to appreciate how much superior to a friend a brother ought to be," *neminem vestrum praeteriret quantum praeferri fratrem amico oporteret*.[42]

---

[39] This collection of rhetorical exercises is probably contemporaneous with or slightly later than the *Institutio Oratoria* of Quintilian, although their language and style does not preclude a date as much as a century later: M. Winterbottom, ed., *The Minor Declamations Ascribed to Quintilian*, xv. [Quint.] *Declamatio* 328, also concerns a case of fratricide; it is a father's defense of one of his sons who is accused of killing the other. The argument is based on the assumption that fratricide is unnatural and therefore impossible as well as morally unacceptable.

[40] Doctor's motives, *Decl.* 321.12–13, 16–19; circumstantial evidence, 20–27; rebuttal, 28.

[41] *Decl.* 321.14, with M. Winterbottom, ed., *The Minor Declamations Ascribed to Quintilian*, 486.

[42] *Decl.* 321.3.

The doctor's greed and self-interest are perceived as a threat to the integrity of his friendship with the deceased, whereas the fraternal relationship is not likely to be threatened by conflicting interests. The fraternal relationship was stronger because its driving affection was grounded in a natural, biological relationship. It is beyond morality, human nature, and beyond biology to kill a brother, because fratricide is tantamount to self-destruction:

> *Fratrem occisuro non succurrit communis uterus, non eadem causa vitae, non una primordia, non illa [consuetudo] quae alienos etiam ac nulla necessitudine inter se coniunctos componere et adstringere adfectibus potest consuetudo actae pariter infantiae, pueritiae studia, lusus tristia ioci? (8) Membra hercule inter se citius pugnaverint et si qua in nobis natura geminavit diversos ceperint adfectus. Nam quid est aliud fraternitas quam divisus spiritus et quae ad tuendos nos natura concessa sunt multiplicata? . . . (9) Huic necessitudini qui dare venenum potest non oculos effodiet suos, non manus in viscera sua armabit? Habet ergo hoc primum (ut parcissime dixerim) admirationem.*

Didn't their shared birth come to the aid of the man who is about to kill his brother, and the same source of life and the shared origins, the familiarity which is able to join in a close emotional bond even strangers who share no interdependence, doesn't the familiarity of shared childhood, boyhood education, joy, sadness, and games? (8) His very arms and legs would sooner fight amongst themselves and take on different conditions as if somehow our nature was divided within us. For what is brotherhood but one spirit distributed between two bodies and the propagation of those things that are granted by nature for our protection. . . . (9) A man who could give poison to someone so essential to his own survival, will he not strike out his own eyes, or turn his hand against his own heart? To say the least, I have the utmost astonishment at this. [Quint.] *Decl.* 321.7–9

The brother envisions fratricide as a battle between his arms and legs, an analogy which recalls the "natural" basis of fraternal *pietas*. As battling limbs are unnatural, so is fratricide, because it is self-destructive; a brother is, after all, a second self. In this sense, fratricide is reflexive. Like the body's limbs, brothers share a life force, *spiritus*, which this brother calls *fraternitas*.[43] Similarly, in the epigram about Bavius and his brother (quoted on the frontispiece) one breath quickens two bodies, *ut aiunt, corporibus geminis spiritus unus erat* .[44] The relationship between brothers was conceived as something at once natural and physical: its

---

[43] A similar illustration of the "natural" basis of fraternity occurs in Plut. *Mor.* 479 A–B where replacing a brother with a friend is like cutting off one's foot and using a wooden leg instead.

[44] Domitius Marsus, *Cicuta* 1.4.

intangible aspects were thought to be rooted in biological kinship and expressed in physical similarity. The strength of this kinship is most evident in the breach: the more dramatic the failure, the more strongly the imperative is asserted.

At least one Roman brother, Cicero, experienced fierce tensions between himself and his brother as just this sort of physical phenomenon. When Pompey and Caesar finally became open enemies, Cicero and his brother Quintus, like other politically active Romans, were faced with the unhappy dilemma of taking sides.[45] Even fraternal *pietas* could not keep the brothers together. Quintus, it appears, felt a stronger obligation to Caesar; his brother, after doing a fair stint of fence sitting, went to Greece with the Pompeians. Quintus and his son expressed hostility to Cicero both in letters to him and in conversations with others. Cicero experienced his brother's hostility as a physical affliction, illness, or torture, and he wished that one of them had never been born.[46] Only by not existing could he have escaped the pangs of his brother's rejection, because their relationship did not dissolve even after they ceased to behave like friends. Conversely, brothers who were unwillingly separated by death might suffer just as keenly. In Catullus' poems on his brother's death, their inborn identity is projected onto the construction of their emotional and spiritual relationship. The poet's fraternal devotion is located within the context of kinship when he describes the funeral ritual as family tradition and laments that his whole house, *domus*, is buried with his brother. The death of a brother separated two people who should not be separated: his brother was wrongfully taken from him, *heu miser indigne frater adempte mihi*.[47] Losing a brother more beloved than life itself, *vita frater amabilior*,[48] is losing a part of one's own life. This loss is poignantly evoked when the poet tells how he tried to talk with his brother's ashes, a futile attempt to sustain fraternal identity. Communication across the grave recurs in an epigram attributed to Seneca where the dead brother speaks to his surviving brothers of their mutual love—they vie to be the more loving ones.[49] Seneca's *Consolatio ad Polybium* also

---

[45] For a case study of Cicero and his brother, see below Chapter 3.

[46] Cic. *Att.* 11.9.3; cf. Cic. *Att.* 11.10.1 and *Att.* 11.9.2. Quintus' son continued to attack his uncle, *Att.* 11.5.4; 11.6.7; 11.8.2; 11.13.2; 11.15.2. See Shackleton Bailey, *Cicero*, 163–64, 179–80.

[47] Catullus 101.6; cf. Catullus 68.20–22, 92–94, with C. J. Fordyce, *Catullus*, 389. This refrain expresses the generic affiliation of the poetry and creates thematic links within and between the poems: his brother's death has made all his poetry into laments (65.12). The burial place of Catullus' brother is also associated with Troy, and Troy itself is a symbol of grief and loss in Poem 68, see C. J. Tuplin, "Catullus 68," *CQ* 31 (1981): 118.

[48] Catullus 65.10, cf. 101.4 for the attempt at communication across the grave.

[49] Epigram 49 = *Anth. Lat.* 441 in *Gli Epigrammi attribuiti a L. Anneo Seneca*, ed. C. Prato, cf. Hor. *Ep.* 1.14.6–8, and Ovid *Tr.* 1.7.17–18. For another perspective on the

elaborates the themes of fraternal identity, *pietas,* and their roles in the family. The death of Polybius' brother is figured as an attack on a most harmonious group, *concordissimam turbam,* and against a house chock full of the best young men, *tam bene stipatam optimorum adulescentium domum.*[50] Polybius and his brother were identically worthy of each other in life and fraternal *pietas* should continue to guide them in death. Out of *pietas,* his dead brother would not want to be a source of pain but of tender longing. In turn, *pietas* should direct Polybius' attention to his surviving brothers in whom he may find solace and for whom he should set an example. Polybius should eschew self-pitying grief as it does not serve *pietas*: his brother's *pietas* in life should convince him that his brother would feel it bitter if he tormented himself with grief. Instead, Seneca urges him to consider, philosophically, not just what his brother has lost in death but what he gained, namely freedom from the cares of this life. The logic of this argument depends on the assumption that his own happiness depends on his brother's, even after one has died. Such enduring devotion may exaggerate but it also conforms to the radical notion of identity shared by brothers. The emotional bond between brothers reconfigures their kinship, translating biological identity into empathy, which guides their behavior and decisions.

Romans understood kinship as an essentially natural, or what we would call biological, relationship. While other kinds of relationships, like friendship, depended on goodwill alone, kinship was the first source of both affection and duty. *Pietas,* the blend of sentiment and duty in kinship, transcended social class and legal categories. Even slaves were assumed to feel *pietas* and Romans were expected to respect the innate necessity of kinship even among men to whom they denied civil rights. Legal relationships, like those created by adoption, were meant to mimic natural kinship and took second place to the real thing. Paul Veyne has written, "the 'voice of blood' spoke very little in Rome,"[51] but the evidence considered here suggests otherwise. Romans did hear the voice of blood kinship and heeded it, even though it may not always have had an unambiguous message. Differences or distance between brothers was a cultural and rhetorical topos that exploited the tension inherent in the relationship between brothers who were both alike and yet separate individuals.[52] The reality of fraternal relationships could be more compli-

---

significance of family terms in general in Seneca, see M. Frank, "The Rhetorical Use of Family Terms in Seneca's *Oedipus* and *Phoenissae,*" *Phoenix* 49 (1995): 121–29.

[50] Sen. *Dial.* 11.3.4, cf.5.2–5, and 9.1–9.

[51] P. Veyne, "The Roman Empire," in *A History of Private Life I,* 17.

[52] E.g. Hor. *Ep.* 1.10.2–5, and 2.2.183–89. Cicero, *Sen.* 65, cites the brothers from Terence's *Adelphoe* as evidence that old age affects men variously. Elsewhere he wrote, men like wine, age differently: old age makes some sour and nasty while others retain their

cated than the idealized notions of *pietas* associated with natural kinship. At the end of Terence's *Adelphoe*, Demea exclaims, *nunc tu germanu's pariter animo et corpore*, "now you are my true brother equally in body and soul," rejoicing that he and his brother have finally found their natural similarity and brought it to life. Demea, the thrifty, harsh brother, has adopted the more liberal, urbane lifestyle of his brother Micio. Yet the path of true kinship, it seems, won't run true. In an aside, just after this exclamation, Demea adds, "I'll stab him with his own sword!" *suo sibi gladio hunc iugulo*,[53] as if to suggest that he was only pretending to be like his brother in order to manipulate the situation. Critics have been troubled by the contradictions in the characters of both brothers and the apparent insincerity of Demea's change of heart.[54] Assume that Demea is feigning *pietas*—his devotion aims to get the best of his brother. The final scenes of the *Adelphoe* raise the intriguing possibility that Romans could and did manipulate each other's assumptions about kinship. Since Romans expected brothers to be similar, assumed that kinship would motivate them to stick together—as the younger brothers in the *Adelphoe* do—then brothers could use these expectations to their own advantage against each other and against others. In an earlier scene, one of the younger brothers, Ctesipho, openly raises this issue with his brother, when he protests that he doesn't want to go on and on about how much he loves his brother, for fear that his brother will think he's insincere: *ah! vereor coram in os te laudare amplius, / ne id adsentandi mage quam quo habeam gratum facere existumes*, "I'm afraid to praise you excessively to your face, lest you suppose that I am doing it more for the sake of flattering [you] than because I am grateful." His brother dismisses his fears: *age, inepte, quasi nunc non norimu' nos inter nos*, "don't we know each other better than that?!"[55] Terence's audience would expect brothers to know each other well, but sometimes perhaps not well enough.

---

appeal. He also describes twin brothers who, although they are identical in appearance, have strikingly different lives and fortunes (*Div.* 2.90, refuting the powers of the Chaldaean prophets). Compare Livy's treatment of Aemulius and Numitor (1.3.10–11) and of Lucius and Arruns Tarquinius (1.46.4–9), and also Plutarch's characterization of the two Gracchi (*TG* 2–3). The twin sons of Antiope, Amphion and Zeuthas, are a traditional representation of the opposition between the contemplative or artistic life and the active or military life: Cic. *Rep.* 1.18.30; Verg. *E.* 2.23; Hor. *Ep.* 1.18.41, *Carm.* 3.11.2, *Ars* 394; Prop. 3.15.29, 43; Sen. *Her. F.* 916, *Ph.* 566 ff.; Ovid, *Met.* 6.101; Stat. *Silv.* 2.2.60 ff., *Theb.* 4.357 ff. The contrasting philosophies represented by these brothers were expressed perhaps most fully in Euripedes' lost *Antiope*.

[53] Ter. *Ad.* 957.

[54] E. Fantham, "*Hautontimorumenos* and *Adelphoe*: A Study of Fatherhood in Terence and Menander," *Latomus* 30 (1971): 970–98, esp. 988–90, and Goldberg, *Understanding Terence*, 211–19.

[55] Ter. *Ad.* 269–71.

Lovers and Brothers

Because natural kinship was thought to endow brothers with a special kind of identity and empathy, Romans distinguished them from other male relatives and friends. But if Romans gave pride of place to fraternal *pietas*, they also understood the fraternal relationship and its emotional identification in symbolic ways. Cousins, friends, and lovers could all be called *fratres*, signalling correspondences Romans saw among different male relationships.[56] Fraternal *pietas* was ascribed metaphorically to other relationships which, for the Romans, had a comparable kind of emotional intimacy and identification. But relationships between brothers, friends, and lovers overlap like imperfect analogies, sharing some qualities and diverging in other respects. This section explores both those areas of overlap and the contested ground at the margins of fraternity, places where fraternal ideology intersects with Roman ideas about sexuality, masculinity, and heroism. Because Romans identified brothers with natural kinship which transcended social categories, fraternal *pietas* could represent sentiments and desires that challenged the dominant political ideology. The following discussion begins by mapping out the overlapping relationships associated with brothers at Rome and moves to an analysis of two literary accounts which explore the varied symbolism of fraternity, the stories of Nisus and Euryalus and of the brothers Pandarus and Bitias in Vergil's *Aeneid* Book 9 and the vicissitudes of the trio, Encolpius, Ascyltus, and Giton in Petronius' *Satyricon*.

Romans described their friendships as fraternal to emphasize closeness and special devotion. During his exile, Ovid described his affection for his friends as brotherly, *ego dilexi fraterno more sodales*, "I loved my friends like brothers."[57] Similarly, when Cicero wanted to express his devotion to Atticus he wrote, *et nos ames et tibi persuadeas te a me fraterne amari*, "love me and believe that I love you like a brother," yet he also wrote in fraternal terms of Lentulus' son, who was surely not as close to him as Atticus. Affection could even make a true friend almost an alter ego, *tamquam alter idem*, according to Cicero, nearly a *frater, ut fere alter*.[58] Even in matters so close to the family as inheritance, friends could be assimilated to brothers through emotional ties, as a striking passage from the *Digest of Justinian* attests:

[56] In approaching this topic, I have drawn on the notion of homosociality from E. K. Sedgwick, *Between Men*. See also J. Boswell, *Same-Sex Unions in Premodern Europe*, 17–18, 64–87.

[57] Ovid, *Tr.* 1.3.65, cf. *Tr.* 4.8.11–12; only his wife was closer, *Tr.* 3.8.7–10, and 4.6.45.

[58] Cic. *Amic.* 80; devotion to Atticus, *Att.* 1.5.8; Lentulus' son, *Fam.* 12.14.8; see below, pp. 104–6, 108–9, 113–15.

Nemo dubitat recte ita heredem nuncupari posse 'hic mihi heres esto,' cum sit coram, qui ostenditur. Qui frater non est, si fraterna caritate diligitur, recte cum nomine suo sub appellatione fratris heres instituitur.

No one doubts that an heir can be properly named in this way 'let this man be my heir,' when it is clear who is indicated. He who is not a brother, if he is loved with brotherly affection, is named heir in his own name with the title of brother. Paul [4 *ad Vitel.*] *D. 28.5.59 pr.*-1

If someone called his heir "brother," when the heir was not really a brother, the will would still be valid, because Romans recognized that fraternal affection could exist between men who were not kin. A Roman could use his last will and testament to express brotherly devotion for a friend, as if making his friend one of the family by granting him a brother's privileged position in inheritance: recall that a brother was the preferred heir in traditional Roman inheritance practice.[59] John Boswell has interpreted this passage as a evidence that Romans used adoption by will to create a union between men analogous to heterosexual marriage.[60] The case above does not, however, need to involve adoption. The connotations of the expression *fraterna caritas* do not allow us to specify the nature of affection, but the usage of *caritas* only indirectly suggests a sexual relationship when it is used of spouses.[61] Literary parallels for the phrase *fraterna caritas* convey the respectful affection that Romans believed arose from natural kinship.[62] The case cited above, where a brotherly friend is named heir, seems to evoke Roman ideas of *consortium* which arose originally through natural kinship among brothers.[63] Adoption could not create what the Romans thought of as natural kinship and did not necessarily engender brotherly feeling. Similarly, as Boswell himself recognizes, the legal relationship between spouses was not primarily a vehicle for emotion. Although Romans did not believe that legal mechanisms could create fraternal affection, they certainly used legal institutions to acknowledge and embrace brotherly sentiment where it flourished among friends.

The extension of fraternal *pietas* to men who were not biological brothers may have resulted from the demographic shape of Roman soci-

[59] See above, Chapter 1, pp. 28–29.

[60] Boswell, *Same-Sex Unions*, 97–106; the passages from the *Digest* that he cites do not seem to support his interepretation, because the legal texts do not reveal the kind of intimacy between adoptive brothers.

[61] For spouses, e.g. Val. Max. 4.6 Ext. 2, and see *TLL s.v. caritas.*

[62] Of real brothers, Val. Max. 2.7.5 (see below Chapter 3, p. 95), 5.5.*praef.*, 5.5.2 and [Quint.] 321.14 (see above p. 72). In Livy, 37.56.7, the Rhodians describe their relationship with the city of Soli as characterized by *fraterna caritas* because both cities shared kinship (*germanitas*) with Argos.

[63] Cf. Arrangio-Ruiz, "Frammenti di Gaio," *PSI* 1182 (1935): 23 at n. 27. These inferences are influenced by a model of kinship relationships in which individual interests are balanced against family duties, see Pitt-Rivers, "Kith and Kin," esp. 101.

ety. Since barely half of Roman men would have had a real brother, the rest would have been likely to forge fraternal ties with other men of their same peer group or *aequales*, whether they were more distantly related, like cousins, or were simply friends. This fraternal intimacy was expressed and complicated through the connotations of the adjective *unanimus*. Bavius and his brother, in Domitius Marsus' epigram (cited on the frontispiece), are *unanimi* in sharing their worldly goods,[64] and a pair of slaves in Plautus' *Stichus* are so tight they even share a girlfriend: when she's with one of them, the other one enjoys her too.[65] An epitaph celebrates a wife who is not just *univira* but *unanima*, as are husband and wife at a moment of sexual intimacy in a Catullan poem.[66] Yet the same poet expresses the depth of his erotic devotion to a woman by comparing his emotions to a father's love for his sons and sons-in-law. Roman epigrams by Martial and Catullus lampoon sexual behavior with allusions to incest that conflate kinship and sexual roles—a lover can be *mater* or *frater*.[67] The intersections among what we might consider different kinds of love is striking: a father's love for his children is comparable to erotic passion; a wife's devotion to her husband matches the bonding between a pair of pals; all of them share the intense identification of *unanimi fratres*.

The potential blurring of distinctions between different kinds of intimacy created a context in which fraternal devotion attained special status. The correlation between brothers and lovers may somehow reflect the familial origins of fraternal *pietas*. As we saw in the preceding discussion of natural kinship, brothers stood alongside husbands and wives at the center of the Roman family, in the closest relationships which generated the strongest sense of *pietas*. A legal definition of marriage as a

[64] Sisters, like brothers, could be *unanimae*, as Dido's sister Anna is, Verg. *A.* 4.8.

[65] Plaut. *Stich.* 731–34, cf. Cic. *Amic.* 92, and *Cluent.* 46. Catullus' description of his friends as *unanimi* in poem 30.1 emphasizes Alfenus' betrayal and lack of unity. The sense of identification can even have political implications, as it does when Livy ascribes fraternal unity, *fraterna unanimitas*, to the brothers Eumenes and Attalus, who ruled together in Pergamum, (40.8.14), and see below Chapter 3, p. 125.

[66] Catullus 66.80, and cf. 72.4. Ringing what seems an odd change on this theme, Cicero says that Ser. Sulpicius Rufus embraces, *osculari*, the law like a daughter, *Mur.* 23. See also M. P. Vinson, "Parental Imagery in Catullus," *CJ* 85 (1989): 47–53.

[67] See, for example, Catullus 100, Martial 2.4, 3.88, 4.16, 8.81, 9.7, 10.65, 10.98, 12.20. I have discussed the overlapping of sexual and kinship identities in Catullus 100, *APAA* (1994) 203. The euphemistic use of *fratres* for male lovers corresponds to the use of *frater* and *soror* for male and female lovers, and assumes a correlation between lovers of the same sex and those of different sexes. In Martial's epigrams especially, and in the Circe episode in the *Satyricon* 126–32, the use of *frater* and *soror* (and other familial terms) implies that there is something wrong with the love affair, that the lovers are somehow mismatched or inappropriate for each other, as the Roman legal rules governing marriage between kin (a kind of incest taboo) indicate that sexual love between real kin was improper and unacceptable. See also the perceptive comments in Boswell, *Same-Sex Unions*, 67–71.

consortium omnis vitae suggests an implicit comparison between fraternal and conjugal relationships.[68] Like spouses, brothers shared a household. Domestic intimacy for spouses entails sexual intimacy, which is in
turn linked to the fraternal relationship and reflected in the euphemistic
usage of *frater* for lover. Calling a lover "brother" drew on Roman assumptions about the domestic and spiritual intimacy that was central to
the relationship between brothers. While Greek patterns assume an unequal pairing of an older and a younger partner, ἐραστής and ἐρώμενος,[69] Roman notions of homoerotic love reflect the "natural" identity of brothers, aptly enough when the lovers are physically alike (of the
same sex) and may engage in interchangeable sexual roles (both lovers
can be active and passive).

Although friends, brothers, and lovers could all be characterized as
fraternal, the sexual relationship between lovers distinguished them from
both friends and brothers. Unlike friends, lovers might live together in
the same household, giving new meaning to the fraternal *consortium*.
Unlike brothers, lovers would not bring their relationship into their public lives: brothers might exploit fraternal devotion to advance their political careers, but homoeroticism entailed political disabilities for Roman
men.[70] The public contexts that framed male relationships at Rome
added political coloring to different kinds of devotion. The Roman elite
who were politically active drew distinctions between different kinds of
fraternal relationships, specifically those that were erotic and those that
were not. In a society where intimacy between men could raise eye-
brows,[71] fraternal intimacy was a safe alternative, a positive paradigm
for men's love for each other. The identification between brothers could
metaphorically mask any inequality in lovers' sexual relationship; that is,
by calling themselves brothers, lovers avoided identifying themselves
with the passive sexual role that was considered unacceptable for Roman
men.[72] The fraternal relationship provided a socially acceptable form of

[68] Mod. [1 *Reg.*] D. 23.2.1. See also Boswell, *Same-Sex Unions*, 53–58, 99–100, and in
general 53–107.

[69] T. W. Richardson, "Homosexuality in the *Satyricon*," *C&M* 35 (1984): 105–27, observes two kinds of homosexual relationships in the *Satyricon*: one based on the Greek
"model," involving an older and a younger partner, ἐραστής and ἐρώμενος, and another
between peers, but does not describe the second kind as fraternal.

[70] A. Richlin, "Not before Homosexuality," *Journal of the History of Sexuality* 3
(1993): 523–73.

[71] A similar restriction on relationships between men exists in twentieth-century western
culture, where the notion of "heterosexual masculinity" has stigmatized same-sex relationships for fear that closeness might suggest homosexuality, see P. M. Nardi, "'Seamless
Souls,'" in *Men's Friendship*, 2.

[72] On the Roman distinction between passive and active male homoerotic behavior and
its social implications, see C. A. Williams, "Greek Love at Rome," *CQ* 45 (1995): 517–39.

male intimacy that complemented the cultural identification of *pater* and *patria*.[73] Fraternal *pietas* embodied the closeness of sexual union without the problematic implications of eroticism. Challenges to these social norms could exploit the overlap between "natural" and erotic fraternity to bring out contradictions in the logic of traditional Roman notions of power and status.

The battle narratives of *Aeneid 9* offer a traditional context for male relationships, especially for the analogous fraternal relationships among soldiers.[74] Vergil pairs two such relationships in a narrative that does more than simply glorify heroic fraternal *pietas*. *Aeneid 9* has two major episodes: the Trojans' night raid on the Latins followed by the Latins' day-time attack on the Trojan camp. Each episode features a pair of men: Nisus and Euryalus in the night raid, Pandarus and Bitias in the defense of the camp.[75] Epic heroes often come in pairs, as David Halperin has noted,[76] a hero and his friend in a relationship that is often unequal and is characterized by both fraternal and conjugal (or erotic) elements. These elements are isolated in the two pairs in *Aeneid 9*. Pandarus and Bitias are brothers; Nisus and Euryalus are, if not lovers, close friends whose intimacy is tinged with eroticism.[77] Parallels in the two episodes, in the characters' motivations and in Vergil's descriptions, generate an implicit comparison between the two pairs of men. Both pairs are stationed guarding the gate to the Trojan camp: both are exceptionally daring[78]—on their own initiative, Nisus and Euryalus undertake a mission to cross enemy lines and recall Aeneas; Pandarus and Bitias stand at the core of the Trojan defense when Turnus storms the camp. In both episodes, when one man is killed, the sight of his fallen comrade incites the survivor to fight back. Within this common framework, Vergil works variations that probe the complexities of fraternal *pietas* among soldiers.

[73] For the conflation of *patria* and *parentem*, Cic. *Att.* 9.9.2, and see also P. Veyne, "La famille et l'amour sous le haut-empire romain," *Annales ESC* 33 (1978): 37–38, 43.

[74] See below, Chapter 4, pp. 140–41, 149–56.

[75] P. R. Hardie, "Tales of Unity and Division in Imperial Latin Epic," in *Literary Responses to Civil Discord*, ed. J. H. Molyneux, 61, observes the parallelism of these episodes.

[76] D. Halperin, "Heroes and Their Pals," in *One Hundred Years of Homosexuality*, 75–87.

[77] In *Aeneid 9*, the relationship between Nisus and Euryalus has been interpreted as a reflection of Greek customs, of the ἐραστής and ἐρώμενος, the older lover and the beautiful young boy, see J. F. Makowski, "Nisus and Euryalus," *CJ* 85 (1989): 1–15, and S. Lilja, *Homosexuality in Republican and Augustan Rome*, 66–67. The prominence of Nisus' Greek patronymic, Hyrtacides, at the start of the second line of the episode (9.177), draws attention to Greek traditions. Their athletic performances in *Aeneid 5* recall the gymnasium as a site for courtship, while the night raid in *Aeneid 9* sets them in the literary tradition of Achilles and Patroclus, a hero and his "pal" who prove their love through military excellence.

[78] Giants, according to P. R. Hardie, *Virgil's Aeneid*, 143–46.

Through a contrast between familial and erotic fraternity, the two episodes show how love can both motivate and compromise heroism.[79] The contrast operates in a charged context, the military, in which the mere intimation of sexuality evoked anxiety in the Romans.[80] The two episodes in *Aeneid 9* resolve tensions surrounding the erotic potential of male intimacy, privileging what Romans saw as natural fraternity as an acceptable paradigm for friendship. Taking the two episodes together also mitigates criticism of the erotic relationship between Nisus and Euryalus because it sets their heroism in an honored context of Roman military valor.

Differences in Vergil's treatment of the two pairs arise at critical moments in each episode. First impressions are telling: inequality is apparent in the first scene between Nisus and Euryalus, whereas the description of Pandarus and Bitias emphasizes equality. Although they share the same passion, *unus amor*, Nisus is introduced first, and Euryalus follows as his companion, *iuxta comes*.[81] Nisus takes the initiative in the mission to recall Aeneas; Euryalus responds with insecurity, not about his own courage, but about their relationship: does Nisus really want him to go along? how could he let Nisus go alone? Euryalus' insecurity conveys the changeability of erotic passions and shows that his heroic ambitions are intimately bound up with his desire to sustain his friendship with Nisus. In contrast, when Pandarus and Bitias are introduced, their names appear together. A simile comparing them to tall oaks refers to them as twins, *geminae*.[82] The oaks are also described as unshorn, *intonsa*, a word that is often used of young men to indicate youth, the time before men shave

---

[79] The Nisus and Euryalus episode has been read as a fable about corrupt heroism, see B. Pavlock, "Epic and Tragedy in Vergil's Nisus and Euryalus Episode," *TAPA* 115 (1985) 207–24.

[80] D. Dalla, *Ubi venus mutatur*, 55ff.

[81] Verg. *A.* 9.176–200, *unus amor*, 9.182, *iuxta comes*, 9.179.

[82] Verg. *A.* 9.677–82, and their names together, 9.672. Servius explains twin, *geminae*, in this simile as meaning not two, as in a pair, but emphasizing the similarity between them, as in identical twins, a brace of oaks rising to the same height. This image of trees as siblings resonates with an episode at the beginning of Book 9, when the Trojans' ships escape from Turnus and are transformed into ocean nymphs, 9.77–122. The ships are identified through their origins as trees on Mount Ida, whose patron, the Magna Mater, *genetrix Berecyntia*, intercedes with her son Jupiter to save them. The interchange emphasizes parent-child devotion and the power that should be accorded to a parent's love: the repetition of *genetrix*, 9.82, 94, 117; the goddess's address to Jupiter begins, *da, nate, petenti, / quod tua cara parens domito te poscit Olympo*, "grant, son, to your mother what your dear parent asks of you, since you have conquered Olympus," 9.83–84. The goddess's care for the trees is associated with her love as a parent, suggesting a metaphorical kinship among trees. When Turnus tells the Trojans to go back to their singing and dancing, that the goddess of mother Ida, *Berecyntia Matris Idaeae*, is calling them, it almost seems as if they share kinship with the trees that come from Mount Ida, 9.617–20.

their cheeks, when they let their hair grow long. The same adjective is used of Euryalus' cheeks, as a sign of his youth and beauty.[83] For Pandarus and Bitias, *intonsa* describes lush unrestricted growth, like a young man's long beautiful hair, and emphasizes their force and freedom. For Euryalus, it describes an attractive lack of growth, the lack of hair that makes young men sexually desirable. Euryalus' smooth cheeks are a sign of his beauty and remind us of the unequal love it inspires. Between the brothers, physical similarity has implications for their heroism: they are equally devoted to their duty to defend the camp. They stand symmetrically to the left and right of the gate, and are united in its defense: Turnus is said to lead the charge: *Dardaniam ruit ad portam fratresque superbos*, "he rushed against the Dardanian gate and the proud brothers," as if their fraternal solidarity stood not just literally for the Trojan forces.[84] They exert themselves equally in fighting on behalf of the Trojans whereas Nisus and Euryalus are unequally motivated by an ambiguous mix of martial and erotic passion, perhaps in an ironic version of the *militia amoris*.

Though the outcome is the same for both pairs of men—they all die—Vergil's narrative focuses on different aspects of the experience of love and heroism. When Nisus discovers that Euryalus has been trapped by the Volscan cavalry, he hides in the trees and takes potshots at the enemy. Only when the Volscans move to kill Euryalus does he come forward hoping to sacrifice himself and save his friend. Nisus' last words, *tantum infelicem nimium dilexit amicum*, "he only loved his unlucky friend too much," could apply to either or both of them, implying that their love for each other motivated their martial boldness.[85] This implication recalls Vergil's earlier description of their shared passion: *his unus amor erat pariterque in bella ruebant*, "they shared a single love and charged side by side into battle." Battle rage and passion are indistinguishable in this friendship, as their death affirms. Euryalus' death is amplified with a simile—his collapsing body is like a languishing bloom—an image of pastoral eroticism that shifts the focus from battle to intimacy. Nisus and Euryalus begin by striving for glory and end up losing the love that unites them in this pursuit: the episode closes as Nisus falls dead on top of Euryalus' corpse in a peaceful embrace.[86]

Pandarus reacts instantly to his brother's death, closing the gate to the camp and pursuing his brother's killer, Turnus. Like Nisus, Pandarus is motivated by the loss of a loved one—he is wild with anger, *demens*, and *mortis fraternae fervidus ira*—but unlike Nisus, he does not seek to die

---

[83] Euryalus' cheeks, Verg. *A*. 9.181, and the oaks, 9.681.

[84] Verg. *A*. 9.695.

[85] Nisus' last words, Verg. *A*. 9.430; Nisus in the trees, 9.399–419; shared passion 9.182.

[86] Embrace, Verg. *A*. 9.444–45, and the simile 9.433–37.

with him.[87] When Pandarus tries to kill Turnus, he is thwarted by Juno, who turns his spear aside and allows Turnus to kill him instead. In a sense, Pandarus is not responsible for the failure, his heroism is untouched. Juno's intervention far from diminishing Pandarus' heroism elevates it; his death is not some erotic corollary of heroism. It is another kind of passion, the dedication that inspires a heroic disregard for the unpredictability of outcomes. The earth itself grieves when these brothers die, as if their kinship and the heroism it inspired were part of the natural order of the world.[88]

Just after Nisus and Euryalus die, Vergil interrupts the narrative to hail the pair, calling them blessed—*fortunati ambo*—and promising them lasting fame, if his song has any power.[89] How are we to understand the apparent whitewashing of their questionable sexuality and its tragic consequences? The qualifying condition, *si quid mea carmina possunt*, "if my song is capable of anything,"[90] may suggest artistic humility, but it also cannot help undermining the promise of lasting memory. If poetry fails, then how will they be remembered? Nisus and Euryalus are renowned for the tragic story of their love and failed heroism—not for any deed they accomplished that helped the Trojans.[91] On the other hand, Pandarus and Bitias and their valiant defense of the gate are memorable, even though they are just two of Turnus' many victims. Turnus remembers, at least, and reminds us. When he is persuading the Latins to renew the war and he wants to prove his merit as a fighter, he mentions by name only Pandarus and Bitias as examples of his victims.[92] These brothers are worthy witnesses to his might because they were worthy opponents in battle. The brothers' deaths earn them the lasting memory that the poet promises to Nisus and Euryalus.

In both pairs, we can see the power of love between soldiers, power to inspire heroism. The story of Nisus and Euryalus emphasizes the passionate experience of love and lost love; whereas, in the case of Pandarus and Bitias, the brothers' love ends in heroic actions for the sake of the community. The story of the lovers reflects Greek literary motifs, like Achilles' love for Patroclus. The brothers' heroism recalls traditional

---

[87] *Demens,* Verg. *A.* 9.728, and *fervidus,* 9.736; Juno's intervention, 9.745–48.

[88] When Bitias falls, the earth moans as it does when a breakwater collapses into the sea, Verg. *A.* 9.708–16, and Pandarus' death, 9.752–55.

[89] Verg. *A.* 9.446–49.

[90] Verg. *A.* 9.446.

[91] Ovid's allusion to Nisus and Euryalus, *Tr.* 1.5.23–24, suggests that he read the passage this way, recognizing that Nisus' glory arises primarily from his devotion to his lover: *si non Euryalus Rutulos cecidisset in hostes, / Hyrtacidae Nisi gloria nulla foret,* "if Euryalus had not died among the Rutilian enemy, there would be no fame for Nisus the son of Hyrtacides."

[92] Verg. *A.* 11.396.

paradigms of Roman martial valor, like the Scipios. Congruities between fraternal and erotic devotion tend to blur distinctions that would lead Romans to condemn the one and to honor the other. In both episodes, motives attributed to the heroes draw on correspondences between brothers and lovers. The brothers' love and valor attains significance by comparison with the ambiguous passion and heroism of Nisus and Euryalus. Conversely, by suggesting a correlation between lovers and brothers, Vergil offsets the negative connotations of an erotic relationship between soldiers. References to brothers and *pietas* recur throughout *Aeneid 9*, raising the fraternal relationship as a backdrop for the larger movements in the action. The names, Remus and Remulus, reminiscent of the foundation myth, occur more often in this book than in any other book of the *Aeneid*.[93] Euryalus' mother is a recurring symbol of *pietas*, which contributes to the fraternal relationship among the soldiers. At Euryalus' request, Ascanius promises to care for her as if she were his own mother, and her grief at Euryalus' death affects the whole army: she begs them to kill her in the name of *pietas*, as if this mother/son relationship embraced the whole army in a broader fraternal *pietas*.[94] Love for a brother, for a lover, and for a fellow soldier are commensurate in their power to inspire devotion, which is manifest in a willingness to sacrifice oneself in battle. The devotion of soldiers who die together matches the fraternal *pietas* and love that echo in laments for a dead brother, such as Catullus' poems and Cicero's laments from exile. A shared death commemorates the intimate devotion among lovers, brothers, and soldiers alike.

Vergil's story of these devoted young men explores the passionate attachments between soldiers, and the power of these emotions to inspire heroism. Roman tradition glorifies martial valor, so we would expect nothing less from the fighting men in an epic of Rome's founding. It may not be surprising to find in Petronius' *Satyricon* different intersections of military roles, fraternal *pietas*, and eroticism. The trio of main characters, Encolpius, Ascyltus, and Giton, routinely refer to each other as *frater* and expect their relationships to conform to the norms of fraternal conduct. But conventions of brotherhood are invoked and undermined revealing the insubstantiality of the bonds between them. These brothers have problems similar to those of Bavius and his brother, in the Domitius Marsus' epigram: their fraternal bliss is disrupted by sexual jealousy and they start a tawdry quarrel, which ends in a violent confrontation, a parody of martial courage. The roles and emotions that these three lovers assume are oriented around fraternal relationships both in the family and

---

[93] *Remo cum fratre*, Verg. *A.* 1.292, and a Rutulian Remus 9.330; Remulus of Tibur 9.360, and a Rutulian Remulus, 9.593, 633; a third Remulus appears at 11.636.
[94] Verg. *A.* 9.493.

among soldiers. Their abuse and misappropriation of the norms of brotherly love recall the sources and the parameters of fraternal *pietas*.

When their sexual jealousy threatens to turn violent, Encolpius and Ascyltus decide to divide their shared household: *hanc tam praecipitem divisionem libido faciebat*, "desire caused this so sudden division."[95] Encolpius resents Ascyltus' sexual involvement with Giton. He wants to end his fraternal relationship with Ascyltus because it threatens his relationship with Giton, so he asks Ascyltus to move out, admitting:

> "*Ascylte,*" inquam, "*intellego nobis convenire non posse. Itaque communes sarcinulas partiamur ac paupertatem nostram privatis quaestibus temptemus expellere.*"
> "I know we can't settle this," I said, "so let's split up our junk and on our own earnings try to keep the wolf from the door." Petr. 10.4

Their household consists of shared baggage, *communes sarcinulas*, itself suggestive of the shared mess among soldiers.[96] In the end, these brothers postpone their separation until, after the dinner at Trimalchio's, jealousy flares up again causing another crisis over dividing the fraternal estate. When Encolpius, wielding a sword, catches Ascyltus in bed with Giton, Ascyltus gathers his belongings saying, *age . . . nunc et puerum dividamus*, "ok, now let's divide the boy, too." Encolpius thinks he's joking,

> *At ille gladium parricidali manu strinxit et, "non frueris," inquit, "hac praeda super quam solus incumbis. Partem meam necesse est vel hoc gladio contemptus abscindam."*
> But he drew his sword with a kin-killing hand and said, "you won't enjoy this prize that you alone are throwing yourself on. I will have my share or I'll lop it right off with this sword!" Petr. 80.1

The description of his hand as "kin-killing," *parricidiali manu*, explicitly compares their relationship to kinship. Ascyltus' intention to divide Giton is a parody of brothers' division of familial property that shows the absurdity of such a division: separating brothers' property is as extreme and futile as slicing a human being in half so that two people can share him.

Giton intervenes, begging his brothers not to turn their cheap hotel room into Thebes, not to pollute the shrine of their affection. He then offers to sacrifice himself and take the blame for destroying their sacred friendship. The description of their relationships as a "well-known shrine of intimacy" and a "rite of friendship"—*familiaritatis clarissimae sacra* and *amicitiae sacramentum*—equates their household and their fraternal

---

[95] Petr. 10.7.

[96] *Sarcinula* is used in a similar context of military and erotic adventure in Catullus 28.2.

devotion with the rituals and sanctity of family cult.⁹⁷ These descriptions along with reference to Thebes—where a pair of real brothers killed each other in battle—establishes an identification between these lovers and brothers in a real family.⁹⁸ The rivalry between Ascyltus and Encolpius has violated a relationship as sacred as kinship, and their willingness to shed blood, and specifically Giton's willingness to die to save this relationship, demonstrates that their devotion is as strong as a bond of blood. Like soldiers, they attempt to resolve their conflict through violence, but the conflict itself arises from a most unmilitary and unfamilial sentiment—sexual jealousy.

After Ascyltus threatens to slice up Giton, Encolpius proposes that Giton be allowed to choose which brother he wants to stay with him. Encolpius expects Giton to choose him. He trusts Giton's devotion to him because he believes that living together has forged a bond between them that is tantamount to kinship: *ego qui vetustissimam consuetudinem putabam in sanguinis pignus transisse, nihil timui*, "I who expect that our long-standing intimacy has been transformed into a blood tie, I have nothing to fear."⁹⁹ Domestic and sexual intimacy merge in their lifestyle. Encolpius and Giton have shared a menage that is not unlike the shared household that was associated with *consortium*. Encolpius expects Giton to feel an appropriately fraternal sense of obligation or *pietas*, but he is disappointed when Giton chooses Ascyltus.¹⁰⁰ The devotion among the brothers in the *Satyricon* has an erotic dimension, which could be considered acceptable, though undesirable, in terms of Roman ideology. While the lifestyle of lovers who live together may closely resemble that of real brothers, their social circumstances and society's judgment of them could diverge. These are not brothers in a respectable Roman family who jointly manage their ancestral property. Rather Giton—his body and his affections—is the fraternal property. Only a slave or a lower-class man would identify himself with such a family. The *consortium*-based ideal reflects the preoccupations of upper-class Romans who were concerned with sustaining family wealth from generation to generation and who competed for political and social laurels. In emulation, or perhaps in parody of the upper classes, these lower-class lovers

⁹⁷ Petr. 80.4, and *clarissimae sacra*, 80.3.
⁹⁸ On Statius' treatment of the Theban brothers, see below, Chapter 5, pp. 182–86.
⁹⁹ Petr. 80.6.
¹⁰⁰ Petr. 80.6–7, cf. 81.1–4. Later in the story, *consortium* is invoked explicitly as a metaphor for a friendship involving Encolpius, Giton, and Eumolpus; this friendship is based on shared literary interests. When Encolpius and Giton are about to die, Encolpius pleads with Eumolpus invoking their partnership: *miserere . . . morientium, id est, pro consortio studiorum commoda manum*, "have pity on us, we're dying, help us in the name of the partnership of our studies," 101.2. Encoplius hopes that Eumolpus will feel if not brotherly affection then at least the duty to save them.

define themselves as a family of brothers and also toy with the role of soldiers. When Encolpius sets out armed to take revenge on Ascyltus, he is mistaken for a soldier by a real soldier who leaves him disarmed and despoiled, revealing the fragility of his identity.[101] Like the pretense of military identity, the use of *frater* for lover is euphemistic, concealing the socially unacceptable erotic component of their relationships and at the same time mocking socially acceptable behavior by suggesting deviant applications of these norms.

The lovers' quarrel ends with a pair of elegiac poems that distinguish real kinship from the pretended fraternity among Ascyltus, Encolpius, and Giton. The first epigram, which is about fair-weather friends, reiterates the comparison between friendship (which can be dissolved) and kinship (which is permanent). Usually this theme is invoked to praise friends who remain loyal even in hard times; this epigram focuses on the calculating sort of friends who run away when things take a turn for the worse. The second epigram compares characters in a book to actors on the stage.[102] It begins with a cast of characters—father, son, rich man—and ends with the assertion that all roles provide only a temporary identity, a disguise for one's real identity.

> Nomen amicitiae sic, quatenus expedit, haeret;
>> Calculus in tabula mobile ducit opus.
> Dum fortuna manet, vultum servatis, amici,
>> Cum cecidit, turpi vertitis ora fuga.

The name of friendship persists so long as it is profitable; a pebble on the counting board does a changeable job. While good luck lasts, you keep your appearance, friend, but when fortune has faltered, you turn away in shameful flight.

> Grex agit in scena mimum: pater ille vocatur,
>> Filius hic, nomen divitis ille tenet.
> Mox ubi ridendas inclusit pagina partes,
>> Vera redit facies, assimulata perit.

The troop [of actors] acts a farce on stage: that one is called "Father," this one "Son," and that one takes the role of "Dives." Soon when the book has closed on the laughable roles, the true face returns, and the contrived vanishes. Petr. 80.9[103]

These two epigrams draw attention to the instability of the metaphors in the preceding scene in which the characters divided up their property like kinsmen splitting an inheritance. Looking back at the scene through the

[101] Petr. 81.6–82.4.

[102] On role-playing in the *Satyricon*, see, in general, N. W. Slater, *Reading Petronius*.

[103] For the accounding metaphor in line 2, the reading *Dum* in line 3, and of *pagina* in line 7, see E. Courtney, *The Poems of Petronius*, 23–24.

second epigram, the characters' division of property seems to be a kind of play-acting in which the lovers take on the roles of brothers and substitute the name *frater* for lover, as if the role of brother could be slipped on and off at will. The first epigram, which sets the permanence of kinship against the changeability of friendship, invalidates the fraternal metaphor or role-playing of the preceding scene. Friends can only play at being brothers; their relationship does not have the security of fraternal *pietas*.

The intersection of fraternal and erotic love in literary depictions of male friendships reveals ambiguities in the nature of fraternal love, ambiguities that challenged Roman stereotypes about masculinity. In Roman society, homoeroticism was often interpreted as a threat to socially acceptable roles. The idealized Roman man was a hardy soldier-farmer whose sexuality was defined through his active role in domination and penetration. Sexual intimacy between men required one partner to take an inferior even shameful role in terms of Roman masculinity. To avoid this predicament, the Romans turned to the fraternal relationship as a model for the emotional intimacy in all kinds of men's friendships. Brotherly devotion provided an overarching structure for a range emotions and behavior—from verbal endearment to sexual intercourse.[104] While fraternal intimacy lacked explicit sexual content, the closeness expected of brothers was thought commensurate with the bond between lovers. Thus, fraternal *pietas* could reconcile a potential ideological rift between intimacy in male friendship and the appearance of unmanly weakness.

The association of lovers and brothers relied on a common element, the intimate devotion in which both relationships are grounded. The Romans understood this intimate devotion as a consequence of brothers' identification with each other. Brothers, like lovers, share their whole lives, not only in the mundane sense of the family *consortium* but also through their emotional experiences. At one time in the Roman past, the legal institution of *consortium* formalized the fraternal relationship. Later, when the institution had become obsolete, Romans still felt that the natural bond of kinship which not only entailed duty but more importantly created a spiritual identity between brothers, a sense of empathy that motivated *pietas*. The emotional intimacy between brothers was comparable to that between friends, or lovers. But because brothers were united in kinship, their bond was stronger, unbreakable, in fact, for better or for worse. Brothers were held up as models of masculine intimacy, as close as lovers, but more in line with traditional male roles such as soldier

---

[104] For such a range of behaviors in male friendships compare K. V. Hansen, " 'Our Eyes Behold Each Other,' " in *Men's Friendship*, ed. P. M. Nardi, 35–58.

and statesman. In Cicero's *De Officiis*, family ties ground public morality. Society is conceived as a group of families that are naturally kin to one another. It is no great leap to move from real to analogous kinship among citizens. In the hierarchy of blood kinship, the relationship between brothers was closely bound to marriage, a cradle of kinship; likewise, in society, fraternal *pietas* generated a paradigm for the duties and devotion that citizens owed to each other.

THREE

IN THE FORUM

P. Rutilius morbo levi impeditus nuntiata fratris repulsa in
consulatus petitione ilico expiravit.
P. Rutilius was feeling a bit unwell, but when he heard
about his brother's defeat in his candidacy for the
consulship, he dropped dead there and then.
(Pliny, *NH* 7.122)

WHILE a brother's electoral defeat might not have affected all Romans so drastically as it did Rutilius, his reaction illustrates, for Pliny as for us, the force of fraternal *pietas* in Roman politics.[1] The forum was the setting for politics at Rome, for speeches and canvassing, a place where reputations were made and tested. When Roman brothers pursued political careers, they brought their relationship into this public arena. The importance of the family in Roman politics has long been recognized and documented in prosopographical studies. This chapter, by analyzing the methods and successes of brothers in Roman politics, offers insight into the complexities of familial politics. At Rome, as in many modern societies, an individual's private life could be a factor in his political career. Having a brother entailed certain duties in a man's public life and offered corresponding advantages.[2] Building on the example of Cicero's and his brother's cooperation in politics, this chapter examines more generally the strategies Roman brothers used to advance their political careers. Fraternal cooperation at home carried over into the forum, where the ideals based in *consortium* fostered cooperation between brothers as they pursued their own ambitions in the changing landscape of Roman politics. The cooperative ideal of fraternal *pietas* offered brothers practical advantages in

[1] On the date of Rupilius' candidacy, see F. X. Ryan, "The Praetorship and Consular Candidacy of L. Rupilius," *CQ* 45 (1995): 263–65. Compare Cicero's description of Murena's brother's joy and dismay, *Mur.* 89.

[2] Despite recent scholarship that downplays the importance of family connections in achieving office, it does seem that a powerful brother could be a significant factor in a man's career. For a reassessment of the importance of the *gens*, see K. Hopkins, *Death and Renewal*, 31–117, and F. Millar, "The Political Character of the Classical Roman Republic, 200–151 B.C.," *JRS* 74 (1984): 1–19. Moreover, given life-expectancy and birth rates, one in four Romans could expect a brother to be alive when he was competing for office, but a father was likely to have passed away; see Saller, *Patriarchy*, 12–69.

financing their political careers and creating networks of powerful and not-so-powerful friends. A brother could also enhance a Roman's public image: appeals to fraternal *pietas* could be an effective rhetorical strategy for winning support, especially from elite Romans whose own political careers were vested in family ties; fraternal symbolism also had a broader appeal because Romans believed that everyone, regardless of class, shared in the ethic of brotherly devotion. The ideal of fraternal *pietas*, or in other words the ideology of fraternity, shaped the rhetoric and the reality of Roman politics both as a dynamic of contemporary events and in literary accounts of Rome's political history. The tension between fraternal devotion and other social norms, such as the duty to observe the rule of law or to respect political traditions, became a focal point for Roman reflections on the changes they observed in their own political system during the last century of the Republican era.

This chapter first offers a general discussion illustrating the scope of fraternal *pietas* in public life: what was possible, what was praiseworthy, what was dangerous. The three other sections focus on three well-known families of brothers, Cicero and Quintus, the Cornelii Scipiones, and the Gracchi. Cicero and his brother are presented as a case study that shows how brothers' home life and public careers are intertwined. The sections on the Scipiones and the Gracchi analyze the ways that Roman attitudes toward fraternal *pietas* influenced historical representations of these brothers.

Fraternal *Pietas* in Public

When Roman brothers entered Republican public life, fraternal *pietas* engaged with the traditional practice of Roman politics in which elites shared power negotiating a flexible array of opportunities and alliances.[3] Tight-knit relationships between brothers and other *aequales* could offset the impediments to political success, which Hopkins describes so persuasively in *Death and Renewal*.[4] Partible inheritance could deplete a family's resources, but fraternal cooperation, on the model of an informal *consortium*, reunited the brothers' inheritance and restored the family's ability to finance a political career for one or even two sons, as Cicero's and his brother's experience illustrates. As a counterbalance to

---

[3] Brunt's discussion of *amicitia* reveals the fertile and flexible networks among friends and relatives, "'Amicitia' in the Late Roman Republic," rev. ed. in *The Fall of the Roman Republic*, 351–81.

[4] Hopkins, *Death and Renewal*, 107–16, and see also Shatzman, *Senatorial Wealth*, 84–94, 143–76.

rising individualism, interdependence among friends and brothers could advance a man's career further than individual ambition. Fraternal *pietas* also had an ideological function in Roman politics, and the ideals based in *consortium* shaped Roman responses to brothers' roles in public life. The way a man treated his brother was subject to public scrutiny and could make or break his reputation for integrity, propriety, and simple human kindness. A man's dealings with his brother were indicative of character, that all-important qualification for a statesman. A man was expected to work with his brother to advance both his own and his brother's careers, but there were limits on this fraternal cooperation. Too much fraternal *pietas* could be perceived as a threat to the status quo and to the built-in fluidity of the system.

Fraternal *pietas* most often manifested itself in two kinds of political activity: cultivating networks of friends and clients, and coordinated efforts to advance each other's careers or to secure their common interest in family prestige. In fact, brothers could share their political inheritance much as they shared their patrimony.[5] For example, the Luculli were famous for the perpetuation of their father's feud with the Servilii. Cicero praises Lucullus and his brother for pursuing their inherited vendetta with equal devotion and energy: *adulescens cum fratre pari pietate et industria praedito paternas inimicitias magna cum gloria est persecutus*, "as a young man, with his brother who was blessed with equal *pietas* and dedication, he pursued his father's enmities."[6] When the Luculli took up their inherited grudge against Servilius, filial *pietas* motivated fraternal cooperation, much as a joint inheritance preserved the family property. Brothers could also inherit political contacts from each other, as Cicero wrote of L. Saufeius, the brother of his friend Appius Saufeius: *nunc credo eo magis quod debet etiam fratris Appi amorem erga me cum reliqua hereditate crevisse*, "now I believe that he will be even more of a friend because, along with the rest of his estate, he's inherited his brother Appius' affection for me."[7] As brothers were expected to provide for each other financially, either in life or by testament, so too, they were expected to share social and political obligations.

While other relatives could and did play a role in a man's political career, no one could be expected to help more than a brother. When a friend goes the extra mile, his devotion is equated with fraternal *pietas*. Cicero describes his own and his friends devotion in terms of brothers in

---

[5] This is in itself not a new idea; see, for example, L. R. Taylor, *Party Politics in the Age of Caesar*, 35, or in general M. Gelzer, *Die Nobilität der römischen Republik*.

[6] L. and M. Licinius Lucullus, Cic. *Ac.* 2.1; cf. Cic. *Off.* 2.49–50, Plut. *Luc.* 1.1–2, with E. S. Gruen, *Roman Politics and the Criminal Courts 149–78 B.C.*, 176–78.

[7] Saufeius, Cic. *Att.* 6.1.10.

order to emphasize the extraordinary degree and nature of their emotions and their actions, as for example when he compares himself to Marcellus' brother:

quod autem summae benevolentiae est, quae mea erga illum, omnibus nota semper fuit, ut vix C. Marcello, optimo et amantissimo fratri, praeter eum quidem cederem nemini, cum id sollicitudine, cura, labore tam diu praestiterim, quam diu est de illius salute dubitatum, certe hoc tempore magnis curis, molestiis, doloribus liberatus praestare debeo.

It was, however, a mark of the exceptional goodwill which I have always felt toward him [Marcellus], as everyone knows, that I would hardly take second place to anyone except perhaps Gaius Marcellus, his best and most devoted brother; since I offered my goodwill with solicitude, concern, and hard work for as long as there was any question about his safety, surely at this time, when I am freed from serious anxieties, troubles, and grief, I ought to come forward. Cic. *Marc.* 34[8]

Cicero could hardly have chosen to compare friends to brothers unless the comparison were positive, since he aims to praise.[9] The grammatical structure of the passage from the *pro Marcello* points to this conclusion. Cicero begins to say that his own goodwill toward Marcellus would almost exceed that of Marcellus' brother, *vix C. Marcello . . .* , and then he corrects himself, *praeter eum. . . .* The resulting anacoluthon emphasizes the assumption that no one could be more devoted than a brother. The promotion of friends to the status of brothers reflects not only the close private relationship, which was explored in Chapter 2, but also corresponds to public, political behavior.

The Romans' expectations of brothers' political careers are oriented around the solidarity and cooperation inherent in *pietas* or the idealized *consortium*. The case of Quintus and Lucius Fulvii Flacci makes an explicit connection between family *consortium* and brothers' cooperation in politics. In the historical sources, Livy, Velleius, and Valerius Maximus, these brothers are called *consortes*, as if they lived in a *consortium*, and the historians expect their public life to conform to this fraternal partnership. When these expectations are foiled, all three historians express outrage. In the very year that Q. Fulvius Flaccus was censor, 174 B.C.E., his own brother was expelled from the Senate for immoral conduct. All three sources emphasize the fraternal relationship and their sta-

<hr>

[8] M. Claudius Marcellus, as consul in 51 B.C.E., initiated legislation condemning Caesar's grant of citizenship to Comum, then had a magistrate from Comum scourged. In 46 he was prosecuted on charges arising from this incident by L. Calpurnius Piso.

[9] Compare Cic. *Inv.* 2.22, where he advises a prosecutor that the defendant will incriminate himself if he mistakes the value of a friend or a brother.

tus as *consortes*. In Velleius: *quippe Fulvii censoris frater, et quidem consors*, "even the brother of the censor Fulvius, indeed his *consors;*" and in Livy: *L. Fulvi, qui frater germanus et, ut Valerius Antias tradit, consors etiam censoris erat*, "L. Fulvius who was full brother and, as Valerius Antius relates, even the *consors* of the censor."[10] Since Livy attributes to the late Republican historian Valerius Antias the identification of Fulvius' brother as his *consors*, the term may be more than metaphorical, if Antias was drawing on family records that accurately reported family practices.[11] The possibility that Fulvius and his brother did form a *consortium* is supported by Valerius Maximus' use of language emphasizing inheritance and family ties. In Valerius Maximus the Fulvii Flacci, as *fratres consortes*, are united in a family partnership—*copulatae societati generis*—and they shared the heritage of their ancestors' prestige—*communioni nominis ac familiae veteris propinquitatis serie cohaerenti*.[12] As *consortium* was a vehicle for the continuity of family property, it was also a metaphor for continuity in the family's political and social status.[13] According to Valerius Maximus, Fulvius expelled his own brother from the senate. His account dwells on the familial situation of the Fulvii in order to show how difficult and yet how virtuous Fulvius' choice was. His description suggests a nexus of conflicting obligations that might have shaped the censor's reactions: responsibility to his fellow citizens to perform the office of censor with integrity, shame before his ancestors and the family tradition of upstanding public service, duty and affection for his brother. Fulvius' duty as censor comes into conflict with his devotion to his brother, *fraterna caritas* (Plutarch adds that the brothers appeared together in public mourning).[14] For Valerius, Fulvius' patriotism was admirable. At least one other brother weighed his priori-

---

[10] Vell. 1.10.6, Livy 41.27.2 = Valerius Antias fr. 50 *hist.*; cf. Plut. *Flam.* 19.1. The sources do not agree on the *praenomen* of Fulvius' brother: L. in Livy, Cn. in Velleius and Fron. *Str.* 4.1.32. Modern scholars have associated him with M. Fulvius Flaccus, the military tribune who served in Spain in 181/80. See T.R.S. Broughton, *The Magistrates of the Roman Republic*, 1:391 at n. 3; H. H. Scullard, *Roman Politics*, 286; F. Münzer, *RE s.v.* "Fulvius (57)" cols. 240–41.

[11] Antias is traditionally dated to the Sullan or Caesarian years and his reliability has been questioned: Livy doubted Antias' accuracy, see 38.56.5 and 39.52.1–6, with T. J. Luce, *Livy*, 93–94, 165–67.

[12] Val. Max. 2.7.5.

[13] "The physical *domus* was an impressive symbol of the glory and continuity of the great Republican lineages." (R. P. Saller, "*Familia, Domus* and the Roman Conception of the Family," *Phoenix* 38 [1984]: 351). See Dixon, *Roman Family*, 110. The *domus* could represent the whole extended family, ancestors included, or it could be associated more narrowly with a group of brothers. *Consortium* can be understood as an equivalent to *domus*, emphasizing a brother's role in the household.

[14] *Caritas* in Val. Max. 2.7.5; public mourning in Plut. *Flam.* 19.1.

ties differently. T. Quinctius Flamininus, who worked closely with his brother Lucius, was in a position to know whether his brother had acted appropriately while on campaign during the Macedonian wars. Yet, when Titus was censor in 189, he did not censure his brother, although the next censor, M. Porcius Cato in 184, not only expelled Lucius from the Senate but also gave a fierce speech denouncing him. Livy's account suggests that Titus may have prevented his expulsion in 189, when he writes that after Cato's speech, *retinere L. Quinctium in senatu ne frater quidem T. Quinctius, si tum censor esset, potuisset,* "not even his brother T. Quinctius, if he were censor at that time, could have kept L. Quinctius in the senate."[15] The historical record is not full enough to tell us what factors might have influenced Quinctius and Fulvius. What both cases demonstrate is the concern to reconcile fraternal devotion with political obligations and also the importance of fraternal *pietas* in creating a public image. Presumably, Fulvius was protecting his own reputation by distancing himself from his brother's unacceptable conduct, whereas Quinctius advanced his status by showing himself a staunch defender of his brother. Part of brothers' shared inheritance was their public image, and they could exploit popular attitudes toward the fraternal relationship to mold public opinion to their advantage.

Even when brothers were not identified explicitly as *consortes*, they were expected to work together in their public lives, as for example, Cicero's contemporaries, the Claudii, who seem to have formed a joint family like a *consortium* to ease the transitions after their father's death.[16] Claudian solidarity is most visible in their united opposition to Cicero. Cicero's letters to Atticus from the years 59–57 B.C.E. portray Appius and his brother Publius allied against Cicero and his brother.[17] Before Cicero's exile, Pompey offered to guarantee that neither Claudius would harm Cicero.[18] During his exile, Cicero worried that his brother Quintus, who was then returning to Rome from provincial duty, would be prosecuted in the *quaestio de repetundis*. The fact that Appius Clau-

---

[15] Livy 39.42.7, cf. 39.42.6–43.5, Cic. *Sen.* 42, Plut. *T. Flam.* 18.2–19.4, Plut. *Cat. Ma.* 17.5–6. On Cato's motives for his expulsion, see D. Epstein, *Personal Enmity in Roman Politics 218–43 BC,* 66–67, and E. M. Carawan, "Cato's Speech against L. Flamininus," *CJ* 85 (1990): 316–29.

[16] See above, Chapter 1, pp. 48–49.

[17] Cic. *Att.* 1–2 passim. The *Bona Dea* affair was a public forum for this enmity, see Shackleton Bailey, *Letters to Atticus,* 1:396; Epstein, *Personal Enmity,* 108–109; Gruen, *Last Generation,* 59; T. W. Hillard, "The Claudii Pulchri 76–84 B.C."; W. K. Lacey, "Clodius and Cicero," *Antichthon* 8 (1974): 75–92; W.M.F. Rundell, "Cicero and Clodius," *Historia* 28 (1978): 301–28; W. J. Tatum, "Cicero and the *Bona Dea* Scandal," *CP* 85 (1990): 202–208.

[18] Pompey's guarantee, Cic. *Att.* 2.22.2; see R. Seager, "Clodius, Pompeius and the Exile of Cicero," *Latomus* 24 (1965): 519–31.

dius, as *praetor*, was presiding over this court only heightened Cicero's anxiety. After Cicero's return from exile, Appius continued to sponsor his brother's attacks, weighing in behind his brother in the battle over Cicero's confiscated property. The two Claudii put up a united front against Cicero, until a reconciliation was achieved in 54, the year of Appius' consulship.[19] The effects of this reconciliation are evident in Cicero's treatment of Appius in his speech in defense of M. Aemilius Scaurus.

In the *pro Scauro*, Cicero discussed Appius Claudius' efforts to promote the election of the third Claudius brother, Gaius, in the consular elections in 54. Cicero's remarks show the workings of fraternal solidarity in politics and offer insight into contemporary attitudes toward such behavior. Scaurus was brought up on a charge of *repetundis*, "extortion," stemming from his administration of Sardinia. According to Asconius, the prosecution was motivated by electoral concerns.[20] The trial was intended to block Scaurus' candidacy in the consular elections of 54. Gaius Claudius was expected to return from his provincial posting to stand for the consulship in these elections as well. In anticipation, Appius Claudius had begun to canvass for his brother and may have been involved in the prosecution of Scaurus as part of this activity. Since this canvassing inevitably arrayed Appius against Scaurus, an ally of Cicero, it could be interpreted as a break in the truce between Claudius and Cicero. Cicero makes a pretense of arguing away any cause for enmity between Appius and himself, including the possibility that in supporting and opposing Scaurus he and Appius were merely carrying out a private feud. Instead, he explained Appius' behavior as a manifestation of fraternal devotion: *nisi hunc C. Claudi fratris sui competitorem fore putasset*, "if he had not thought that he [Scaurus] would be his brother Gaius Claudius' opponent." Appius worked so assiduously for his brother, Cicero suggested, because it was a matter of personal and family honor that his brother not lose the election to a man of lesser social standing while he himself was consul: *se consule neque repelli fratrem volebat. . . .* , "he

---

[19] Appius Claudius presiding over *quaestio de repetundis*, Cic. *Att.* 3.17.1, cf. Dio 39.6.3; Cicero's confiscated property, Cic. *Att.* 4.2.3–4, 4.3.3–4. Pompey facilitated the reconciliation between Appius Claudius and Cicero, according to a lost letter of Cicero's, cited in Quint. *Inst.* 9.3.41: *ego cum in gratiam redierim cum Ap. Claudio, et redierim per Pompeium*, "I got back on good terms with Appius Claudius, and I did it through Pompey." On the date of the reconciliation, see Shackleton Bailey, *ad Familiares*, 1:308, who calls it "recent" in December 54; cf. E. S. Gruen, "Pompey, the Roman Aristocracy and the conference of Luca," *Historia* 18 (1969): 103 at n. 145, dating the reconciliation to 50.

[20] Asc. *Scaur. Arg.* Oddly enough, M. Cicero was joined by P. Clodius on Scaurus' defense team; Scaurus had six advocates, an unusually large number, according to Asconius. On the political orientations and motives of Scaurus' supporters, see B. A. Marshall, *A Historical Commentary on Asconius*, 155–56.

did not want his brother to be defeated while he was consul."[21] And this is nothing more than what Cicero himself would have done for his own brother: *praesertim qui quid amor fraternus valeat paene praeter ceteros sentiam*, "especially I who feel the force of brotherly devotion almost more than others."[22] Despite pointed barbs about patrician and plebeian status, Cicero condoned Appius' canvas for his brother as conventional behavior that was socially acceptable and politically sensible. Appius, as consul in 54, was ideally positioned to help his brother to election. It was common enough for a man to win election in the year when his brother held office and for brothers to hold the consulship in successive years. And consider the exceptional year 179 B.C.E. when four (and possibly six) of the ten highest magistracies were held by three pairs of brothers: the consuls were the two sons of Q. Fulvius Flaccus; Valerius Laevinus, also praetor, was the half-brother of one of the censors, M. Fulvius Nobilior; and two Mucii Scaevolae were praetors.[23] In fact, if a brother couldn't get someone elected, Romans might suspect electoral corruption.[24]

Appius' behavior takes on a different appearance, however, once it is

[21] Cic. *Scaur.* 33, 34. Since only one patrician could be elected, it was in Appius' and his brother's interest to eliminate Scaurus, also a patrician, from the running, Schol. Amb. *Sc.* 34, and see Marshall, *Commentary on Asconius*, 124. This regulation on patricians and plebeians in consular elections lends a note of piquancy to Cicero's banter. But his remarks could also be taken as referring to P. Clodius' adoption into the plebeian branch of the family, but cf. Asc. *Sc.* 33, as emended by T. Stangl, *Ciceronis Orationum Scholiastae*, 2:27, where the remarks are aimed at C. Claudius.

[22] Cic. *Scaur.* 35; compare a similar promise to Ser. Sulpicius Rufus, *Mur.* 10. And although Cicero does not mention it, fraternal *pietas* seems to have been involved on Scaurus' side as well, so it would hardly suit his case to reject all brotherly sentiment. Asconius, *Argumentum*, tells us that Scaurus' brother, who was quaestor at the time of the trial, played some role in the pretrial negotiations; unfortunately, a lacuna in the text of Asconius prevents us from knowing the scope of his brother's actions. Asconius also includes his brother in the list (at the end of his comments) of those who served as character witnesses, *unus praeterea adulescens laudavit, frater eius, Faustus Cornelius, Syllae filius.*

[23] Sources for the Magistrates of 179 are collected in Broughton, *Magistrates of the Roman Republic*, 1:391–94. Brothers who held the consulship in consecutive years: M. Fabius Buteo in 245 and N. Fabius Buteo in 247; Ap. Claudius Pulcher in 185 and P. Claudius Pulcher in 184; Cn. Baebius Tamphilus in 182 and M. Baebius Tamphilus in 181; M. Popilius in 172 and C. Popilius in 171; Q. Caecilius Metellus Macedonicus in 143 and L. Caecilius Metellus Calvus in 142; C. Aurelius Cotta in 75 and M. Aurelius Cotta in 74; L. Licinius Lucullus in 74 and M. Licinius Lucullus in 73; P. Cornelius Lentulus Spinther in 57 and Cn. Cornelius Lentulus Marcellinus in 56; M. Claudius Marcellus in 51 and his brother Gaius in 50 (cf. also his cousin in 49). See also Gruen, *Criminal Courts*, 23, and *Last Generation*, 102–104.

[24] So Livy, 4.44.1–5, in an account of elections of 420: when only patricians were elected quaestor, the tribunes cried foul, because A. Antistius' son and Sex. Pollius' brother were not elected.

known that his brother will not be a candidate in 54.[25] Apparently, Appius had blamed the Sardinians for instigating the attacks on Scaurus. The Sardinians, Cicero parries, stood to gain from the election of Appius' brother to the consulship.[26] Cicero shifts the blame back to Appius, implying that Appius had offered incentives to the Sardinians. So long as his brother was a candidate, Appius' behavior was not only a conventional but laudable demonstration of fraternal *pietas*. But once his brother was out of the running, his involvement with the Sardinians was nothing but electoral bribery, an unacceptable display of clout. Cicero then turns the tables on fraternal devotion, claiming that he himself is only acting like a good brother in helping Appius to see the true nature of his actions.[27] Appius' determination to see his brother elected conforms to precedent, but Cicero's ironic attribution of brotherly devotion to Appius raises questions about these precedents. Cicero claims to have defended Appius' behavior as if he himself were Appius' brother, in effect, giving an example of what Appius might have done for Gaius. Is the pot calling the kettle black? If Cicero's defense of Appius was accepted as honest and valid, Appius' canvas for his brother must also have been upright and acceptable. However, the suggestion of irony undermines the validity of brotherly love as a motive for political behavior in both cases. While in principle the extension of the ideal to political behavior was not only acceptable but traditional, it was open to abuse. Cicero's irony implies that Appius had gone too far in claiming fraternal devotion as a motive for attacking Scaurus. It might have been all well and good for brothers to help each other to advance to glory and magistracies, but there were limits on this kind of help.[28]

Norms of civic duty and Roman ideas about law provided one limit to

[25] Cic. *Scaur.* 35–37. Appius continued with the prosecution of Scaurus with L. Domitius Ahenobarbus, perhaps as part of a plan to promote two other candidates, C. Memmius and Cn. Domitius Calvinus, cf. Marshall, *Commentary on Asconius*, 124. For Appius' motives see Epstein, *Personal Enmity 218–43 BC*, 7–8, 90–91; Gruen, *Last Generation*, 332–33; E. Courtney, "The Prosecution of Scaurus in 54 BC," *Philologus* 105 (1961): 151–56.

[26] Cicero's characterization of the Sardinians, *Scaur.* 42–44, as "ferocious, unattractive brigands and congenital liars" (to borrow Balsdon's words) is surely intended to impugn their reliability as witnesses and to appeal to Roman prejudices. For the stereotypes about Sardinia, see J.P.V.D. Balsdon, *Romans and Aliens*, 64, 221, 248.

[27] Cic. *Scaur.* 37.

[28] Livy's description, 39.32.10–13, of an earlier generation of Claudii and the elections of 195 reveals a similar ambivalence: canvassing for a brother is expected, but within certain bounds, cf. Cicero's sarcasm about M. Antonius' election practices, *Phil.* 8.27, and below pp. 000. On the tension between family solidarity and individual ambition in the late Republic, see Gruen, *Last Generation*, 58–59. Compare the courts in Classical Athens where kinship could be used for "excusing behavior that did not conform strictly to the standards of the public sphere" (S. Humphreys, "Kinship Patterns in the Athenian Courts," *GRBS* 27 [1986]: 88).

the exploitation of brotherly love in politics. The case of Cornelius Sulla and his half brother L. Caecilius Rufus, tribune of the *plebs* in 64, recounted in Cicero's speech for P. Cornelius Sulla, offers a test case for the tensions between fraternal and civic duty. After a successful consular candidacy, Sulla was prosecuted and convicted of *ambitus* under the *lex Calpurnia*, which prohibited him from holding office again.[29] In the next year, his brother, L. Caecilius, was elected tribune and, when he took office, he proposed a bill that would ease the penalty imposed on his brother as a result of this conviction. Since the bill was defeated, it not only failed its immediate purpose of facilitating Sulla's return to politics, but became a political liability for Sulla, two years later, when he was prosecuted for complicity in the Catilinarian conspiracy under the *Lex Plautia de vi*. Sulla's prosecutors appear to have alleged that Caecilius' initiative in raising the bill was not only improper but illegal. Cicero responded to these allegations and justified Caecilius' initiative as fraternal devotion: *pietas et fraternus amor propulisset*, "familial devotion and brotherly love had driven him."[30] The collocation of *fraternus amor* and *pietas* is reminiscent of the motivations underlying *consortium*. Moreover, Caecilius is praiseworthy because he attempted to use his political office to foster his brother's political career. But, the prosecution argued, Caecilius' support for his brother conflicted with his duty, as tribune, to the state and people. Cicero neutralized this charge with agreement. If Caecilius had neglected his civic duty for the sake of his brother, Cicero, too, would have condemned him: *recte reprehendis . . .* "you rightly rebuke him . . ." Caecilius' moderate proposal, not overturning the conviction but easing the penalty, satisfied his duty to both state and brother. A specious argument, perhaps, but an argument that would appeal to the jurors' assumptions about brotherly devotion: *peterem veniam errato L. Caecili ex intimis vestris cogitationibus atque ex humanitate communi*, "I would ask you to find it in your own hearts and in your human sympathies to forgive Lucius Caecilius' misplaced devotion."[31] He expects his audience to identify with Caecilius' feelings for his brother and to condone his actions as right and moral and within the bounds of civic duty. Such tension between personal and public interest became a persistent issue,[32]

[29] Prior to the *lex Calpurnia*, those convicted of *ambitus* were barred from seeking office for ten years. The *lex Calpurnia* imposed harsher penalties: a monetary fine and a lifetime prohibition on seeking office, Schol. Bob. *Sul.* 17. Caecilius' bill sought to grandfather his brother's conviction, so that he would pay the penalty under the earlier law not the later *lex Calpurnia*.

[30] Cic. *Sul.* 64, 62–63; for the prosecution of Sulla, Schol Bob. *Sul.* 92.

[31] Cic. *Sul.* 64.

[32] See, for example, Sall. *Hist.* 1.11, and Appian *BC* 1.1–5. Cf. D. Earl, *The Moral and Political Tradition of Rome*, 23. The issue was prominent in formulations of the conflict between Pompey and Caesar, see R. Syme, *The Roman Revolution*, 35, 45–46, 48, 51, and Taylor, *Party Politics*, 163.

which took on added significance in the late Republic, as an explanation for the deterioration of the *mos maiorum* and for the causes of civil war. Although the main players in Cicero's speeches belonged to the political and social elite, his speeches appealed to a broader audience, the mixed audience of the *corona*, whose votes might matter to these elite protagonists.[33] Appeals to fraternal *pietas*, one of the emotional arguments recognized as central to the orator's art, could reach this broader audience, because Romans believed that fraternal *pietas* crossed class boundaries.

Brothers were expected to cooperate in their political activities, advancing their own careers and the family's reputation, much as they did in the household or in a fraternal *consortium*. While brothers might not always have achieved perfect equality in their public careers, they might seek to project an image of fraternal *pietas* to the Roman public, if it seemed politically expedient. Cicero's rhetorical appeals to brothers' devotion demonstrate the power of fraternal imagery in the political arena. There could, however, be too much of even a good thing. While Romans might have been pleased to invoke brotherly love on their own behalf and felt virtuous in praising and accommodating fraternal *pietas*, they recognized the risks of nepotism among their competitors for political prestige. Fraternal *pietas* needed to be carefully couched in patriotic motives: brothers who used their fraternal *consortium* in behalf of Rome earned the highest praise, so long as their ambitions did not threaten the established balance of power among senatorial contenders.

Cicero and Quintus: A Case Study

tibi vero, frater, neque hortanti deero, neque roganti, nam neque auctoritate quisquam apud me plus valere te potest, neque voluntate.

I won't fail you, brother, whether you urge me or ask me [for something], for no one, in either his influence or his wish, could mean more to me than you.

Cic. *De Orat.* 1.4

---

[33] F. Millar, "Politics, Persuasion and the People Before the Social War (150–90 B.C.)" discusses the power of oratory to express public opinion and mobilize Roman assemblies behind tribunician laws. Cicero's *De Oratore* provides insight into Roman assumptions about the rhetorical exploitation of emotions. The speakers in the *De Oratore* assume that appeals to emotion are the most powerful weapon in the orator's arsenal, see, for example, Cic. *De Orat.* 2.178. Because of the Roman belief in the natural basis of fraternity, appeals to brotherly devotion fall into this category. The crowd reacts instinctively to an orator's words, *quodam quasi naturali sensu*, "as if by some innate capacity," through some inherent, "natural" capacity that all humans share—*in communibus infixa sensibus, De Orat.* 3.151, 159–97. Court cases are not weighed in a goldsmith's balance but in common, ordinary scales—*populari quadam trutina,* Cic. *De Orat.* 2.159, cf. 1.219–24, 3.122, 3.147. And after all, "is there anyone who doesn't know what's praiseworthy about people?" *quis est qui nesciat quae sint in homine laudanda?* Cic. *De Orat.* 2.45.

Cicero dedicated the *De Oratore* to his brother Quintus, as if answering a request or fulfilling an obligation underwritten by emotional attachment. Such formal statements of fraternal *pietas* are rare in Cicero's writings, and yet his speeches and letters offer us a fuller picture of the fraternal relationship than any other ancient source.[34] These letters provide some of the most complete, if subjective, evidence about brothers in late Republican Rome. Although some of these letters were written under the extraordinary circumstance of his exile, they offer insight into the rather more ordinary aspects of the brothers' relationship. His words and actions are engaged with fraternal *pietas*; he interprets events, guides his own behavior, and explains his motivations in ways that reflect the sentiment and morality associated with *consortium*. It is unfortunate that only one letter from Quintus survives,[35] yet on the basis of Cicero's own writings, we can reconstruct a fairly complete account of the ways that these brothers managed their personal and public lives. The details of this case study confirm and add nuances to the more general picture that arises from other legal and literary sources. Cicero's fraternal relationship operated within a larger context of friends and family. Quintus was not the only or even the most steadfast partner in Cicero's life. His wife Terentia, their children, as well as his friend Atticus, whose sister was married to Quintus, were all part of the immediate circle in which fraternal *pietas* operated. The relationship between brothers was both like and unlike these other relationships. Juxtaposing the behavior and sentiments of different people—a wife, a friend, a brother—clarifies both what is common to all these close relationships and what is distinct about brothers.

Cicero's letters to his brother contain descriptions of his and his brother's activities, reactions to public and private events, advice, and affection. The letters are full of the minutiae of family life. How is Quintus getting along with his wife?[36] What are their sons learning in school?[37] What about plans for Tullia's marriage?[38]

[34] The three books of Cicero's letters to his brother comprise twenty-seven letters. Most of these letters were written when Quintus was away from Rome, while he was provincial governor in Asia, 62–59 B.C.E. (*Q. Fr.* 1.1 and 1.2), legate to Pompey in Sardinia, 56 (*Q. Fr.* 2.1–2.7), and on campaign with Caesar in Gaul, 54 (*Q. Fr.* 2.13–3.7). Several of the letters were written while they were both residing at Rome or nearby at one of their villas (*Q. Fr.* 2.8–2.12). Two were written from exile (*Q. Fr.* 1.3 and 1.4). For a good biographical sketch of Quintus, especially focusing on his younger years, see W. C. McDermott, "Q. Cicero," *Historia* 20 (1971): 702–17.

[35] Cic. *Fam.* 16.16. This letter does not reply directly to any of Cicero's letters; it celebrates the manumission of Tiro, his brother's indispensable assistant.

[36] These matters were really too confidential for letters: *Pomponia autem etiam de te questa est. sed haec coram agemus*, "Pomponia, however, also complains about you. But we'll deal with this in person," *Q. Fr.* 2.6(5).2–3.

[37] Progress reports on young Quintus: *Q. Fr.* 2.4.2; 2.6(5).3; 2.13(12).2; 3.1.14, 19; 3.3.4. Reports to Quintus about his own son *Q. Fr.* 3.4.6; 3.6(8).2; 3.7(9).9.

[38] *Q. Fr.* 2.4.2 and 2.6(5).1.

Negotia se nostra sic habent, domestica vero ut volumus. Valent pueri, studiose discunt, diligenter docentur; et nos et inter se amant.
Our public business is in such a condition, and things at home are as we want them to be. The boys are healthy, they learn eagerly and are carefully instructed; they love us and each other. Cic. *Q. Fr.* 3.3.1

The brothers and their families were close, emotionally and physically. Cicero's son loved Quintus' son like a brother, and Cicero rivals his brother in devotion to young Quintus.[39] When Cicero bought a house on the Palatine, he gave their paternal home in Rome to his brother, and later, the brothers built houses next door to each other: *domus utriusque nostrum aedificatur strenue. . . . spero nos ante hiemem contubernalis fore,* "both of our houses are being built quickly . . . I hope that we will be under the same roof before winter"[40]—all this without sharing a household. Their physical proximity and cooperation seems to have been the product of affection rather than any economic interdependence.

For the elite, like Cicero, his brother, and Atticus, who traveled overseas and were engaged in a wide net of interpersonal relationships as patrons, clients, and friends, having a partner in the family could be an advantage. Two could manage the demands of travel and social relations better than one. While one brother was abroad, the other could manage property, business, and personal matters at home. Cicero and Quintus discussed finances, household repairs, and the purchase of new property, including acquisitions for their library. During Quintus' tour with Caesar in Gaul, Cicero took responsibility for management of Quintus' property. He supervised new construction of buildings and renovations, plans for roads and plumbing, arrangements for slaves and hired personnel.[41] Cicero was enthusiastic about some of the projects, with a zeal that suggests a more than casual interest in the property, but he deferred to his brother's opinions about building projects on his brother's land and consulted him to make sure things were to his liking. Despite all this cooperation, there is no evidence of joint ownership: while children are *nostri* "ours" or *tuus meusque,* "yours and mine together,"[42] houses, land, and cash are "yours" or "mine."[43] Cicero consistently refers to Quintus'

[39] *Q. Fr.* 1.3.3 and 3.1.7; cf. *Att.* 6.3.8. Tullia seems to have been quite attached to her uncle, *Q. Fr.* 2.4.2.

[40] *Q. Fr.* 2.4.2; on their paternal home, see Plut. *Cic.* 8.3.

[41] Construction on Quintus' property: *Q. Fr.* 2.4.2; 2.6(5).3; 3.1.1–6, 14, 23–24; 3.2.3; 3.3.1; 3.4.5; 3.5.6; 3.7(9).4, 7. Cicero also makes occasional mention of his own building projects, *Q. Fr.* 2.5.1(4.3).

[42] Cic. *Q. Fr.* 1.3.10; 2.4.2; 2.6(5).2; 2.7(6).2; 2.9(8).1; 2.13(12).2; 3.1.19; 3.3.4.

[43] Yours v. Mine, *Q. Fr.* 3.1.14; 3.3.1. When Marcus discusses Quintus' negotiations with a certain Anicius concerning the purchase of property, Marcus says specifically that Anicius is buying property for Quintus, *Q. Fr.* 3.1.23, though when Marcus pays Quintus' contractor, he does not specify with whose money, Q. *Fr.* 2.4.6.

property with forms of *tuus*, implying that he made a clear distinction between what was his own and what belonged to his brother. Cicero and his wife maintained a similar separation of property, as his letters from exile demonstrate.[44] Yet both wife and brother took on financial responsibility for Cicero during his exile. Terentia took care of the children while Quintus supported his brother.[45] Cicero was, however, eager to repay his brother as soon as he could, so eager that he borrowed money from other friends to do so.[46] Cicero's efforts to avoid financial dependence imply that he wanted and expected to be economically independent from his brother.

While the brothers maintained separate accounts, they pooled their responsibilities for child-rearing. While Quintus served with Caesar in Gaul, Cicero took great interest and an active role in educating young Quintus together with his own son, as is attested by his frequent progress reports to Quintus.[47] In addition, Cicero was quite concerned about the choice of the boys' tutor, so much so that he finally took over the job himself.[48] The fraternal *pietas* between Cicero and Quintus seems to have been strengthened through their attachment to each other's children, much as the son in Seneca *Controversia* 1.1 hopes he can unite his uncle and father.

Atticus, linked to the family not only by his friendship with Cicero but also through his sister's marriage to Quintus, was practically a third brother. In much the same way as Cicero consulted with Quintus about finances, he also made arrangements with Atticus.[49] When Cicero wrote to Atticus of *mulieribus nostris*, "our womenfolk," he included Atticus' sister Pomponia, Quintus' wife, along with his own wife and daughter.[50] Cicero's attachment to Atticus drew him into the family, and he regarded their friendship as fraternal: *et nos ames et tibi persuadeas te a me fraterne amari*, "please love me and believe that I love you like a brother."[51] Yet in another letter, he wrote that only his brother and his immediate

---

[44] *Fam.* 14.2.3, 14.1.5.

[45] Terentia, *Fam.* 14.1–4, with S. Dixon, "Family Finances," in *The Family in Ancient Rome*, ed. B. Rawson, 95–102. Quintus, *Q. Fr.* 1.3.7: when his assets were confiscated, Cicero drew funds from the state treasury against the funds set aside as reimbursement for the expenses of Quintus' provincial governorship.

[46] *Q. Fr.* 1.3.7, and *Att.* 4.3.6. Cf. Shackleton Bailey, *Letters to Atticus,* 2:179; Dixon, "Family Finances," 101; W. W. How, *Cicero: Select Letters,* 2:142.

[47] See above p. 102 note 37.

[48] Tutor, *Att.* 8.4.1–2; 9.12.2; 9.15.5; *Q. Fr.* 2.13(12).2; 3.3.4; cf. Shackleton Bailey, *Cicero,* 160–61.

[49] Discussion of finances with Atticus, for example, *Att.* 6.7.1; 7.13a.1; 7.18.4; 7.26.3; 10.11.2; 10.15.4; 11.2.2.

[50] *Att.* 7.14.3; 7.18.1; cf. 6.5.4; 7.22.2.

[51] *Att.* 1.5.8, cf. *Att.* 1.18.1.

family were closer to him than Atticus. Indeed, Atticus took care of Tullia during her pregnancy in 49 (though she gave birth with her own family).[52] While Cicero was in exile, both Quintus and Atticus looked out for his wife and children.[53] Cicero's repeated entreaties to Atticus to help his brother drew his friend more closely into the fraternal network.[54] Though Cicero entrusted his family to both his brother and his friend, his description of Quintus' role suggests a distinction between the two: Cicero wrote that his children would not be orphans so long as his brother was alive, *te incolumi orbi non erunt.*[55] In effect, Quintus was a surrogate father, the very role he would play as *tutor legitimus* to Cicero's children, the preferred guardian for a brother's children. Though Cicero distinguished between brother and friend, both were intimately involved in the care and education of the next generation.

In raising Quintus' son, Atticus seems to have played the same range of roles as Cicero: both loved the boy and believed that discipline would train his native talent into proper and productive expression.[56] According to anthropological models of kinship, we might expect maternal uncle (Atticus) and paternal uncle (Cicero) to have different roles, and Bettini has made the case that at Rome paternal uncles were strict while maternal uncles were indulgent. Recently, Saller has argued that these models do not work for the Roman evidence,[57] and Cicero and Atticus are just one more case that defies the stereotypes. In this particular family, the two uncles saw eye to eye about what young Quintus needed. Their unity of opinion contrasts with Cicero's disagreements with his brother over how to handle his son.[58] The behavior and attitudes of Cicero and Atticus can be better explained as the product of circumstance and personality rather than through a rule-based system of kinship identity. Cicero explained some of the trouble with young Quintus as a product of the

---

[52] Tullia with Atticus, *Att.* 10.1a.1, and 10.8.9 with Shackleton Bailey, *Letters to Atticus*, 4:410. For the birth, *Att.* 10.18.1, cf. *Att.* 6.1.10; 6.8.1–2; 6.9.5.

[53] Cicero entrusted his family to his brother during exile, *Q. Fr.* 1.3.10, and to Atticus, *Att.* 3.6; 3.19.2–3; 3.23.5; 3.27. Cicero sends Atticus Terentia's thanks, *Att.* 3.5; 3.8.4; 3.9.3. See Shackleton Bailey, *Cicero,* 72. Also during the troubled years of 49–47, Cicero consulted with Atticus about the safety of his wife, children, and brother, *Att.* 7.12.6; 7.13.3; 7.16.3; 7.17.1; 7.18.4; 8.3.5.

[54] *Att.* 3.11.2; 3.13.2; 3.19.3.

[55] *Q. Fr.* 1.3.10, cf. Drusus' care for Germanicus' children, Tac. *Ann.* 4.4 and 8 and below Chapter 5, p. 180.

[56] The two uncles corresponded about young Quintus' education while the elder Quintus was in Gaul: *Att.* 5.20.9; 6.1.12; 6.7.1. Cicero shared his concern for the boys' future with Atticus, *Att.* 7.13.3; 7.19; 7.26.3; 10.4.5. The civil war brought out the difficulties with governing young Quintus: *Att.* 10.5.2; 10.6.2; 10.7.3; 10.10.6; 10.11.3–4; 10.12.3; 10.12a.4; 10.15.4; cf. 6.6.4 for an early hint of trouble.

[57] "Roman Kinship," in *The Roman Family in Italy.*

[58] For example, *Att.* 10.4.6, and 10.6.2.

generation gap,[59] an explanation that perhaps inadvertently points to one source of fraternal solidarity: brothers might stand together in response to paternal discipline, might feel *pietas* that affirmed a sense of generational identity.

Such sentiments are conveyed in the formal features of the letters—salutations and closings that express conventional courtesy, enhanced at times by genuine affection.[60] Yet the affection between Cicero and his brother seems to be wider and deeper than convention implies. Shared intellectual interests, specifically literary pursuits, seem also to have drawn them together.[61] The brothers shared wit and pride,[62] and at other times vented their anger, frustration, and disappointment.[63] Occasionally, Cicero describes his or his brother's attitude as *fraterne*, "brotherly," and contexts attach several meanings to this adverb. It can mean candid, as in give me your honest opinion, be straight with me, φιλαληθῶς *et, ut soles, [scribere] fraterne.*[64] Brotherly can also imply gentleness and indulgence: in one letter, Cicero apologizes for an angry letter written in haste and begs Quintus' forgiveness for his rashness. The angry letter is *parum fraterne* and *non fraterne scriptae*, "too little brotherly" and "not written in a brotherly way."[65] Likewise, he calls the forgiveness he expected from Quintus *fraterne*, "brotherly." Fraternal *pietas* can absorb and endure unbrotherly behavior, but it must be repaired and restored through brotherly behavior. Such shared emotional reactions attest to an intimacy which corresponds to the reciprocity of *consortium* and to poetic expressions of brotherly love.

Cicero's exile put fraternal *pietas* to the test; we have already seen how Quintus and Atticus adjusted their roles in care-taking at this time. Exile also exerted stress on their emotional attachments, stress which in the

[59] *Att.* 10.11.3.

[60] There are several examples of formal courtesy in letters, polite apologies, *Q. Fr.* 2.2.1; 2.16(15).1; 3.3.1 (for letters written by a scribe instead of himself); *Q. Fr.* 2.15(14).1 (for poor penmanship); *Q. Fr.* 3.1.8 (for an erroneously dated letter). Variations in closing formula reflect genuine affection: fondness for a wooden lampstand built by Quintus, *Q. Fr.* 3.5.9(7.2); concern for dangers of winter sailing, *Q. Fr.* 2.1.3; 2.2.4; 2.3.7; 2.5.5(4.7); eager to see him soon, *Q. Fr.* 2.2.4; 2.6(5).4; reference to their sons, *Q. Fr.* 2.6(7).2. Similarly, requests for letters seem to be conventional, yet they occasionally have special emphasis, suggesting more than perfunctory anticipation of a letter: conventional request, *Q. Fr.* 2.3.7, 2.5.5(4.7); special emphasis, *Q. Fr.* 2.11(10).5; 2.7(6).1.

[61] Literature was a frequent topic in the letters, *Q. Fr.* 2.8(7).1; 2.10(9).3; 2.12(11).4; 2.13(12).1; 2.16(15).4; 3.1.11, 13, 25; 3.4.4–5; 3.5.1–2, 6–7.

[62] Wit, *Q. Fr.* 2.10(9).2; 2.11(10).2–3, 5; 2.12(11).1; 3.7(9).5. Pride, *Q. Fr.* 2.1.2–3; 2.3.6 (cf. 2.4.1); 2.5.5(4.7); 2.14(13).1; 3.1.11; 3.4.2.

[63] Anger, *Q. Fr.* 2.9(8).1; 3.6(8).1. Frustration, *Q. Fr.* 3.1.12–13; 3.3.1; 3.5.2. Disappointment, *Q. Fr.* 3.5.4; 3.7(9).1–3.

[64] *Q. Fr.* 2.16(15).5.

[65] *Q. Fr.* 1.2.12.

end revealed the strength of fraternal *pietas*. Quintus' devotion is a recurring theme in Cicero's letters from exile and in the speeches he delivered to the Senate and the People on his return. In these writings, Cicero sets his brother's devotion in the context of other relationships: Quintus manifests variously the devotion of a son, father, and brother.[66] Like a father, he offers advice and assistance, *consilium* and *beneficium*. Like a son, he is devoted in *pietas* and *obsequium*. His status as brother is marked by affection, *amor*, and pleasure *suavitas*. Yet, as brother he combines all three. There is an interesting difference between the formulation of these roles in the public speeches and in his letters to Quintus. Fathers offer advice in both public and private. Sons, however, offer *obsequium*, obedience, in private but *pietas*, devotion in public: *obsequium* is the product of asymmetry, filial respect, whereas *pietas* implies symmetrical duty.[67] Perhaps in private Cicero felt the need to shore up his brother's sense of duty under circumstances that threatened Quintus' personal and political security.[68] In public, Cicero used the term *pietas*, to express the symmetrical devotion associated with brothers in *consortium*. Similarly, in a private letter to Atticus, Cicero affirmed his love for Quintus and connected their affection to *pietas*. Cicero singled out his brother and daughter from among his close family as those especially devoted to him, setting the fraternal relationship firmly at the center of familial love. Years later, Cicero described Quintus expressly as his *consors* at the time of his exile: *consorti mecum temporum illorum*, "a partner with me in those times."[69] In Cicero's writings, Quintus is a portrait of fraternal *pietas*, manifesting the emotional identification and mutuality implicit in *consortium*. By invoking an idealized form of fraternal *pietas* Cicero crafted a powerful medium for praising Quintus and expressing his gratitude.

The cooperation between Cicero and his brother in domestic matters carried over to their public and political activities.[70] Cicero's letters to his brother show that they worked together in cultivating a network of friends and clients and in exploiting these connections for their own political advancement. In addition, they shared the vicissitudes of each other's political status and reputation: *etiam illud debes cogitare, non te*

[66] Cic. *Red. Pop.* 8; *Red. Sen.* 37; *Q. Fr.* 1.3.3, cf. 2.3.7. Compare Cicero's portrayal of Murena's brother's reaction to his exile, *Mur.* 89. On the social context surrounding Quintus' public display of grief, see A. W. Lintott, *Violence in Republican Rome*, 16ff.

[67] Saller, *Patriarchy*, 123.

[68] Cicero's anxieties about his brother's safety during his own exile: *Q. Fr.* 1.3, and 1.4 passim; *Att.* 3.8.4; 3.23.5; 3.27.

[69] Cic. *Mil.* 102. Affection and *pietas*, *Att.* 4.1.4, and singling out his brother and daughter, *Att.* 4.2.7.

[70] Almost every letter contains news of politics and the courts; Cicero's repeated promises to write to Quintus suggest that Quintus expected these reports and was interested in the news, *Q. Fr.* 2.11(10).5; 2.10(9).1,4; 2.13(12).3; 3.1.10; 3.5.9 (7.2).

tibi soli gloriam quaerere, "you ought to keep this in mind, that you are not pursuing glory for yourself alone."[71] Such sentiments may have motivated Quintus to pen the *Commentariolum Petitionis*, a short handbook, dedicated to his brother, outlining the best strategies for campaigning. Although the *Commentariolum* does not indicate the precise role a brother should play in the campaign, the details and scenes that Quintus describes suggest firsthand knowledge of the election process, experience that he may have gained while helping Cicero campaign.[72] Two specific political challenges—Cicero's exile and the brothers' interactions with Julius Caesar—dramatize the advantages and the disadvantages of brothers' association in Roman political life.

For Cicero and Quintus, exile threatened not only political success but personal safety. Though desperate emotions may have magnified the disaster for Cicero, his exile posed a real danger to Quintus because it increased the chance that he would be prosecuted on a charge arising from his term as governor of Asia, probably *de repetundis*.[73] Cicero's letters to Quintus from exile express remorse for ruining his brother's career and his fortune; the situation is so desperate that suicide seems the only remedy. Writing to his wife, Cicero says that he will try to keep living for the sake of their children. Atticus, it seems, had no truck with such maudlin protestations, though Cicero sought consolation from and seems to have taken more comfort from his friend than from his relatives.[74] Cicero relied on Atticus to give him straight answers about his chances for recall, the kind of open communication associated with

---

[71] *Q. Fr.* 1.1.44, cf. 1.2. Cicero's second letter to Quintus, written during Quintus' stint as provincial governor of Asia in 61–60 B.C.E., demonstrates the importance of reputation and how it could be created and manipulated. Cf. T. P. Wiseman, "The Ambitions of Quintus Cicero," *JRS* 56 (1966): 110.

[72] The *Commentariolum Petitionis* is associated with Cicero's campaign for the consulship in 64 B.C.E., but it may well have been revised or published later, as the treatment of Catiline (§ 9–10) could be read as *ex post facto* justification of Cicero's opposition to Catiline.

[73] Desperate emotions, *Q. Fr.* 1.3.1–4; 1.4.1. Compare his letters to Atticus, for example, *Att.* 3.7–3.20, which are full of despair, pessimism, and self-pity. See D. Stockton, *Cicero*, 190. Concern about a charge *de repetundis*, *Q. Fr.* 1.3.4; 1.4.5; *Att.* 3.9.1; *Pis.* 34–35; cf. Shackleton Bailey, *Letters to Atticus*, 2:145. On the Claudii see above, pp. 96–99.

[74] Suicide, *Q. Fr.* 1.3 passim; 1.4.4–5; for the sake of the children, *Fam.* 14.4.5; Atticus' remonstrations, e.g. *Att.* 3.10.2, 3.11.2. Cicero avoided a meeting with Quintus, because he feared that it would be too painful and that Quintus would not be able to leave him, *Q. Fr.* 1.3.1; *Att.* 3.9.1. Letters to Atticus also repeatedly express Cicero's desire to see him, *Att.* Book 3 passim. In less dramatic situations, Cicero felt responsibility for his brother's public career, *Q. Fr.* 1.2.13, and even after the two had split in the war between Pompey and Caesar, *Att.* 11.9.2.

brothers, except in this situation, where Quintus' affection interfered with candor.[75] He also enlisted Atticus to assist in protecting Quintus, which also seems to indicate that the effect of his exile on Quintus' political situation was real and serious.[76] In this extraordinary situation, wife, brother, and friend each evoked different emotional reactions and played different roles in resolving the crisis. Wife and marriage sustain his children. Friendships, fraternal and otherwise, straddled both public and private spheres: personal anguish is interwoven with political strategy in letters to both Quintus and Atticus. But, Atticus, since he did not pursue a political career, was able to distance himself from the fallout; Quintus could not. After Cicero's return from exile, when Clodius' mob drove away the workmen who were rebuilding Cicero's house, they also threw stones at Quintus' house, under construction next door, and set fire to it.[77]

Quintus played a crucial role in negotiating his brother's return to Rome, especially through contacts with P. Sestius and Pompey.[78] Writing to his brother, Cicero emphasized Sestius' devotion: *tu nobis amicissimum Sestium cognosces*, "you will find that Sestius is a very close friend of ours," for he stood by him as if he were a brother *iuxta ac si meus frater esset*.[79] When later Cicero described his energetic and successful defense of Sestius, he claimed to be repaying a debt of gratitude to Sestius, on both his own and Quintus' behalf. In order to obtain Pompey's backing for Cicero's recall, Quintus gave him a pledge guaranteeing his brother's good behavior on his return.[80] A year or so later, Quintus was called upon to stand by his pledge. In April of 56, Cicero arranged for a senatorial debate of Caesar's disposition of the Campanian land. Pompey was not pleased. Although he did not express his displeasure to Cicero, he made Quintus responsible for reining in his

[75] Straight talk from Atticus, *Att.* 3.24.1, cf. 3.22.3. Quintus too kind for candor, *Att.* 3.18.2.

[76] References to requests for Atticus' help, above, p. 105, n. 54. Even if his brother's exile had not damaged Quintus' standing, it prevented Cicero himself from working to help Quintus avoid prosecution, and would have deprived him of Cicero's oratorical skill if the case had come to trial: *non enim gladiis tecum, sed litibus agetur*, "for the case will not be decided by the sword but in court" (*Q. Fr.* 1.4.5).

[77] *Att.* 4.3.2; *Sest.* 75–77; Plut. *Cic.* 33. The same mob also damaged the portico of Catulus' house. See Stockton, *Cicero*, 192, and Wiseman, "Ambitions of Quintus," 111. On Cicero's efforts to protect himself from Clodius' attack, see W. J. Tatum, "Cicero's Opposition to the *Lex Clodia de Collegiis*," *CQ* 40 (1990): 187–96.

[78] On Quintus' role in general, see Stockton, *Cicero*, 191–93.

[79] *Red. Sen.* 20, and *Q. Fr.* 1.4.5, cf. *Q. Fr.* 1.4.3. Cicero kept his brother apprised of the progress in Sestius' trial, *Q. Fr.* 2.2.1; 2.3.5–6; 2.4.1.

[80] *Fam.* 1.9.9–10, with Shackleton Bailey, *ad Familiares*, 1:310.

brother.[81] In a letter to P. Lentulus Spinther written two years later, Cicero described how Pompey had leaned on Quintus when he met him in Sardinia, where Quintus was serving on his staff. In persuading Quintus to control his brother, Pompey invoked his own *beneficia* as well as fraternal *pietas*, he reportedly said to Quintus:

> *'Te' inquit 'ipsum cupio; nihil opportunius potuit accidere. Nisi cum Marco fratre diligenter egeris, dependendum tibi est quod mihi pro illo spopondisti.' Quid multa?*
> "I want to see you!" he said, "What a stroke of luck. If you do not work attentively with your brother Marcus, you'll have to repay what you promised me on his behalf!" What more is there to say? Cic. *Fam.* 1.9.9

By opposing Caesar's legislation and acting contrary to Pompey's wishes, Cicero endangered not just himself but also his brother. Pompey exploited this interdependence to enforce both Quintus' guarantee and his brother's compliance. In this situation, Quintus was in the position of greater influence: he could offer the advice, which Cicero so praised in his letters from exile, and expect it to be heeded.[82] In the same letter to Spinther, Cicero described his position after receiving Quintus' report: he was in a tight spot, caught between his own principles and his duty to Quintus. Cicero framed this dilemma as a conflict between fraternal *pietas* and his duty to the *res publica*.[83] The rhetorical elaboration of this issue, then, grows out of shared assumptions about brothers' roles in public life. The obligation to comply with his brother's advice, which is in their interest, was a given: Cicero weighed his responsibility to his brother, *fides fratris*, against other claims and found it more compelling. When Quintus arranged for his brother's recall, he not only restored his brother but he renovated their shared status and demonstrated that both brothers had a role to play in their mutual political survival.

The interaction between the Ciceros and Julius Caesar further demonstrates the mechanics of fraternal cooperation in politics. Cicero's letters to Quintus, especially during his service in Gaul, contain frequent consultation and reports about Caesar, indicating close cooperation. When Cicero undertook to compose an epic for Caesar, Quintus served as a kind of literary agent, encouraging Cicero, providing information about Brit-

---

[81] Cicero, *Q. Fr.* 2.6(5).3, reports a friendly meeting with Pompey, just before Pompey's less friendly encounter with Quintus. On Cicero's relations with Pompey, see Stockton, *Cicero*, 207–209.

[82] Cf. *Q. Fr.* 2.7.(6).2. "The events of 58–57 had placed them on a less unequal footing, and as guarantor to Pompey Quintus could and did offer political advice, which was well received" (Shackleton Bailey, *Cicero*, 92).

[83] *Fam.* 1.9.10. For this same conflict in other speeches, see pp. 97–101, 132–34.

ain, and reporting Caesar's reactions to the work.[84] Quintus' role in encouraging his brother to foster their ties with Caesar is described as *fraterne*; in another letter, the use of the word *mandata* to describe Quintus' advice suggests the substratum of duty underlying fraternal cooperation. Cicero uses *mandata* as he reassures Quintus that he was doing his part, as was Quintus, *tu quem ad modum*. These reassurances suggest that Quintus was motivating him to do so.[85] The need to assert cooperation explicitly suggests that compliance was not automatic, but depended on a perception of mutual interest or an observance of duty. There seems to have been a delicate balance between expectation of and actual compliance: both Cicero and Quintus expected to work together, but other factors, e.g. individual interests and situations, also affected their ability to do so. In the case of Caesar, their combined efforts brought *dignitas* to them both.[86]

During Quintus' service with Caesar in Gaul, the Ciceros appear to have focused their efforts and interest on one particular goal: a consulship for Quintus.[87] At home, Cicero offered hospitality to Balbus and his entourage, associates of Caesar, when they came to Rome. Eager for news, Cicero drew Atticus into the brothers' political schemes. As for Quintus, his service with Caesar was boosting the brothers' shared political capital, and his brother was quick to praise his efforts.[88] When Quintus conferred with his brother early in 54 about the possibility of returning to Rome, Cicero replied with a discussion of their mutual interests and political connections. Addressing his brother as *mi optime et suavissime frater*, "my sweetest and best brother," Cicero promised candid advice, not necessarily what Quintus wanted to hear but what would be in fact to his advantage. Though Cicero himself would rather have had Quintus back at home with him, he deferred to his brother's wishes:

> qua re [si] suavitatis equidem nostrae fruendae causa cuperem te ad id tempus venire quod dixeras, sed illud malo tamen quod putas magis e ⟨re⟩ tua.

[84] Epic, *Q. Fr.* 3.1.11; 3.4.4; 3.5.4; 3.6(8).3; 3.7(9).6. Britain, *Q. Fr.* 2.14(13).2; 2.16(15).4. Reactions, *Q. Fr.* 2.16(15).5. Cooperation in general, *Q. Fr.* 2.11(10).4; 3.1.18; 3.5.3; 3.7(9).3–6.

[85] *Fraterne*, *Q. Fr.* 2.14(13).2, and *Mandata*, *Q. Fr.* 2.13(12).2–3, cf. *Q. Fr.* 2.2.2; 2.3.6; 2.4.1; 2.11(10).5; 2.12(11).1; 2.16(15).1; 3.1.9; 3.4.2; 3.5.5. There is also evidence that Cicero did not in fact always comply; see, for example, *Q. Fr.* 3.7(9).1; 2.7(6).2. See also Shackleton Bailey, *Cicero*, 72, 81–82.

[86] Shackleton Bailey, *Cicero*, 92.

[87] For this interpretation of events, see in general Wiseman, "Ambitions of Quintus." Stockton, *Cicero*, 220–22, suggests more general aims of gaining Caesar's friendship and political protection.

[88] Entertaining Balbus, *Q. Fr.* 3.1.12, and drawing in Atticus, *Att.* 4.14.2. Quintus' service with Caesar, *Q. Fr.* 2.14(13).1, cf. *Att.* 4.19.2.

For this reason [if] for the sake of enjoying your pleasant company I would like you to come at that time which you named, but I prefer nevertheless that you come at that time which you think is more in your interest. Cic. Q. Fer. 2.15(14).3

Cicero balanced his affection for his brother against their common political interests: if it had been simply a matter of individual desires, of course both Quintus and his brother would have preferred to be together at Rome. But as it was, their common political goal, election of Quintus to the consulship, superseded affection. Later in the year, Cicero reiterated the principle, urging Quintus to stick it out with Caesar. In both passages, he explicitly stated that Quintus' service with Caesar garnered *dignitas* for both of them: *communi dignitati* and *ad omnem statum nostrae dignitatis*, it was part of a joint plan, *consilium nostrum*.[89] Both passages attest to the brothers' mutual interest in cultivating their connection with Caesar. Circumstances required redefinition of their interests to achieve this common goal. As Cicero enunciated this principle, he emphasized that he was speaking honestly, without prejudice, in a word, *fraterne*, like a brother, linking their political goals to fraternal *pietas*.

The events of 49–47 and the war between Caesar and Pompey tested not only the Ciceros' friendship with Caesar but also the fraternal alliance between Cicero and his brother. Cicero's almost daily letters to Atticus document his own deliberations and the growing tensions between the brothers.[90] Cicero himself was undecided for a long time over whether to leave Italy and follow Pompey or to remain neutral but stay in Italy. At first, Cicero believed that his brother was willing to follow his lead; he felt that his brother was identifying with his own dilemma: *iacet in maerore meus frater neque tam de sua vita quam de mea metuit*, "my brother is prostrate with grief and he fears not so much for his own life as for mine."[91] Quintus did, it seems, spend some time with Cicero in Pompey's camp during 48, but his interests appear to have diverged from his brother's. The sticking point may have been Quintus' allegiance to Caesar, and Cicero himself was aware of this issue at the time.[92] Even after the fact, Cicero attempted to shore up Quintus' ties to Caesar, by writing to him that Quintus was not in any way responsible for their

---

[89] *Q. Fr.* 3.6(8).1, balancing affection and political goals, *Q. Fr.* 2.15(14).3. Cicero's status and influence may have been Quintus' most important political asset: Wiseman, "Ambitions of Quintus," 111.

[90] For example, *Att.* 8.3.5; 8.4.1; 8.11D.1, 3; 8.14.1–3; 10.4.5–6; 10.11.1–4; 11.5.4; 11.6.7; 11.8.2; 11.15.2; and see Shackleton Bailey, *Cicero*, 163–66; Stockton, *Cicero*, 261–62.

[91] *Att.* 10.4.6, cf. 9.6.4.

[92] *Att.* 9.1.4.

decision to leave Italy.[93] This effort on Cicero's part to promote his brother's political connections conforms to the expectation of fraternal cooperation, but it was not without self-interest. Cicero would not want Caesar to think that he had not made his own decision to leave Italy, and moreover, generosity to his brother might earn him points in Caesar's book and advance his own rapprochement with the general.[94] In this case, Cicero's observance of his fraternal duty coincided with his own self-interest; Quintus' interests appear however, to have been, somewhat different.

Already on their return to Italy in the autumn of 48, Cicero was aware that a storm was brewing: *Quintus aversissimo a me animo Patris fuit*, "Quintus was very antagonistic to me at Patrae." The lingering bitterness blossomed as the brothers began to reconstruct their relationship with Caesar in the new political context. Quintus' son was instrumental in bringing the conflict into the open. Quintus sent his son to Caesar not only to speak in defense of his father but also to accuse his uncle. Cicero wrote to Atticus that no other event of those difficult years was so bitter.[95] Quintus seems to have believed that his brother's decision to join the Pompeians damaged his own alliance with Caesar and that he himself had stronger ties to Caesar than his brother. Cicero's friends thought otherwise: Caesar's goodwill toward Quintus had been motivated primarily by his respect for and rapport with his brother. Quintus was in disrepute with Caesar, for what reason it is uncertain, but Caesar seems to have thought Quintus was somehow responsible for the brothers' decision to join the Pompeians.[96] Quintus may also have attacked his brother

---

[93] *Att.* 11.12.1–2, cf. Stockton, *Cicero*, 263. For Quintus with Cicero during 48, see Shackleton Bailey, *Cicero*, 167, cf. 162–63. Cicero has Quintus in the *de Divinatione* (1.68) call him (Cicero) to witness a true prediction before the battle at Dyrrachium, cf. Stockton, *Cicero*, 263.

[94] Shackleton Bailey, *Cicero*, 181, puts it rather more elegantly: "[l]eaving aside the implication that the virtue of magnanimity was alien to the first century B.C., and without denying that Cicero here showed more than a trace of it, one may fairly remember that the opinion he contradicted was unflattering to his own *amour propre* ('the last thing I wanted Caesar to think was that on such a matter I had followed anybody's judgement but my own'), and that a generous attitude was more likely to impress Caesar favorably than the contrary."

[95] Storm brewing, *Att.* 11.5.4, and young Quintus' attack, *Att.* 11.8.2. Quintus' son continued to attack his uncle see, for example, *Att.* 10.7.3; 10.10.6; 10.11.1, 3; 11.10.1, cf. Shackleton Bailey, *Cicero*, 163–64, 180.

[96] Caesar's opinion of Quintus, *Att.* 11.9.2, 11.12.1. In his letters of early 49, Cicero frequently used "the first person singular about things which concerned them jointly, for example, what to do with the boys. In letters from correspondents (Caesar, Pompey, Caelius, Sulpicius, Mescinius, Antony, Dolabella) all in one way or another canvassing Cicero's attitude and conduct in the crisis, Quintus' name never occurs. Seemingly (despite a con-

because he felt stranded in the new political configuration: Cicero was invited to return to Italy through the mediation of his son-in-law Dolabella, whose letter of invitation makes no mention of Quintus.[97] Judging by his active animosity toward Cicero, Quintus did not think that his own interests were compatible with his brother's or even that his brother was taking his interests into consideration.

Quintus' hostility was a source of grief for Cicero. He described his reactions to accounts of the young Quintus' behavior as torture, *excruciant*, and his grief over his brother makes him physically ill.[98] When he first learned of his brother's anger, he wished that one of them had never been born:

> *Haec ad te die natali meo scripsi; quo utinam susceptus non essem, aut ne quid ex eadem matre postea natum esset! plura scribere fletu prohibeor.*
> I write this letter to you on my birthday. Would that I had not been taken into the family, and that nothing had been born from my mother afterwards! Tears keep me from writing more. Cic. *Att.* 11.9.3

Only by not existing could he escape the pangs of his brother's rejection, because their relationship was rooted in kinship and did not dissolve even after they ceased to behave like friends. This is a far cry from the sense of unity and shared fortune that Cicero had expressed at the time of his exile. Quintus seems to have felt that their interests were polarized, and then acted in such a way as to intensify their opposition. Nevertheless, Cicero did not abandon the attempt to preserve their connection; he invoked Caesar on behalf of his brother, despite Quintus' angry accusations. In comparison to this breach in fraternal devotion, Cicero's friendship with Atticus survived even though the civil war brought them disagreements. Atticus took up Cicero's case with Quintus—even then, it seems, Atticus could not bring himself to hate Quintus, though he apparently chastised him for his harshness to his brother. Atticus' efforts to

---

trary opinion later attributed to Caesar) they made no account of him as a factor influencing Cicero's decision. . . . An impression of passivity amounting to almost paralysis on Quintus' part is supported by the few passages in which his future is specifically mooted. . . .[Cicero seems to have taken Quintus' acquiescence] for due confidence and loyalty. In reality (to judge from what was to follow) it was a line of least resistance, travelled in frustration, helplessness, and interior disgruntlement. When Quintus set out for Pompey's camp, he let his hard work in Gaul go for nothing and said good-bye to hope of favour from Caesar. Why did he not take an independent course, neutral or Caesarian? Perhaps from republican principle, perhaps from lack of enthusiasm for Caesar personally or dislike of his entourage, but chiefly, one imagines, from the habit of a lifetime which made dissociation from his elder brother at such a turning-point a psychological impossibility" (Shackleton Bailey, *Cicero*, 182).

[97] *Fam.* 9.9, cf. Shackleton Bailey, *Cicero*, 162–63.

[98] *Att.* 11.10.1, 11.9.2, cf. Shackleton Bailey, *Cicero*, 179. See above Chap. 2, p. 74.

achieve a reconciliation between the brothers failed, while his own friendship with Cicero increased in closeness: only after Cicero broke with his brother did he write that Atticus was his only resort, the only person to whom Cicero could entrust the care of his daughter; thus friend succeeded brother in familial intimacy.[99] Quintus continued to upbraid his brother in letters, expressing what he thought was justifiable anger. Cicero was unsympathetic to his brother's complaints, and perhaps unaware of their causes, proving that he was unable to put himself in his brother's position, unable truly to be a second self. The circumstances of civil war may have caused this inability—in other desperate situations, Cicero's exile for example, the brothers stuck together. Or perhaps the tensions created by civil war unmasked a fault deep within this relationship, revealing places where the norms of fraternal *pietas* did not apply.[100] Quintus may have been aware on some level all along that Cicero's rhetoric of fraternal *pietas* did not always correspond to his motives and decisions. In the context of civil war, even a brother could not be trusted to keep his own interests from harming his brother, and fraternal *pietas* could lose its power to sustain the affection that motivates reciprocity among brothers.

This case study of Cicero and Quintus has illustrated the complex interplay of fraternal *pietas*, personal ambition, and political events in the public and private lives of elite brothers. Cicero and Quintus adopted the spirit of cooperation associated with *consortium* in managing property and raising their children. Cicero's wife Terentia also shared these family responsibilities with Cicero and his brother, though her first duty seem to have been to their children, whereas Quintus could be expected to take care of Cicero, too. Cicero's letters to his brother are full of the affection that was the counterpart of duty in fraternal *pietas*. In public life, even though Cicero was the more famous and accomplished of the two, both brothers had a role to play in securing their shared reputation and success. Cicero's exile put Quintus in a stronger position where he was more responsible for the brothers' continuing political influence. The civil war

---

[99] Atticus and Quintus, *Att.* 11.13.2, and 11.10.2–3; Atticus as last resort, *Att.* 11.9.3.

[100] Other issues that may have persistently rankled include Quintus' marriage to Pomponia, Cicero's dislike of his freedman Statius, disappointments in Gaul and in their hopes for the consulship, incidents in Cilicia, Cicero's loan of the money from Cilicia to Pompey. "Grudges of long standing, probably unsuspected by the elder brother and in part perhaps not consciously realized by the younger, will have lain beneath an eruption which so thoroughly shattered the surface of family concord. That seems to have been Cicero's own belief, implicit in his words to Atticus after reading Quintus' letter of accusation: 'he would not have flaunted his hatred of me either now or previously were it not that he sees I am totally ruined' (*Att.* 11.13.2). If Quintus would have concealed his hatred in different circumstances, it looks as though (in Cicero's opinion) he had concealed it before the circumstances of 48 existed" (Shackleton Bailey, *Cicero*, 182–83).

between Caesar and Pompey tested and ultimately broke the fraternal *pietas* that had mediated Cicero's and Quintus' differences for many years. Throughout these years, Cicero's friend Atticus was a close companion, almost another brother, who shared in his domestic duties and advised him about politics. The similarities between Cicero's friendship with Atticus and his relationship with his brother show why the Romans' ideas about brothers were so easily transferred to close friends who might take the part of a brother both in public and in private. The civil war brought out critical differences in these two relationships. Atticus was Cicero's refuge when his relationship with Quintus deteriorated in 48–47, yet, despite the hostility between him and his brother, Cicero still felt an attachment to Quintus of an almost physical nature. The brothers were held together even when their feelings for each other had changed, whereas the friends sustained their affection in spite of events that might have divided them. Both brothers and friends could be invaluable assets in a Roman's political career: even though a friend might at times prove more devoted than a brother, a brother was closely and permanently identified with a man through their shared public and private lives.

Scipio Africanus and Scipio Asiagenus

The Scipiones were central players in Roman military expansion during and after the Second Punic War. Through four generations this family attained prominence in politics and achieved exceptional success in winning high office: in three of the four generations, at least one Scipio was consul—in contrast to Hopkins' analysis, which predicts that only about half of the consuls ought to have a consular son.[101] The Scipiones' success began with the brothers Cnaeus (cos. 222) and Publius (cos. 218), who fought the Carthaginians in Spain while Hannibal ravaged Italy.[102] In the next generation, another pair of brothers and a cousin were active in politics: Cnaeus' son, P. Cornelius Scipio Nasica, and the more illustrious sons of Publius, P. Cornelius Scipio Africanus and L. Cornelius Scipio Asiagenus.[103] All three were elected consul. Nasica seems to have

[101] Hopkins, *Death and Renewal*, 55–69.
[102] For Cnaeus, see *PWRE s.v.* Cornelius 345, and Publius, *PWRE s.v.* Cornelius 330. Cnaeus probably served as his brother's legate when the consul was sent in 218 B.C.E. to cut off reinforcements to Hannibal's army and to drive the Carthaginians from Spain. Publius followed Hannibal to the Rhône. After failing to stop Hannibal in Gaul, P. Scipio returned to Italy, where he fought and lost two battles against Hannibal in the fall of 218 at the Ticinus and at the Trebia. During the next seven years, the brothers led the Roman forces in Spain and both died in battle in 211, Publius on the upper Baetis and Cnaeus at Ilorici.
[103] Nasica, *PWRE s.v.* Cornelius 350, Africanus, *PWRE s.v.* Cornelius 336, Asiagenus, *PWRE s.v.* Cornelius 337.

been too young to participate in the Second Punic War, but both sons of Publius Scipio were active in the campaigns against Hannibal. Historians, both ancient and modern, have tended to dismiss Asiagenus as a lesser light than his brother. But it cannot have been easy being the brother of Scipio Africanus, and Asiagenus' career is more likely to represent that of a typical senatorial brother than his more illustrious sibling's—in other words, his brother's reputation hurt him as much as it helped him in politics. Africanus' friend Gaius Laelius also figures in the history of these brothers.

Throughout the Second Punic war, Laelius worked more closely with Africanus and to a far greater extent than his brother Asiagenus did.[104] For example, when the fleet sailed from Sicily in 205 B.C.E., Laelius led twenty warships on the left wing, half the Roman forces, while Africanus led the other half; Asiagenus sailed along with his brother.[105] Laelius' prominence may reflect his abilities as well as a personal relationship with Africanus. We might compare this pair of friends with a pair of brothers, T. and L. Quinctius Flamininus, who defeated the Achaean Confederacy in 198–197 B.C.E. When Titus was consul in 198, the Senate appointed his brother to command the fleet. While the consul was besieging Elatia, his brother, relying on the consul's authority, began negotiating a peace treaty. Both brothers' powers were extended through the next year by the Senate, and together they clinched a deal with Attalus.[106] Comparison between the Flamini and the Scipiones reveals the flexibility in relationships among men of the same generation. Where a brother was present, willing, and able, he would be a man's partner in his military career. The Senate's appointment of L. Quinctius indicates formal, public acknowledgment of such a partnership.

Africanus' brother appears only occasionally in Livy's narrative of the Second Punic War, although Asiagenus does make several trips to Rome to report his brother's progress. It may be that Asiagenus was much younger than Africanus: he was the only one of three delegates to Rome in 202 who had not yet been elected to office.[107] Given his junior status, Asiagenus

---

[104] Africanus valued Laelius' support so much that he was reluctant even to begin a campaign without him, Livy 27.17.8. On an early mission, Laelius appears to have been the only officer who was privy to his commander's plans, Livy 26.42.5. He regularly shared duties of command with Africanus, in various capacities, e.g. as *praefectus classis*, 29.25.10, and as *quaestor extra sortem*, 29.33.9. Laelius went as Africanus' advance man in Africa, Livy 29.1.14–16 and 24.5, and was instrumental in the negotiations that finally brought the Second Punic war to a close, Livy 30.16.1 and 17.1–14.

[105] Livy 29.25.10.

[106] Appointment of L. Quinctius to command the fleet, Livy 32.16.2; his negotiations, 32.19.1, 5–6; both brothers proroged, 32.28.9, 11; deal with Attalus, 32.39.7–10.

[107] Livy 30.38.4; the two other delegates were L. Veturius Philo (cos. 206), Livy 28.10.2, and M. Marcius Ralla (pr. urb. 204), Livy 29.13.2.

may have been included in this mission because of his relationship with Africanus, as if to represent the commander in a more personal way than the senior delegates. Africanus himself was only in his mid-twenties when he first went to Spain in 211 and he may have brought his brother along, as elder relatives often did to prepare the young men of the family for a career in public service. It is an attractive hypothesis to explain Asiagenus' absences from his brother's campaign through the notion of *consortium*: while Africanus was abroad, Asiagenus may have used his visits home to take care of family matters on behalf of both brothers.

After the war, when the brothers and Laelius were back in Rome, their relationships continued to intersect in election politics in the years 193–190 B.C.E. Elections were a prime occasion for brothers to bring their relationship into the public eye. Canvassing provided a wide field for appeals to fraternal *pietas* and rich prizes for those whose brothers could make their devotion pay off in votes. Because of the openness of the Roman political system, competition could be stiff in consular elections, especially in years where more than one patrician was in the race,[108] and a famous brother could make the difference. A new player joined the group at the time, Scipio Nasica, the cousin of Asiagenus and Africanus. Again, the Quinctii Flaminini brothers provide a point of comparison.

The elections for 192–190 B.C.E. took place against the backdrop of Africanus' victory over Hannibal and T. Quinctius Flamininus' successful campaigns in Greece. Livy's account of the elections for 192 reveals the singular power of a brother's sponsorship in a hotly contested race. Livy focuses on the competition between L. Flamininus and Scipio Nasica. Africanus was campaigning for his cousin Nasica, Titus Flamininus for his brother Lucius. Africanus and Flamininus were almost equally influential backers: Flamininus had just won victory in Greece and Africanus was still lionized for defeating Hannibal. Against all odds—backed by his cousin, the entire Cornelian *gens*, and with L. Cornelius Merula as consul—Nasica lost.[109] Whatever factors actually influenced the outcome of the election for 192, Livy at least credits fraternal *pietas* as a powerful strategy for winning votes. Flamininus was a more compelling advocate, Livy explains, because he was campaigning for his brother, not his cousin, *pro fratre germano non patrueli*,[110] and a brother who as prolegate had done his part in waging the war in Greece. Both a cousin and a brother could be called *frater*, but apparently the relationship between sons of one or both the same parents was accorded more signifi-

---

[108] For a dramatic ship of state metaphor for the unpredictability of elections, see Cic. *Mur.* 35–36.

[109] Livy 35.10.9, cf. 2–7; for Merula's consulship, see Livy 34.54.1; it is not clear from the sources what relation Merula was to the Scipiones, see *PWRE s. v.* Cornelius 270.

[110] Livy 35.10.8.

cance than the more distant relationship between cousins. The outcome of the elections for the next year tends to confirm this conclusion in an indirect way. The elections for 191 again pitted a cousin against a brother, this time Africanus' brother Asiagenus and his cousin Nasica, in a competition among three patricians. Nasica was elected, and Livy explains his success as a result of his own reputation.[111] Africanus' brother Asiagenus does not seem to have been helped by fraternal *pietas*. Some Romans were apparently jealous of Africanus' success, and this hostility may have hurt his brother's chances in the elections for 191.[112]

Asiagenus was finally elected consul for 190 and his colleague was his brother's friend Laelius. One of the consuls for this year would have the privilege of taking on the war against Antiochus. Instead of choosing a commander by lot, as was usual, the Senate was to assign provinces and anticipated a contest because the coming war was bound to be glorious and lucrative. For the politics of this decision, we have the testimony of both Livy and Cicero. Romans were, Livy suggests, eager for a rematch between their champion Africanus and Hannibal, who was now advising Antiochus.[113] Though Asiagenus and Laelius were consuls, all attention was focused on Africanus when the question came up in the Senate. According to Cicero, the Senate was prepared to award Asia to Laelius, because Asiagenus did not have enough gumption, *parumque in eo putaretur esse animi, parum roboris.*[114] But then when Africanus offered to serve as his brother's legate, his brother was a shoo-in. Cicero suggests that the Senate asked Africanus to accompany his brother as a shadow commander. By securing the command for his brother, Cicero implies, Africanus defended the family honor as well as his brother's virtues. The choice between friend and brother may well have caused Africanus a conflict in loyalty, yet fraternal *pietas* was more powerful than the duty of friendship, at least as Cicero and Livy saw it. Whether or not Asiagenus was as incapable as the Senate feared, this case shows that an illustrious man like Africanus could accomplish quite a lot in the name of fraternal *pietas*, even for a brother whose abilities were dubious. In the event, Asiagenus won the decisive battle against Antiochus at Magnesia while his brother lay ill at Elea, far from the fray.[115]

[111] Livy 35.24.5.

[112] Livy 35.10.5.

[113] Livy 37.1.9–10.

[114] Cic. *Phil.* 11.17, and *Mur.* 32, cf. Val. Max. 5.5.1. Appointment of a legate of consular rank was unusual, but did occur "especially where there [was] a family relationship between *legatus* and commander" (G. M. Paul, *A Historical Commentary on Sallust's Bellum Iugurthinum*, 92). Cicero expected it, *Att.* 13.6.4.

[115] Livy 37.37.6 and 45.3. Africanus did play a role in negotiations with Antiochus, Livy 37.34–36 and 45.3–21.

The Scipiones' cooperation in military campaigns shaped their public image back at Rome. Political prosecutions, like elections, could also bring out fraternal *pietas*. Livy's account of the trials of the Scipiones is notoriously vexed; without unraveling all the problems, my discussion will draw attention to several details that reflect the power of fraternal relationships to shape Roman historical and political traditions. In the first phase of the trials that Livy records, Africanus was brought to trial on charges relating to luxury at his headquarters in Syracuse, to his acquittal of Pleminius, and to his role in negotiating the peace with Antiochus.[116] Africanus avoided trial first by leading the Senate in a day of visiting the temples, and then because of illness. When Asiagenus petitioned the tribunes to accept his brother's plea of illness, Tib. Sempronius Gracchus (one of the tribunes whose unanimous vote was needed) superseded legal requirements, saying that his brother's excuse should be enough, as if a brother's word were worth as much as proper procedure.[117] Livy attributes to Gracchus a fiery speech defending Africanus, in which he describes Africanus as a partner in his brother's victory, *fratrem consortem huius gloriae*. The term *consors* underscores a continuity between the private, domestic duties of brothers and their partnership in military campaigns.

After Africanus death, Livy's account continues, the Q. Petillii (two tribunes with the same name) proposed an investigation into the money that was collected from Antiochus, attacking the Scipiones' reputation and influence in the Senate: *Petillii nobilitatem et regnum in senatu Scipionum accusabant*.[118] Asiagenus spoke in his own defense against the Petillii's proposal, against what he framed as a posthumous attack on his brother. He claimed that he was only being prosecuted as a sacrifice to his brother's reputation. Asiagenus was accused of receiving a payoff in exchange for granting Antiochus more favorable terms of peace, one of the same charges that had been brought against his brother. Livy, in an attempt to exonerate Asiagenus, explains how a bookkeeping error could account for what looked like a payoff.[119] At this point in his account, Livy relates an episode involving Africanus: before his death, when the senate had demanded the same amount from him, he had had his account books brought into the Senate and dramatically tore them to shreds, indignant that anyone would question his integrity.[120] Livy's connection of these two episodes shows that the reputation of these two brothers was intertwined in the historical tradition.

[116] Livy 38.51.1–4, for luxury 29.19.12ff., and for Pleminius at Locri, 29.8.6 ff.
[117] Gracchus' exception, Livy 38.52.9–10; Africanus avoids trial, Livy 38.51.7–52.11.
[118] Livy 38.54.6, and for Asiagenus' speech, 54.8–11.
[119] Livy 38.55.6–10.
[120] Livy 38.55.10–12.

Halfway through his account of the trials, Livy considers inconsistencies in the historical sources for Africanus' death and in the speeches attributed to the parties in these trials. He then posits an alternate version of the trial based on the speeches. In this reconstruction, Asiagenus was prosecuted for misappropriating the revenues from the victory over Antiochus while Africanus was still alive and on a mission in Etruria. When Asiagenus was arrested, his brother rushed to the rescue snatching him forceably from the tribunes who were leading him to prison; he acted *magis pie quam civiliter*, "more out of devotion to his brother than civic duty."[121] The hostility so dominant in his sources, Livy concludes, must have arisen from this event alone, from Africanus' use of excessive force to rescue his brother, his only act that went beyond the law and his rights as citizen. Some Romans probably did react negatively to the Scipiones' public fraternal *pietas*, interpreting their solidarity as evidence of dangerous ambition.[122] Like other relatives, brothers, too, had to adjust their personal relationships to serve Rome: *pietas* should not endanger devotion to the ultimate father figure, the *patria*. It may be no coincidence, then, that when (toward the end of Livy's account of the trials) their cousin Scipio Nasica speaks in defense of Asiagenus, he recalls the family history of defending Rome, equating Asiagenus' victory over Antiochus with Africanus' defeat of Hannibal.[123]

The equation of Asiagenus with his successful brother recalls a theme from Livy's battle narratives from the Second Punic War. In Livy's account, when Africanus awarded the highest praise to his officers, he would say that they were equal to himself. His brother Asiagenus and his friend Laelius earn the same praise, but not so other officers. A pair of battle narratives at the beginning of Livy's Book 28 points up this contrast. In the first, the propraetor M. Silanus earned warm praise, *conlaudato benigne Silano*, after he routed the Carthaginians in Celtiberia. Then, when Asiagenus sacked Orongis, Africanus measured his brother's achievement against his own: *Scipio conlaudato fratre cum quanto poterat verborum honore Carthagini ab se captae captam ab eo Orongin aequasset . . .* , "Scipio gave his brother as great a compliment as he could, saying that the capture of Orongis was equal to his own capture of New Carthage."[124] In both cases, Livy expresses the praise in an ablative absolute introducing Africanus' next move. The praise of Asiagenus,

---

[121] Livy 38.56.9; cf. 38.56.11–12 and 51.1–5. Livy's reflection on the sources, 38.56.1–7.

[122] For a discussion of other social and political factors that might have contributed to the opposition to the Scipiones, see E. S. Gruen, *Studies in Greek Culture and Roman Policy*, 132–37.

[123] *Consors gloriae*, Livy 38.53.3; cf. 38.54.10, and Nasica's speech, 38.58.10.

[124] Praise for Silanus, Livy 28.2.14, and for Asiagenus, 28.4.2.

however, was more than a simple circumstance of the commander's strategy. Livy expands the praise of Asiagenus with a clause that describes him as equal to his brother, the famous general. Livy draws attention to this form of praise, when he says that Scipio gave his brother as great a compliment as he could. The juxtaposition of the two battles and two commendations—the first of Silanus, the second of Asiagenus—invites comparison between brother and colleague, and the comparison privileges the brother. Whether out of merit or brotherly sentiment, Scipio appears to have lavished richer praise on his brother than on Silanus. When Asiagenus is praised as equal to his brother, the phrase resonates with Roman assumptions about fraternal *pietas* and brothers' roles in the family. These assumptions could be transferred to a close friend, such as Laelius, whom Africanus praised as his equal after the capture of New Carthage. After rewarding the soldiers according to their merit in battle, Scipio singled out Laelius: *ante omnes C. Laelium praefectum classis et omni genere laudis sibimet ipse aequavit et corona aurea ac triginta bubus donavit*; "in front of everyone [Scipio] both likened C. Laelius, the prefect of the fleet, even to himself with every kind of praise and he bestowed him with a gold crown and thirty cattle."[125] The emphatic particle "-met" suggests how extraordinary such praise was, even for a tried and true companion like Laelius. In the private context, friends were like brothers because they shared a similar kind of emotional attachment. In the public context of a military campaign, friends and brothers achieved the same status not through emotion but by their actions.

The military exploits of brothers could influence political events long after the battle. Nasica's speech for Asiagenus was so persuasive that he was released from prison amidst great public rejoicing.[126] The Romans were ready to believe that a man whose competence the Senate had questioned had won the war and deserved glory equal to one of the greatest generals ever. What makes this apparently impossible claim credible? The success of Nasica's appeal relies on a powerful subtext of assumptions about the fraternal relationship. Because he was Africanus' brother, Romans expected Asiagenus to be like him, endowed with similar capabilities which lead him to commensurate success. And (or?) because his brother had done so many glorious deeds for Rome, Asiagenus should be given the benefit of the doubt, and his errors should not be allowed to besmirch the reputation of his brother and the rest of the family.[127]

Fraternal traditions are harder to trace in the next generation of Scip-

---

[125] Livy 26.48.14.

[126] Livy 38.60.3–7.

[127] We might compare Plutarch's advice to brothers to profit from each other's strengths and compensate for and not condemn the other's weakness, *Mor.* 482A–483C, 484D–486F. Livy's treatment of the Scipiones seems to do just that.

iones: neither Asiagenus' son nor either of Africanus' sons left much of a mark on the historical record. But in the third generation, adoptions created a new context for fraternal *pietas*. Fraternal relationships center on the biological sons of L. Aemilius Paullus and their adoptive brothers. Africanus' elder son adopted one of L. Aemilius Paullus' sons, Scipio Aemilianus. An otherwise obscure Q. Fabius Maximus adopted another, Fabius Aemilianus, and also one of the sons of Cn. Servilius Caepio, Fabius Servilianus. Servilianus also had two natural brothers, Cnaeus and Quintus.

Although the sources are not as rich for the Servilii as for the others, there is a recognizable pattern of fraternal cooperation in their military careers during the campaigns against Viriathus in Spain, 145–140 B.C.E. In 145, Fabius Aemilianus was the first consul sent against Viriathus. When his successor Q. Pompeius was unsuccessful, Aemilianus' adoptive brother Fabius Servilianus was sent to carry on the fight.[128] Perhaps surprising is the apparent cooperation between Fabius Servilianus and Fabius Aemilianus, men who are brothers *only* by adoption. Among the natural brothers in this family, however, fraternal *pietas* seem to have been less of a factor. Q. Servilius Caepio, as consul of 140, took over the command as successor to Fabius Servilianus, his natural brother. Caepio renewed hostilities against Viriathus, rejecting the treaties that Servilianus had made as unworthy of the Romans: ὁ γὰρ ἀδελφὸς Σερουιλιανοῦ, τοῦ ταῦτα συνθεμένου, Καιπίων, διάδοχος αὐτῷ τῆς, στρατηγίας γενόμενος, διέβαλλε τὰς συνθήκας καὶ ἐπέστελλε Ῥωμαίοις ἀπρεπεστάτας εἶναι, "for, when Caepio, Servilianus' brother and his successor in the province, took up this command, he discredited the treaties and sent word that the treaties were unbecoming to the Romans."[129] This difference in opinion about the treaty with Viriathus may have grown out of previously existing rivalry between Caepio and Fabius Servilianus; but in any case, events of the next year tend to confirm that these two natural brothers did not always cooperate. In 139, Q. and Cn. Servilius Caepio prosecuted Q. Pompeius for extortion, *res repetundae*; Fabius Servilianus does not seem to have joined his brothers in this lawsuit. Fabius Servilianus had succeeded Q. Pompeius in Spain and they both suffered losses against Viriathus, in contrast to Caepio, who defeated Viriathus and engineered his assassination. Perhaps lingering rivalry over the campaign in Spain led Fabius Servilianus to distance him-

[128] His legate, C. Fannius, who was brother-in-law to Laelius adds a double connection to Aemilianus, because this Laelius was a friend of Aemilianus (Scipio's natural brother) and the son of Africanus' friend, Laelius.

[129] App. *Iber*. 70. For the whole campaign, App. *Iber*. 63–75, and Livy *Epit*. 52–54. On the prosecution of Q. Pompeius (dating it to 139), see Gruen, *Criminal Courts*, 36–38, cf. 19–20.

self from his brother's prosecution of Q. Pompeius. Cicero characterizes Q. and Cn. Servilius as men driven by *cupido* and *inimicitia* when he refers to their prosecution of Pompeius.[130] Quintus' rejection of his brother's treaties may be another example of his ambition, though in his report to Rome, Quintus cached his personal motive in patriotic rhetoric that obscured the role that fraternal rivalry might have played in his decision.

Adoption could generate fraternal cooperation, as it did between the adoptive sons of Fabius, and it might interfere with relations among natural brothers, as it may have done among the Servilii in the preceding case. But adoption did not necessarily interfere with the devotion of natural brothers who were adopted by different fathers. The sons of Aemilius Paullus were famous for their fraternal *pietas*. Their behavior at the critical moment of their father's death reflects the norms associated with *consortium*. The brothers inherited their father's estate together. But then Scipio ceded his share to Fabius because Fabius needed the money more.[131] Cicero praised his generosity: Scipio's virtue in sharing with his brother was of far greater value than the property itself: *haec profecto quae sunt summarum virtutum pluris aestimanda sunt quam illa quae sunt pecuniae*, "undoubtedly, these deeds, which involve the greatest virtue, should be valued more than those that involve money."[132] This example of fraternal *pietas* is even more compelling because it reflects the Romans' belief in the biological basis of fraternal kinship. Even though Scipio and Fabius, sons of Aemilius Paullus, had each been adopted by different fathers, their fraternal bond remained untouched by the new legal relationships created through adoption.[133] As if to commemorate the transcendence of fraternity, the brothers staged Terence's *Adelphoe* at their natural father's funeral games. Though it was Fabius' idea, Scipio put up half the expenses.[134]

The Scipiones continued to be a powerful example of Roman fraternal and military glory in Livy's history even after they ceased to be actively involved in political events. When king Philip V of Macedon wanted to teach his sons a lesson about brotherly love and the responsibilities of royalty, he brought forward historical examples. In the speech that Livy

[130] Cic. *Font.* 23, 27.
[131] Polyb. 31.28.1–4, Plut. *Aem.* 39.5.
[132] Cic. *Parad.* 48.
[133] Scipio and Fabius appear in Cicero's *De Amicitia* as a model of friends, *Amic.* 69, as do the Gracchi, Cic. *Amic.* 38–39.
[134] Ter. *Ad. Didascalia* Codex Bembinus, and on the finances, Polyb. 31.28.5. Scipio and Fabius were following a tradition of sons offering games for their father: the earliest recorded gladiatorial show in Rome was given by D. Junius Brutus Pera and his brother in 264 for their father, Val. Max. 2.4.7, and see Hopkins, *Death and Renewal*, 4 with n. 3, and G. Boyer, "Le droit successoral Romain dans Polybe," *RIDA* 4 (1950): 179.

ascribes to Philip, the king admonishes his sons to settle their differences and secure a peaceful kingdom.[135] Brothers who are divided against themselves only ruin the state they rule and bring about their own demise. They should emulate the kings of Sparta and of Pergamum, who rule in tandem, and also Roman brothers, who though not kings, stand together in support of their country. Livy follows Polybius in general in this speech but changes the emphasis to bring together the personal and the political. Polybius' version focuses on the contrast between tyrannical monarchy and the constitutional monarchy in which the two kings cooperate in governing with the ephors,[136] whereas Livy emphasizes the fraternal relationship between these two rulers. Several details of Livy's account introduce Roman ideas about fraternal *pietas* into this political situation. First, the cooperation between the Spartan kings is characterized as a *sociabilis consortio*, "allied partnership."[137] The term *consortio* recalls the fraternal *consortium*; though its connotations are more general, *consortio* conveys the metaphorical extension of *consortium* from a family partnership to abstract ideas.[138] Second, Livy attributes the Attalids' success to *fraterna unanimitas*, namely unity in purpose, concord, and shared responsibility to respect each other—all ideals consonant with *consortium*.[139] The political significance of this fraternity corresponds to Polybius' description of the Attalids, which almost seems to gloss *consortio*: διὰ τὴν πρὸς αὑτοὺς ὁμόνοιαν καὶ συμφωνίαν καὶ τὸ δύνασθαι καταξίωσιν ἀλλήλοις διαφυλάττειν, "on account of their unanimity and agreement and of their being able to safeguard each other's reputation."[140] Philip urges his sons to act like partners; they are metaphorically *consortes*, in that they will share a patrimony, that is, their father's kingdom. Finally, to the two Greek examples in Polybius, Livy adds Roman brothers: T. and L. Quinctius Flamininus, P. and L. Cornelius Scipio, and their father and uncle, Cn. and P. Cornelius Scipio. These Roman brothers mobilized fraternal *pietas* to their own and

---

[135] Livy 40.8.7–20.

[136] Polyb. 23.11.1–8. The passage refers to the "abolition of the ephorate and transformation of the dual kingship into a μοναρχία that characterized Cleomenes' rule as tyranny" (F. W. Walbank, *A Historical Commentary on Polybius*, 3:234–35), cf. Polyb. 2.47.3, 4.81.14. See also Gruen, "The Last Years of Philip V," *GRBS* (1974): 240–41.

[137] Livy 40.8.12.

[138] Usage of the related term *consortio*, though rare, also reflects the metaphorical significance of *consors* and *consortium*. *Consortio* appears first in a fragment of Lucilius 818–19M, which is too short to provide context useful for establishing its connotations: *deierat se non scripsisse, et post non scripturum: redi / in consortionem*, "he swore that he didn't write and that later he would not write that he returned to the partnership." Cf. Cic. *Off.* 3.26, on which see below pp. 162–63, and *OLD s.v. consortio*.

[139] Livy 40.8.14.

[140] Polyb. 23.11.6–7.

Rome's glory. The elder Scipiones together died a glorious death for
Rome, a death that also manifested their unity: *perpetuam vitae concor-
diam mors quoque miscuit*, "their death was the culmination of the ev-
erlasting harmony of their life."[141] Brotherly love is correlated with political stability in the word *concordia*, a buzzword of late Republican
political rhetoric. When brothers were as devoted to Rome as to each
other, their city would be safe and strong.

The political significance of brothers at Rome went beyond the success
of individual families, and this broader significance is evident in two of
Livy's narratives of the conflict between the orders in the early Republic,
where the political community is likened to a fraternal *consortium*. In
455 B.C.E., the *plebs* sought the right of intermarriage with patricians and
the right to elect one plebeian consul each year. These rights are the basis
of the social contract, which Livy describes as *consortio* and *societas*.[142]
This political alliance relies on equal rights to marry and to hold the
consulship, rights which underlie the alliances that create common interests in political, economic, and social life. *Consortio* also appears in
Livy's account of the dispute in the year 368 B.C.E., when the military
tribunes again tried to obtain the right to elect one plebeian consul per
year. In this case, the debate turned on the balance between self-interest
and the common good. Livy gives Ap. Claudius an emotional speech
opposing this reform, arguing that the plebeians' demand was a dangerous expression of self-interest—dangerous, that is, to the unity of society. His outrage emerges in a rhetorical question: *quaenam ista societas,
quaenam consortio est*, "what sort of alliance is this? Is this any kind of
partnership?"[143] In both incidents, *consortio* represents the political reconciliation of self-interest and the common good in a metaphor that resonates with fraternal *pietas*.

Livy was not idiosyncratic in associating fraternal unity with Rome's
success. The relationship between brothers had its roots in the structure
of the Roman family and in Roman inheritance practices, but it extended beyond the home to the forum and to historical accounts of politically prominent brothers like the Scipiones. Fraternal cooperation
could subtly influence the Romans' view of brothers' political careers,
or it could be used overtly to justify or praise their successes. The historical traditions surrounding the Scipiones reflect Roman assumptions
about brothers' political behavior. If one brother were more talented or
successful, he would use his skills and influence to help his brother to
get ahead.[144] Both brothers would then share the risks and fruits of this

[141] Livy 40.8.15.
[142] Livy 4.5.5.
[143] Livy 6.40.18.
[144] Cf. Plut. *Mor.* 484D–490B passim.

success. Africanus' prominence was a double-edged sword: it could advance Asiagenus's career by securing the command against Antiochus, or it could make him liable to public prosecution as a scapegoat for his brother's enormous influence, which might appear as a threat to civic liberty. But ambition could also be cloaked in claims of fraternal devotion. A Roman audience was susceptible to the moral claim of fraternal duty and to the emotional appeal of brotherly affection. Confusion in the historical accounts of the trials of the Scipiones reflects the interchangeability and identification between brothers. The arguments put forward in their defense, and the success of these arguments, attest to the importance of fraternal *pietas* in Roman political life. In the case of the Scipiones, this fraternal *pietas* was strengthened by an association with patriotism. The brothers created a public image in which brotherly devotion was central to their military service earning glory for Rome.

Tiberius and Gaius Gracchus

An undercurrent of Roman anxiety about brothers' political collusion runs throughout Roman historical traditions, but it bursts forth in reactions to the Gracchi, especially Gaius, because his political career was so openly constructed around his relationship with his brother. Roman reactions to the Gracchi illustrate the precarious balance between fraternal and patriotic duty. Plutarch's biographies of the Gracchi, along with the various references to them in Cicero's writings, demonstrate the interplay of brotherly love and political vicissitudes, allowing us to understand how fraternal *pietas* became implicated in the Roman perceptions of social and political morality. Sallust identified the Gracchi as a focal point of the declining morality and increasing violence in the last hundred years of Republican politics; Cicero, too, considered the Gracchi suspect because Gaius Gracchus' appeals to fraternal *pietas* had led to political violence. Because the Gracchi were associated with the civic violence that arose around them, their fraternal *pietas* was implicated in larger political changes.

The norms of fraternal complementarity color historical portraits of the Gracchi. In Plutarch's biography, the brothers have contrasting personalities and styles of oratory.[145] Where Tiberius is gentle and sedate, Gaius is intense and vehement. Tiberius stands still, speaking with clear diction and sweet cadences, evoking pity. His brother's sparkling style is so passionate that he stirs terror in his audience as he strides around the

---

[145] Plut. *TG* 2. Plutarch introduces this section with a reference to Castor and Pollux; cf. the opening of his Περὶ Φιλαδελφίας, *Mor.* 478B.

platform, toga falling loose around him. Despite these differences, the brothers exhibit traditional Roman virtues and follow nearly identical career paths.[146] In the end, both die attempting to enact laws perceived as revolutionary by their opponents. Their difference in age, projected from their record of office-holding, seems to have freed them from rivalry. In fact, Gaius built his career on his brother's reputation, beginning with the notorious anecdote, which Gaius himself popularized, that his brother appeared to him in a dream and urged him to run for the tribunate.[147] The ability to communicate through dreams suggests a spiritual connection or empathy that transcended the grave.[148] In the case of the Gracchi, spiritual communication not only implied affection but it galvanized fraternal *pietas* in their political careers.[149] In this dream, Tiberius encouraged his brother by promising him the same fate as he himself had had. On the face of it, this advice is hardly encouraging. Why would Gaius desire the same violent death as his brother? Metaphorically, the Gracchi, like true *consortes*,[150] share the same fate, both during their lives—serving as tribune and advancing reform legislation— and in their deaths—violence stopped them when their methods violated tradition.[151] But this is getting ahead of the story.

Gaius followed his brother's advice and was elected tribune of the *plebs* in 123. The evidence for Gaius' career, scattered throughout the ancient sources, indicates that he made his brother and fraternal *pietas* an important part of his political activity. He published a pamphlet recount-

---

[146] For the pattern of these careers, see C. B. R. Pelling, "Plutarch and Roman Politics," in *Past Perspectives*, ed. I. S. Moxon, J. D. Smart, and A. J. Woodman, 169–70.

[147] Cic. *Div.* 1.56 = Coelius Antipater fr. 49 *hist.* cf. Val. Max. 1.7.6. Plutarch, *CG* 1.6, tells us that directly after Tiberius' death, Gaius withdrew from public life, perhaps to avoid his brother's fate. On Gaius' reaction to Tiberius' death, see P. Fraccaro, "Ricerche su Caio Gracco," in *Opuscula*, 2:26. On C. Gracchus' early career, see Plut. *CG* 2, and D. Stockton, *The Gracchi*, 94–98.

[148] See above Chapter 2 on Catullus' epitaph for his brother, Poem 101.

[149] The dream has been interpreted by scholars in two ways: it was sent either to motivate Gaius to undertake a public career or to encourage him specifically to run for the tribunate, where he could truly replicate his brother's career. See A. S. Pease, *Cicero De Divinatione Libri Duo*, 193–94, and Stockton, *The Gracchi*, 179.

[150] Cf. Varro's etymology of *sors*, above Chapter 1, pp. 19–20.

[151] Tiberius breached tradition in two ways: he exceeded his constitutional powers as tribune when he arranged the disposition of the will of Attalus III, flouting the authority of the Senate, and he challenged the practice of annual succession of magistrates by seeking a consecutive tribunate: E. Badian, "Tiberius Gracchus and the Beginning of the Roman Revolution," *ANRW* 1, no. 1 (1972): 709–22. Tiberius may have also set forth a more wide-ranging reform package for his second tribunate and ousted the tribune C. Octavius, who vetoed his agrarian plan, all of which made him appear even more of a threat to the *status quo*. See Stockton, *The Gracchi*, 73–74, 81–84, 114–61, 184–85, 195–98; A. E. Astin, *Scipio Aemilianus*, 212, 214–16, 350–51; K. Richardson, *Daggers in the Forum*, 72–79, 136–37.

ing how Tiberius was inspired by the desolation of the Italian countryside to reform landholding legislation.[152] Fragments from two of his speeches show Gaius making political capital out of his brother's death. Gaius gave a dramatic description of his brother's death in a speech in support of his *lex de provocatione*, and took every opportunity to remind the Roman public of his brother.[153] This law can be connected with Gaius' attack on Popillius Laenas, who, as consul in 132 B.C.E., presided over the summary trial and execution of many of Tiberius' supporters.[154] The law was, it appears, retroactive, and Laenas was forced into exile under threat of prosecution and then outlawed.[155] Gaius' invocation of his brother's murder implies that he connected the law with his brother's death and was using his legislative power as tribune to carry out a personal vendetta that satisfied fraternal *pietas*. In this speech, after invoking fraternal *pietas*, Gaius compared the Romans' treatment of tribunes in the past to the neglect and disrespect that had led to Tiberius' death, and he implored the crowd to return to their traditional respect for the tribunes. Alternatively, Gaius may have had other reasons to want Laenas out of the way, and his brother's death may have been a convenient pretext. In either case, his appeal to fraternal *pietas* was an effective strategy for moving legislation, as we have already seen, in Cicero's treatment of Sulla's brother Caecilius.

Gaius used the same strategy in a speech supporting Papirius Carbo's law allowing reelection to the tribunate in successive years. His speech on the question, the *pro Rogatione Papiria*,[156] drew attention to the similarities between himself and his brother:

[152] Plut. *TG* 8.7. Stockton, *The Gracchi*, 6, describes this pamphlet as "an interested invention on Gaius' part." On propaganda in the sources, see Badian, "Tiberius Gracchus," 678. In any case, the existence of such a pamphlet shows public awareness of a link between Gaius and his brother.

[153] Plut. *CG* 3.2–3, and Gaius Gracchus fr. 31 *orat.*: the only direct speech attributed to Gaius Gracchus in Plutarch's *Lives of the Gracchi* can be associated with this legislation.

[154] Stockton, *The Gracchi*, 118–20.

[155] The sources offer conflicting evidence for Laenas' exile. Diodorus 34/35.26 says that Gaius relied on massive bribery to achieve Laenas' exile and that Laenas' exile was mourned by the people. Cicero's reference to the event suggests otherwise, *Leg.* 3.26: *si nos multitudinis furentis inflammata invidia pepulisset tribuniciaque vis in me populum, sicut Gracchus in Laenatem incitasset, . . . ferremus*, "if the passionate hatred of a raging mob had forced me and if tribunician power had roused the people against me, just as Gracchus roused the people against Laenas, . . . I would have endured it." In 121, the tribune L. Calpurnius Bestia passed a bill allowing Laenas to return to Rome, which he subsequently did. See Stockton, *The Gracchi*, 90–91, 119–20.

[156] Carbo, as tribune, sponsored the bill in 131 or 130, Livy *Epit.* 59, with Stockton, *The Gracchi*, 92, 218. The speech was eloquent, according to Cic. *De Orat.* 1.154, 3.214, 225, cf. *Orat.* 233, *Brut.* 296, 333. See also J.-M. David, "L'action oratoire de C. Gracchus," in *Demokratia et aristokratia*, ed. C. Nicolet, 103–16.

pessimi Tiberium fratrem meum optimum interfecerunt. Em! videte quam par pari sim.

The worst of them killed Tiberius, my best of brothers. Now see how I settle the score. Gaius Gracchus fr. 17 *orat*.

With the accounting metaphor, *par pari*, Gaius implies that he is his brother's equal, drawing on connotations that resonate with the ideal of *consortium*.[157] Although the fragment is cited out of context, other evidence allows for conjecture. Since Carbo's bill concerned reelection to the tribunate, it is likely that Gaius at some point in his speech referred to his brother's bid for reelection and the tragic results. This fragment can be interpreted as an emotional conclusion to such an account. After describing his brother's past tragedy, Gaius returned to the present, and asked the crowd to imagine that he, like his brother, could suffer the same fate. In a fragment of another speech, the *de legibus promulgatis*, Gaius refers explicitly to this possibility:

> . . . *si vellem apud vos verba facere et a vobis postulare, cum genere summo ortus essem et cum fratrem propter vos amisissem, nec quisquam de P. Africani et Tiberi Gracchi familia nisi ego et puer restaremus, ut pateremini hoc tempore me quiescere, ne a stirpe genus nostrum interiret et uti aliqua propago generis nostri reliqua esset: haud ⟨scio⟩ an lubentibus a vobis impetrassem.*
>
> Since I have come from a most illustrious family and since I have lost a brother on your account, and there was no one left from the family of P. Africanus and Tib. Gracchus except myself, and I was a still a boy, if I wanted to make a speech to you and to obtain from you by entreaty that you would leave me in peace at that time, lest our family perish from the root, and so that some scion of our family would be left: I scarcely [know] whether I would have obtained my request from you willingly. Gaius Gracchus fr. 47 *orat*

In what is clearly a plea for the audience's goodwill, Gaius attests to his devotion to the people: he has lost a brother for the sake of the people, will they now demand his life also? In this appeal, fraternal *pietas* appears in the context of family reputation and continuity; the plant imagery suggests that brothers' role in carrying on the family's public reputation arises from their natural relationship. By stirring up sympathy for his personal loss and risk, Gaius earned support and protection for his political agenda.[158] The comparison to his brother in his speech for Carbo's bill had the same rhetorical force. Like his rhetoric, his agenda also ex-

[157] *OLD s.v. par*[1] 2b for the accounting metaphor, *par*[2] an equal or a partner, *par*[3] for a pair.

[158] Compare Cicero's emotional plea on behalf of Q. Ligarius, esp. *Lig.* 33–37, which is based largely on the assumption that Ligarius could not have been disloyal to Caesar because he would not have differed with his brothers, who were staunch supporters of Caesar.

pressed his affiliation with his brother.[159] Carbo's bill would have prevented other tribunes from facing the opposition which ultimately led to Tiberius' death.[160] Gaius' support of this measure could be seen as an attempt to redress, through legitimate political channels, the lawless murder of Tiberius which ended their fraternal relationship. Gaius Gracchus' appeals to fraternal devotion depended on Roman assumptions about fraternal *pietas*; his success attests to the power of these assumptions.

An incident narrated in one of the early books of Livy offers an interesting parallel for Gaius Gracchus' political exploitation of fraternal *pietas*.[161] In 461 B.C.E., the tribunes attempted for the second time to pass the Terentilian law to limit consular power. K. Quinctius led the senatorial opposition. The tribunes had brought charges against him in order to blunt his opposition; he was charged with the death of the brother of a certain M. Volscius Fictor. When Fictor told the crowd how Quinctius caused his brother's death, the people went wild and nearly killed Quinctius. In this incident, an appeal to fraternal *pietas* was used to bolster an attack on a political opponent, in much the same way as it was used by C. Gracchus. Livy's account of the prosecution of Quinctius may reflect the tribunician agitation of 52 B.C.E..[162] Similarly, Cicero and Sallust associated the Gracchi with the spiral of civil unrest in the late Republic. The popular legislation advanced by the Gracchi and their means of persuasion, including appeals to fraternal *pietas*, were implicated in the decline in political morality that they believed was responsible for the increasing violence. Whether or not Gracchus' speeches were inflammatory, Cicero and other Romans saw them as a sign of dangerous changes in Roman politics.[163] The potential conflict between fraternal *pietas* and civic duty shaped Roman reactions to the Gracchi and their politics. Where Plutarch introduced sentimental tragedy into their story,[164] Roman writers tended to be preoccupied with the political ram-

---

[159] Richardson, *Daggers in the Forum*, 118–19.

[160] The continuity between brothers' political agendas need not be so dramatic. Compare, for example, the activities of the Popilii, Livy 42.10.10. In 172, the consul C. Popilius blocked public business in order to prevent the legislation enacted by his brother in previous year from being overturned.

[161] Livy, 3.13.1–3.

[162] R. M. Ogilvie, *A Commentary on Livy, Books 1–5*, 418. Earlier cases of tribunician violence may also have shaped Livy's account, and the emphasis on the fraternal relationship would suggest the Gracchi as a possible influence. The prosecution of Milo evoked fraternal *pietas* at one generation removed: two sons of Clodius' brother Gaius (both named Appius) brought the charges against Milo, Asc. *Milo Arg.* p. 32 Stangl.

[163] Gracchus' speeches and political agenda may have been more rhetorical than substantive, despite how they may have appeared to Cicero. See C. Nicolet, "La Polémique Politique au II siècle avant Jésus-Christ," in *Demokratia et aristokratia*, ed. C. Nicolet, 37–50.

[164] For example, the emotive scene between Gaius Gracchus and his wife before he left for the forum on that fateful day, when she reminded him of his brother's fate, Plut. *CG*

ifications of this brotherly duo. Cicero's attitude toward the Gracchi is flexible and various, but it nearly always centers on the intersection of brotherly love, political ambition, and civic responsibility.[165]

Among Cicero's treatments of Gaius Gracchus, the most favorable occurs in the *pro Rabirio Perduellionis Reo*, where fraternal and patriotic duty seem to coalesce. In this speech, Cicero compares the prosecutor, T. Labienus, to C. Gracchus.[166] Charges were brought against Rabirius in 63 B.C.E. for his involvement in the death of Saturninus in 100 B.C.E.. Rabirius was among the men who besieged Saturninus and his followers on the Capitol and subsequently killed many of them. Labienus, it seems, had personal motives for the prosecution, because his uncle was killed with Saturninus. Gaius Gracchus provided a limiting case for both the legal issues and the personal motives. Since Labienus' relationship with his uncle could not compare with the intimate bond between the Gracchi brothers, he was hardly justified in comparing his prosecution of Rabirius to C. Gracchus' attacks on his brother's enemies.[167] For Cicero, justifiability varies not just much with the degree of kinship but also with the depth of the emotional attachment.[168] This view affirms the importance of affection in establishing the norms of fraternal *pietas*. Fraternal devotion was, however, more than a personal motive in Cicero's case: it was implicit in the legal issues.

Rabirius was charged with unlawfully putting to death a Roman citizen. Cicero maintained that Rabirius was immune from prosecution be-

15.2–3. On Plutarch's use of sources hostile to the Gracchi, see B. Scardigli, *Die Römerbiographien Plutarchs*, 63 with the literature cited there.

[165] On Cicero's treatement of the Gracchi see J. Béranger, "Les jugements de Cicéron sur les Gracques," *ANRW* 1, no. 1 (1972): 732–37, 744–46, and R. J. Murray, "Cicero and the Gracchi," *TAPA* 97 (1966): 291–98.

[166] T. Labienus served with Caesar for nine years in Gaul earning rank and riches, Cic. *Att.* 7.7.6. He is perhaps to be identified with the "*mentula*" in Catullus' poems, on which see T. Frank, "Cicero and the Poetae Novae," *AJP* 40 (1919): 396. Despite service with Caesar, Syme argued that Labienus was an old Pompeian, who accompanied Caesar as Pompey's representative, and then showed his true colors by backing Pompey in 49, see R. Syme, "The Allegiance of Labienus," in *Roman Papers*, ed. E. Badian, *et al.*, 1:62–75.

[167] Cic. *Rab. Perd.* 14–15, where Cicero also justifies Gaius Gracchus on the grounds of fraternal devotion. Cf. Cic. *Har.* 43: *C. autem Gracchum mors fraterna, pietas, dolor, magnitudo animi ad expetendas domestici sanguinis poenas excitavit*, "his brother's death, pietas, grief, and his greatness of spirit roused C. Gracchus to seek revenge for the shedding of his family's blood." See W. Blake Tyrrell, *A Legal and Historical Commentary to Cicero's Oratio pro C. Rabirio Perduellionis Reo*, 95.

[168] Cic. *Off.* 1.59, where Cicero asserts that claims of social relationships vary by degree and circumstance, but when the chips were down, close kinship and affection counted: *ut vicinum citius adiuveris in fructibus percipiendis quam aut fratrem aut familiarem, at, si lis in iudicio sit, propinquum potius et amicum quam vicinum defenderis*, "you might sooner help a neighbor than a brother or a friend in gathering the harvest, but if there were legal dispute in court, you would rather defend a relative or a friend than a neighbor."

cause he had acted under a *senatus consultum ultimum* directing the restoration of public order. Such senatorial authorization traditionally provided legal sanction for the violent suppression of threats to public safety, even if it led to the death of citizens.[169] According to Cicero, Labienus argued that Rabirius was outside this authority and was thus subject to condemnation for unlawfully killing a citizen. Cicero turns this argument on its head: it was Labienus who was attempting not merely to convict but even to condemn Rabirius *iniussu populi*, "without an order from the people's assembly."[170] Labienus was threatening the very freedom of Roman citizens by doing this, because their freedom depended on their right to protect themselves from arbitrary violent suppression. Moreover, Labienus, who was threatening the people, was tribune in 63, the magistrate specially charged with representing the people's interest. The right of the people to approve or reject the execution of a citizen was encoded in the *lex Sempronia de provocatione*, the law with which C. Gracchus sought revenge on his brother's murderers. Under the *lex Sempronia*, Gaius was justified in avenging his brother's death, and however personal his love for his brother, he pursued his vengeance in a way that was compatible with the interests of the Roman people. The *lex Sempronia* was not simply a vehicle for vengeance, it provided lasting legal protection for all Romans. Cicero's argument would have appealed to both *populares* and *optimates* in his audience. The implicit distinction between Gracchus' and Saturninus' tribunician violence would have satisfied *populares* who idealized the Gracchi. Conservative senators could find Gaius' devotion to his brother praiseworthy because it did not interfere with the performance of his duties as tribune to represent the people's interest. In other respects, Gaius' political activities and his exploitation of fraternal *pietas* were problematic for Cicero.[171]

Although Cicero admired Gaius' eloquence, he seems to have thought that he went too far in his rhetorical exploitation of fraternal devotion. In

[169] Cicero rightly understood the indictment of Rabirius as an attack on the authority of the Senate and the legality of the *senatus consultum ultimum*, Cic. *Orat.* 102, *Pis.* 4, cf. Lintott, *Violence*, 169. Even more is at stake for Cicero himself in this case, since his suppression of the Catilinarians was also protected by this point of law. For a discussion of the constitutional development of the *SCU* and the issues surrounding Cicero's use of it in 63, see T. N. Mitchell, "Cicero and the *Senatus Consultum Ultimum*," *Historia* 20 (1971): 47–61.

[170] Cic. *Rab. Perd.* 12–17, and for the *Lex Sempronia*, see Cic. *Catil.* 4.4.

[171] Though Cicero praises their rhetorical ability, the Gracchi are only politically correct in comparison with other troublesome characters, for example, Catiline, *Catil.* 1.3,29 and 4.4, Clodius, *Dom.* 82, and Antony, *Phil.* 1.18. In the right context, their agrarian laws are invoked as precedent for reform, *Leg. Agr.* 2.10, 31, but elsewhere Cicero acknowledges the potential danger in their politics, *Verr.* 2.4.108, *Sest.* 103–105. The Gracchi are compared to their disadvantage with their father, Tib. Sempronius Gracchus, Cic. *Catil.* 1.4, *Prov.* 18, *De Orat.* 1.38, *Fin.* 4.65, *Off.* 2.43; cf. Tac. *Dial.* 40.4.

the *Brutus*, he wrote, *utinam non tam fratri pietatem quam patriae prae-stare voluisset*, "if only he hadn't wished to put his love for his brother before his love for his country."[172] In the *De Officiis*, Cicero ranks the Gracchi among such demagogues as the Spartan kings, Agis and Cleomenes, perhaps setting the model for Plutarch's pairing of the Grac-chi with these kings.[173] The Gracchi represented political movements that destabilized the conservative values of the senatorial class and the elusive *concordia ordinum*. Either Gaius was duplicitous, cloaking policy in emotive appeals to fraternal *pietas*, or his sincere devotion to his brother eclipsed all other concerns. For Cicero, putting the welfare of Rome second to anything was tantamount to treason, and his attitude is a consistent if extreme example of traditional Roman ideas about the ethics of citizenship.[174] Cicero disagreed with the Gracchi's political pro-gram, yet he was sympathetic with Gaius Gracchus' fraternal *pietas*.

Roman sources for the Gracchi betray a specific fear of the conse-quences of giving too much importance to personal motives in political activities. For Cicero, the Gracchi were responsible for the increase in civic violence, and Gaius' appeals to fraternal *pietas* were also impli-cated.[175] In Sallust's treatment of the Gracchi, there is less emphasis on fraternal symbolism than on the problem of excessive violence. When Sallust digresses, in the *Bellum Iugurthinum*, on the causes of moral de-cline and political violence, he cites the Gracchi twice to illustrate the troubles that began after the defeat of Carthage. First in Memmius' speech, he relates how the Gracchi died attempting to defend *libertas* for the *plebs*. After the death of both Tiberius and Gaius, the *nobiles* inflicted punishment—prosecution and imprisonment—on the *plebs*. These pun-ishments resulted not from law but from wanton exercise of power: *utri-usque cladis non lex, verum ludibo eorum finem fecit.*[176] Later, in his

[172] Cic. *Brut.* 125–26, cf. 103–104.

[173] Cic. *Off.* 2.80. Plutarch, *Agis* 2.11, describes the politics of the Spartan kings as follows: ἀδελφοὶ μὲν οὖν οὐκ ἦσαν ἀλλήλων οἱ Λάκωνες, συγγενοῦς δὲ καὶ ἀδελφῆς ἥψαντο πολιτείας, "even though they were not brothers of each other, they took up kin-dred and brotherly forms of government." Plutarch, like Cicero, is concerned with the danger of demagogues, but the over-riding themes of these *Lives* is metaphorical fraternity, the sharing of kindred political goals, *Synkrisis Agis/Cleom.* Polybius also compares the political systems of Rome and Sparta, 6.43. It may be that Plutarch started with the Gracchi and then went looking for a suitable Greek pair, see J. Geiger, "Plutarch's Parallel Lives," *Hermes* 109 (1981): 90–94. Still valuable on Plutarch's sources is H. Peter, *Die Quellen Plutarchs in den Biographieen der Römer*. On the importance of Spartan models for Roman political thought, see E. Rawson, *The Spartan Tradition in European Thought*, 99–106.

[174] Cf. Val. Max. *5.6.praef.* Cicero's views on this subject often involve contemporary events, e.g. *Att.* 9.6.7, 8.11.1, *Fam.* 16.11.2, 16.12.1, with P. A. Brunt, "Cicero's *Officium* in the Civil War," *JRS* 76 (1986): 12–32, esp. 21.

[175] E. g. Cic. *Amic.* 39, 41.

[176] Sal. *Iug.* 31.7, cf. 42.3–5, and *Hist.* 1.11, 12, 17; App. *BC* 1.2. See R. Syme, *Sallust*, 170–71, 183, and, in general, E. Badian, "Tiberius Gracchus."

own voice, Sallust presents the Gracchi as victims of their own excessive ambition, but he mitigates what might seem a harsh judgment by saying that they were victims in a good cause. For Sallust, the political violence surrounding the Gracchi epitomized Rome's descent into moral anarchy. If these brothers were not exactly the beginning of the end, their fate signaled the demise of social and political life as the Romans knew it in the Republic.

To be or to have a brother was an advantage in Roman politics. The combined efforts of several brothers could influence political events, and an appeal to fraternal devotion could move the Romans as they decided the fate of their country and/or passed judgment on their leaders. A Roman's duties to his brother in public life were oriented around the norms inscribed in *consortium*: as in managing the family property, so with political capital, brothers were expected to share an equal interest in maintaining and enhancing their social and political status. The roles of brothers fit into the familiar structure of Roman politics articulated by family connections and reciprocal *amicitia*. Romans acknowledged a man's obligation to help his brother; they might even praise him for fulfilling it. The general acceptance of fraternal devotion as a factor in politics left room for abuse: an appeal to fraternal devotion could be merely a pretext concealing less worthy interests, perhaps even interests that threatened the stability of the state or challenged powerful individuals. In those cases where the norms for fraternal behavior collided with other social priorities, most often the ideal of patriotic sacrifice for Rome emerged as an imperative to which fraternal *pietas* should yield. Brothers could transcend this conflict of norms by devoting their joint efforts to Rome, thereby melding the two ideals and serving both their own interests and those of Rome. As civil war followed civil war in the late Republic, Roman writers began to examine what happened when fraternal *pietas* failed to exercise a normative function in political morality, and fratricide became a motif of civil strife.

FOUR

ON THE BATTLEFIELD

*"Duos," inquit, "fratrum manibus dedi; tertium causae belli
huiusce, ut Romanus Albano imperet, dabo."*
"I dedicated two [Curatii] to the shades of my brothers," he
said, "I will devote the third in the name of this war, so that
Roman may rule Alban."
(Livy 1.25.12)

THE STORY of the Horatii and the Curiatii illustrates the inter-
relationship between fraternal *pietas* and Roman patriotism.
During one of Rome's wars against Alba, the two sides agreed to
settle the dispute in a battle of champions: two pairs of triplets, one from
Alba and one from Rome, Curiatii and Horatii, fought to the death. The
Roman Horatius lost his two brothers but survived to claim victory for
Rome. Livy's version of this story moves toward Horatius' return to
Rome, where he killed his sister because she grieved more for her lost
fiancé, one of the Curiatii, than for her brothers who died for Rome.
Commentators likewise glide over the fraternal relationship in this episode, perhaps because it seems so central, so obvious a part of Roman
civic and military life. How different would Livy's story be if the three
fighters from each side were not brothers? Roman traditions allow for
two different answers. On the one hand, the story could be just as compelling since soldiers who fought together felt bound by a kind of fraternity. On the other hand, the real kinship among these triplets intensified
the experience of war and the courage inspired by fraternal *pietas*.

The battlefield tested brothers; it was a venue for devotion, loss, and
conflict. Battle narratives offer poets and historians the opportunity to
dramatize fraternal *pietas*. Pliny the Elder reports that Ennius added a
sixteenth book to his *Annales* to commemorate the deeds of T. Caecilius
Teucer and his brother.[1] Traditionally, war was an occasion for brothers
to exercise their fraternal solidarity for their own glory and for Rome's,
as for example the Scipios. Valerius Maximus treats in the same chapter
pietas toward parents, brothers, and country.[2] Brothers set the paradigm

---

[1] Pliny, *NH* 7.101. On the troublesome identity of these brothers, see Gruen, *Studies in Greek Culture*, 120–21.

[2] Val. Max. 5.4. Compare Livy's assimilation of *pietas* to father and to fatherland, see T. J. Moore, *Artistry and Ideology*, 59, cf. 56–61.

for the relationship between fellow soldiers, but the association between brothers and soldiers was more than a battlefield analogy; its roots lay deeper in Roman political culture and had broader significance in Roman ethical and rhetorical discourse. As we saw in Chapter 3, elite brothers could use their relationship to affect Roman politics, and fraternal *pietas* was a powerful trope in political rhetoric. Because relationships between brothers could have a real influence on political and military events, the symbolic weight of the relationship between brothers was grounded in Romans' experiences in the forum and on the battlefield. Fraternal *pietas* was a traditional counterpart to patriotic devotion to Rome, an expression of solidarity with one's fellow citizens and soldiers. When, in the later years of the Republic, wars became civil and brothers sometimes found themselves fighting on opposite sides,[3] fraternal *pietas* took on new metaphorical dimensions. Instead of emphasizing the fraternal solidarity of soldiers, civil war narratives focused on brothers fighting brothers, and dramatic scenes of fratricide came to epitomize the experience of civil strife.

Romans traced the beginnings of civil strife in the late Republic to the destruction of Carthage. During the next hundred years, Romans experienced a series of civil wars—the so-called Social Wars of 90–88 B.C.E., the civil wars of the 80s involving Cinna and Sulla and thirty years later between Pompey and Caesar—which ended with Octavian's defeat of Antony and Cleopatra in Egypt in 30 B.C.E.. Toward the close of this period, a number of writers began to reflect on the effects of this protracted civil strife, on the ways that war changed human relationships and moral expectations. The literature of the triumviral period expressed a profound anxiety about the loss and change incurred in civil war, changes that Romans perceived as a breakdown in traditional morality and social system.[4] These reflections often formulate social and moral questions in terms of fraternal *pietas*. As in the emotional attachment between brothers, so also in political symbolism fraternal *pietas* conveyed the strongest message in its absence. As the civil wars ran their course, fratricide came to mean *the* fratricide, Romulus' murder of his brother Remus at the moment when Rome was founded. Romans saw in this original fratricide a paradigm for the civil wars which eroded what we might call the social contract among Roman citizens and the fraternal sentiments that united them. But the foundation story did not present a simple fable of discord. Because the twins' story involved both fraternal cooperation and fratricide, the foundation myth represented both the good and the bad in Rome's political experience. During the middle Re-

---

[3] See, for example, App. *BC* 1.5.
[4] P. Jal, *La guerre civile à Rome*, 391 ff.

public when the familiar features of the Romulus and Remus story developed, the twins were idealized as paradigmatic Romans. The civil wars of the late Republic brought out the dark side of the myth, and allusions to the foundation story or retellings of it in the literature of this era exploit its inherent duality, juxtaposing the twins' partnership with the fratricide to dramatize their experience of violence and loss. Poets writing under Augustus, whose rise to power brought the civil wars to a close, cultivated a careful ambivalence that avoided the critical issue of fratricide.

This chapter first establishes the metaphorical significance of brothers in Roman ideas about citizenship and soldiering, and then examines how fraternal *pietas* was adapted in the literature of the triumviral era to express both the personal and political dilemmas of civil strife. In the second section, we turn to battle narratives of the Roman civil wars where brother faces brother on the battlefield, their confrontation dramatizing the disruption of the *mos maiorum* and *pietas*. The chapter ends with a reevaluation of the Romulus and Remus story and its resonance in the literature of the triumviral and Augustan eras.

Stipata Cohors: Brothers and the *Mos Maiorum*

In Roman political culture, brothers could earn the most glorious distinction by putting their devotion to work for Rome, fighting side by side on the battlefield. Prosopographers have long recognized the importance of fraternal relations in the network of Roman political alliances, and the idea of brothers fighting together for the sake of Rome is fundamental to the Romans' identity as citizen-soldiers. A man might begin his military career as a military tribune by his father's side, but he would share the rigors of camp life with men of his own generation, including his brother if he had one.[5] By winning military glory, brothers could restore or enhance the family reputation and serve Rome at the same time. In turn, military devotion to Rome could express fraternal *pietas*: in the wake of the civil war against Antony in 44, Cicero urged men who had lost brothers in battle to seek consolation in being like their brothers, following them into war.[6] Such fraternal devotion is prominent in political image-making and in literary accounts of the Roman past.

[5] For example, L. and Sp. Mummius, Cic. *Att.* 13.5.1 and 6.4; L. and M. Licinius Lucullus, Cic. *Ac.* 2.1; L. Murena and his father, Cic. *Mur.* 11–12; Sp. and Aul. Albinus, Sal. *Iug.* 37–40; Q. and M. Fabius, Livy 9.36.2; Cn. and C. Fulvius Flaccus, Livy 27.8.12, and Fulvius' consular colleague Fabius brought his son along, 27.8.13; Cn. and L. Manlius, Livy 38.20.7; Q. and M. Fulvius Flaccus, Livy 40.30.4–5; Q. and M. Fulvius Nobilior, Livy 40.41.8; C. and M. Lucretius, Livy 42.48.6 and 56.1; P. and C. Licinius Crassus, Livy 42.58.12.

[6] Cic. *Phil.* 14.34.

The Fabii were exemplary brothers in the military annals of early Rome. Three Fabii distinguished themselves in a battle at Veii in 479: M. Fabius, as consul, and his brothers Quintus (consul of the previous year) and Kaeso (consul two year before). The family fought, according to Livy, with special distinction, *Fabium nomen maxime enituit*, and their military brilliance won the support of the Roman *plebs*.[7] Heedless of his own safety, Quintus charged ahead and was killed. His death so demoralized the troops that they would have fled if his brother, Marcus the consul, had not rallied them as he sprang to defend his brother's body:

> " 'Hoc iurastis,' inquit, 'milites, fugientes vos in castra redituros? Adeo ig-navissimos hostes magis timetis quam Iovem Martemque per quos iurastis? (6) At ego iniuratus aut victor revertar aut prope te hic, Q. Fabi, dimicans cadam . . .' "

> "Is this what you swore, soldiers," he said, "that you would return to camp as runaways from battle? Are you more afraid of this most cowardly enemy than you are of Jupiter and Mars by whom you swore? I, though unsworn, will either return as victor or fall fighting side by side with you, Quintus Fabius." Livy 2.46.5–6

Marcus melds fraternal devotion with patriotism: while other soldiers swore a general oath not to desert, Marcus promised not to desert his brother. The natural fraternal *pietas* among the Fabii is equated with the patriotic fraternity that unites all Rome's soldiers. His brother Kaeso, rebuking Marcus, shifts the focus away from this metaphorical fraternity to the actions that make it real:

> "Verbisne istis, frater, ut pugnent, te impetraturum credis? (7) Di impetra-bunt per quos iuravere; et nos, ut decet proceres, ut Fabio nomine est dig-num, pugnando potius quam adhortando accendamus militum animos." Sic in primum infensis hastis provolant duo Fabii totamque moverunt secum aciem.

> "Do you think your words, brother, have the power to make these soldiers fight? The gods they swore by will make them fight. Let us exhort our soldiers not with exhortation but by fighting as befits leaders, as is worthy of the name Fabius." Then the two Fabii rushed forward against the front line into the hostile spears, leading the entire battle line forward with them. Livy 2.46.6–7

In their actions the Fabii show themselves true brothers, soldiers, and patriots. Fraternal posturing is empty without risk and victory in battle. After the Fabii had led Rome to a victory, the Senate decreed a triumph for the consul Marcus Fabius; his colleague Cn. Manlius had died in battle. Fabius refused to celebrate his triumph because both his family

[7] Livy 2.45.16, cf. 2.46.2–4.

and Rome were in mourning; Rome's loss doubled his own private grief. The refusal of a triumph was even more glorious, says Livy, than a triumph would have been, since it acknowledged the public and private value of fraternal *pietas* and patriotism.[8] Fabius gave a eulogy for his brother and for his colleague, and, to generate a sense of unity among the Romans, he assigned to patricians the care of wounded soldiers. The Fabii themselves took in the greatest number of the wounded and gave them the best care, literally bringing their fellow soldiers into their home like brothers.[9] Fabius' policies, his personal bravery, and sentiments reveal the interconnections between individual fraternal relationships and the symbolic power of fraternal *pietas* to unite soldiers and citizens. In the following year, the Fabii again demonstrated patriotic *pietas*; three hundred from the extended clan volunteered to protect Rome from Veii, making public duty their own private business.[10] When families or brothers undertook special duty for Rome, their solidarity represented the fraternal sentiments that could bring Roman soldiers and citizens together on the battlefield.

Patriotic solidarity among brothers-soldiers like the Fabii was assimilated to the fraternal solidarity that could develop among soldiers who fight together. As brothers were responsible for protecting the home, soldiers belonged to a civic home, which they were bound to defend like brothers.[11] The analogy works in both directions. In Seneca's *Consolatio ad Polybium* on the death of his brother, Polybius and his brothers are cast as soldiers repelling an attack on their home, *tam bene stipatam optimorum adulescentium domum*, "a home so chock full of the best young men."[12] This fraternal defense of the *domus* corresponds to brothers' roles in the family and at the same time mirrors their role as citizen-soldiers. The custom among Roman legionnaires of calling their messmates *frater* presumes an identification between brothers and soldiers. Army life was conducive to fraternal relationships: soldiers shared tent and mess so that they, too, came to think of each other as brothers. Through the perils of battle, fraternal empathy could arise among soldiers, a sense of identity that made them willing to sacrifice themselves for each other.[13] In the *Aeneid*, fellow soldiers are *unanimi*, like brothers,

[8] Livy 2.47.9–11, cf. 2.47.1–7, and Val. Max. 5.5.2, who contrasts Fabius' *pietas fraternae caritatis*, "the devotion of brotherly esteem," with *tantus amplissimi honoris fulgor*, "the so great glory of the most fulsome honor."

[9] Livy 2.47.12.

[10] Livy 2.48.8–9, and 49.1–8, and see K.-W. Welwei, "Gefolgschaftsverband oder Gentilaufgebot? Zum Problem eines frührömischen familiare *bellum* (Liv. II.48.9)," *ZRG* 110 (1993): 331–69.

[11] Cf. the truce in Sen. *Con.* 1.1.

[12] Sen. *Dial.* 11.3.4–5; see above Chapter 2 p. 75.

[13] R. MacMullen, "The Legion as Society," *Historia* 33 (1984): 442–44.

friends, and lovers, but their devotion underlies a united front in battle.[14] The *ius fraternitatis*, "law of brotherhood" that provided a foundation for the legal notion of partnership suggests a parallel for the extension of fraternal ideals to soldiers. As fraternal intimacy was the model for other affections among men, so the fraternal *consortium*, with its balance between self-interest and the common good, provided the Romans with a model for military ethics, for the proper relations between fellow soldiers. Since Romans derived their civic identity from serving as soldiers— the traditional citizen-soldier is the idealized Roman male identity—all Romans could conceive of themselves as brothers.[15] Thus, the fraternal relationship served as a paradigm not only for personal relationships, but also for bonds among citizens and for the social morality that governed Roman public life.

The fraternal relationship served as a metaphor for the social bonds between friends and citizens and for the *mos maiorum*, the attitudes and behaviors that Romans traditionally associated with a healthy, moral society. As Seneca puts it in a letter outlining the foundations of philosophy, *quid mihi prodest scire agellum in partes dividere, si nescio cum fratre dividere?* "What good does it do me to know how to survey a field if I don't know how to share the field with my brother?"[16] The division of land among brothers is not so much a question of surveying as of morality. While fraternal *pietas* was a sign of personal moral virtue, it could also represent Roman civic values. Fraternal *pietas* could represent the political notion of *concordia*, that power to achieve consensus and maintain social stability,[17] as it does, for example, in Livy's account of the sons of Philip V of Macedon, discussed in Chapter 3. Since Romans grounded their sense of citizenship in military service, all Romans could feel a fraternal bond with their fellow citizens, their comrades in arms, with whom they might literally have served in the field defending their common home, or at least on whom they depended for defense.[18] Sallust's account of Jugurtha's rise to power in Numidia and his influence

---

[14] Verg. *A.* 12.264–82. These brothers are, like Nisus and Euryalus, united by a common passion, and see above Chapter 2 pp. 81–85.

[15] Cicero invokes their common kinship to rouse outrage at Verres' abuse of Roman citizens in Sicily, *Ver.* 2.5.172.

[16] Sen. *Ep.* 88.11.

[17] As described, for example, by Badian, "Tiberius Gracchus," 697. For an analysis of late Republican politics as general conflict, see J. Plescia, "*Patria Potestas* and the Roman Revolution," in *The Conflict of the Generations in Ancient Greece and Rome*, ed. S. Bertman, 143–69.

[18] Fraternal imagery characterizes the alliance between the Aedui and the Romans in Caes. *BG* 1.33.2, Cic. *Att.* 1.19.2, and Tac. *Ann.* 11.25, though this sole example of metaphorical fraternity in foreign relations may reflect the lost customs of the Aedui rather than Roman ideas.

at Rome weaves together fraternal *pietas*, social morality, and political stability, as Jugurtha pursues his ambitions in rivalry with his adoptive brothers, Hiempsal and Adherbal, the sons of Micipsa. Jugurtha is their cousin, the illegitimate son of Micipsa's brother, Mastanabal; although he had been excluded from the succession to the throne, Micipsa raised him in the palace alongside his own sons.[19] After Jugurtha proved his merit on the battlefield, Micipsa adopted him and named him as joint heir with his own sons to the kingdom. Even though the three cousins were, in a broader sense, *fratres*, "cousins," even before the adoption, the creation of legal kinship formalized their duty to behave like brothers.

In a dramatic deathbed address, as Sallust recreates it, Micipsa instructs Jugurtha to share power with his adoptive brothers emphasizing the importance of the fraternal *pietas* in securing the kingdom. He beseeches them to cherish their brothers, holding no one closer. This fraternal relationship has political implications because power resides in blood ties:

> *obtestorque te, uti hos, qui tibi genere propinqui, beneficio meo fratres sunt, caros habeas neu malis alienos adiungere quam sanguine coniunctos retinere.*
>
> I adjure you to hold dear these men who are your relatives by birth, your brothers by my blessing; do not prefer alliances with strangers to the ties of kinship. Sal. *Iug.* 10.3

Fraternal *pietas* turns out to be the strongest basis for power, *quis autem amicior quam frater fratri*, "for who is a better friend than a brother to a brother?"[20] As in Philip V's address to his sons, fraternal *pietas* could symbolize and realize political *concordia*: if Jugurtha would work with his brothers, Numidia would be politically stable and successful, otherwise, fraternal discord will lead to political strife. Predictably, Jugurtha violated fraternal *pietas* and Rome was implicated in this immorality.

After Micipsa's death, the brothers failed to follow his advice and instead of working together, they divided their inheritance: *propter dissensionem placuerat dividi thesauros finisque imperi singulis constitui*, "on account of their disagreement, it was decided that their moneys should be divided and territories should be assigned to each to rule individually."[21] One kingdom becomes three; the brothers' inheritance is divided, just as in the epigram about Bavius. Then, in the course of negotiating the divi-

---

[19] Sal. *Iug.* 5.6–7, 6.2–3, and 9.3–4.

[20] Sal. *Iug.* 10.5, cf. 10.6. Micipsa's expectations were sadly unrealistic: G. M. Paul, *A Historical Commentary on Sallust's Bellum Iugurthinum*, 46, and E. Tifou, *Essai sur la pensée morale de Salluste à la lumière de ses prologues*, 473.

[21] Sal. *Iug.* 12.1, cf. 12.3–9. On the chronology see Paul, *Historical Commentary*, 40–42.

sion, Jugurtha had one of his brothers, Hiempsal, murdered. When the brothers first met to plan their joint rule, Jugurtha suggested that Micipsa's decrees from the previous five years be declared invalid. Hiempsal agreed; Jugurtha's adoption had occurred during that time. Hiempsal's agreement undermined Jugurtha's claim to power, since the adoption legitimized this claim. From then on, Jugurtha harbored ill-will toward Hiempsal and began plotting his murder. Both Jugurtha and Hiempsal were vying for sole power, each advancing himself at the expense of his brother: no fraternal *consortium* here. Jugurtha, however, killed his brother, demonstrating that nothing, not even a brother, could stand in the way of his ambitions. After the murder, according to Sallust, the majority of Numidians supported Adherbal (Hiempsal's brother) against Jugurtha, who was backed by most of the army, a smaller but more powerful group.[22] The majority support for Adherbal implies a condemnation of fratricide: only the army, the agent of force, implicitly condoned fratricide through its backing of Jugurtha. The balance of power between those condoning and those condemning fratricide is a sign of the moral climate: might makes right in Numidia, when fraternal *pietas* falls victim to an immoral balance of power.

In the aftermath of Hiempsal's murder, both Adherbal and Jugurtha sought aid from Rome. Sallust recreates Adherbal's address to the Senate, in which he begged for help in ousting Jugurtha. Sallust characterizes Adherbal as a loyal ally of Rome, following in the footsteps of his father and grandfather, and now expecting a return on past *beneficia*. In this role, he invokes traditional political practices and the personal relationships that support political power, *amicitia* and *societas*. Adherbal asserts that the only basis he has for his claim is his belief that Rome's dignity will not suffer such deeds: *tamen erat maiestatis populi Romani prohibere iniuriam neque pati quoiusquam regnum per scelus crescere*, "the sovereignty of the Roman people has the power to prevent this injury and not to allow anyone to increase his power through crime."[23] Adherbal looks to Rome for justice and moral standards. While Adherbal addressed the Senate in person, Jugurtha sent emissaries, who went to work even before Adherbal made his plea. Jugurtha, afraid that Rome would turn against him, appealed to the greed of the *nobiles*. He sent gifts to his old friends and courted new friends with bribes. Although his plan did not succeed in turning the tide of public opinion, his bribes won over enough senators to secure his own claims and to discredit Adherbal. Only

22 Sal. *Iug.* 11.5–6, 13.1–2.

23 Sal. *Iug.* 14.7, with Paul, *Historical Commentary*, 31, 55, and 59. Cf. Sal. *Iug.* 14.5–6 and 8–9. See also K. Büchner, *Sallust*, rev. ed., 182, 185–87. The pathos of Adherbal's pleas also emphasized the degree of corruption at Rome, see Tifou, *Essai sur la pensée morale*, 474.

a few men who valued good and right more than money, *quibus bonum et aequom divitiis carius erat*, continued to argue Adherbal's case.[24] The Senate decided to send ten envoys to Numidia to negotiate a settlement between the two brothers. By similar means Jugurtha won over these men and the leader of the delegation, L. Opimius:

Eum Jugurtha, tametsi Romae in inimicis habuerat, tamen adcuratissume recepit, dando et pollicendo multa perfecit uti fama, fide, postremo omnibus suis rebus commodum regis anteferret. (4) Relicuos legatos eadem via adgressus plerosque capit, paucis carior fides quam pecunia fuit.

Jugurtha nevertheless received him [Opimius] most carefully, even though at Rome he had considered him among his enemies; by giving and promising him [Opimius] many things he brought it about that he gave the king's interest precedence over his own reputation, loyalty, and in the end over all his own affairs. Jugurtha won over most of the envoys, after he had approached them in the same way: to a few men loyalty was more dear than money. Sal. *Iug.* 16.3, 4.

Thus Jugurtha obtained for himself the better part of the kingdom.

Sallust casts Rome as arbiter of justice and morality in this episode. His narrative sets out the two sides of the case. Adherbal represents traditional Roman practices, the *mos maiorum*, human relationships based on *fides* and reciprocity, and the proper working of social morality. Jugurtha embodies self-interest out-of-control: greed and ambition for political power drive him to kill his brother and throw his kingdom into turmoil. The Senate's decision and the actions of the ten commissioners reflect the state of Roman morality. It is the Romans' own greed and self-interest that leads them to this choice.[25] Although Sallust may be aiming this attack primarily at the *nobiles*,[26] his narrative reflects moral standards that are not necessarily restricted to any particular class of Romans. Arrogance caused the Romans and Jugurtha alike to ignore the obligations of traditional relationships, that is, to ignore social morality. Fratricide represents the corruption of these human relationships and the values on which they rest. Jugurtha committed the fratricide, but the Romans are complicit in the crime through their tolerance. As Jugurtha was driven by greed to kill his brothers, so too the Romans are moved by greed to let him go unpunished. Such tolerance of immorality and the consequent breakdown of social relations are, for Sallust, among the causes of civil

[24] The uncorruptable few, Sal. *Iug.* 15.3; Jugurtha's old and new friends, 13.5–6; discrediting Adherbal, 15.2, 16.1; winning over the Senate commission, 16.2–4. The fact that Jugurtha does not speak himself adds to the emphasis on his pure lust for power: Büchner, *Sallust*, 182.

[25] R. Syme, *Sallust*, 175.

[26] Sal. *Iug.* 4.7–8.

war. Sallust wrote his monograph on Jugurtha after the war between Caesar and Pompey, at a time when Romans were keenly attuned to the vicissitudes of a civil war waged by ambitious men. Without arguing for any kind of simple correspondence between contemporary and historical figures, I would suggest that Sallust's historical study of Jugurtha had contemporary resonance. The historical situation of Jugurtha's rivalry with his brothers provided a framework for probing the dynamics of greed, ambition, and political morality. Because brothers were prominent in Roman politics, Sallust's audience would have a familiar context against which to read his account of Jugurtha, ready standards for assessing his treatment of his brothers as well as the Roman reaction. Because Sallust implicates the Romans in Jugurtha's fratricide, his narrative invites Roman readers to put themselves to the test, to ask how they would have acted if faced with Jugurtha's choices. If they had been in the Senate when Adherbal made his plea, would they have refused Iurgurtha's bribes, or would they have been complicit in fratricide? Such questions could also pertain to the recent civil wars fought by Romans who understood citizenship in fraternal terms.

Roman poets ring variations on this theme when they respond to changes in late Republican society. Lucretius pairs civil war, *sanguine civili,* with fratricide, *crudeles gaudent in tristi funere fratris,* as the ugly evidence of societal corruption.[27] This image recurs in two other poems. At the end of poem 64, Catullus catalogues the varieties of violence and deviant sexuality all situated within the family. Fratricide heads the list with the gruesome image of brothers washing their hands in each other's blood, *perfudere manus fraterno sanguine fratres.*[28] This from the poet who felt his brother's death as his own. In the lines preceding, Catullus remarks that the gods do not walk the earth as freely as they used to but they only appear on the battlefield, now that the earth is imbued with evil and justice has been banished by greed. The juxtaposition of battlefield and fratricide suggests civil war driven by rampant self-interest.[29] In

[27] Lucr. 3.68–73. J. Kenney, *De Rerum Natura. Book 3*, 85: "'C'est du Salluste en vers' (Martha 188)." These invocations of fratricide are part of a larger rhetorical trope, the sequence of ages or the Golden Age mythology. The corruption of kinship, including fratricide, is a conventional feature of the degenerate age already in Greek literature beginning with Hesiod, *Op.* 109–201, cf. Arat. *Phaen.* 100 ff. See also C. J. Fordyce, *Catullus*, 322–23, and M. L. West, *Hesiod: Works & Days*, 200.

[28] Catullus 64.399. On the poems about his brother, see above Chapter 2 p. 74.

[29] Catullus 64.394–98. The mythological narratives in this poem are similarly ambiguous, see J. C. Bramble, "Structure and Ambiguity in Catullus LXIV," *PCPS* 16 (1970): 25–27. Such ambiguity undercuts a simple contrast of past and present. The poem refuses to idealize the past; instead it charts continuity between past and present corruption, in the end, noting a difference only of degree. Cf. J.E.G. Zetzel, "Looking Backward," *Pegasus* 37 (1994): 21–22.

Vergil's *Georgics* as well fraternal discord marks the corrupt society. In *Georgics* Book 2, Vergil sets an idealized "Golden Age" against a society that resembles contemporary Rome. In the ideal world, the farmer does not feel jealous desire because the earth satisfies his needs. He is ignorant of political power, both republican and royal, and the fraternal discord that both entail.[30] On the other hand, contemporary society is intoxicated with politics and forensic dispute, and spattered with brothers' blood, *gaudent perfusi sanguine fratrum*.[31] As good relations between brothers could indicate the moral nature of an individual, so too, by extension, a society's attitude toward fraternal *pietas* emblemmatized social morality. The death of a brother was not only a sign of corruption but also an occasion to mourn the loss of shared community values. At the end of *Georgics* Book 3, a plague ravages the natural world, a plague that is associated with the other destructive forces in the poem, including civil war.[32] An appropriately pastoral image of fraternal *pietas* conveys some sense of the emotional reaction to the plague, the destruction of the Golden Age, and the civil wars which eroded the Romans' faith in their own past. Among the victims of the plague Vergil draws attention to the pathetic death of a young bullock, yoked to his mate in the field. After the bullock dies,

> . . . *it tristis arator*
> *maerentem abiungens fraterna morte iuvencum,*
> *atque opere in medio defixa reliquit aratra.*
> *non umbrae altorum nemorum, non mollia possunt*
> *prata movere animum, non qui per saxa volutus*
> *purior electro campum petit amnis; at ima*
> *solvuntur latera, atque oculos stupor urget inertis*
> *ad terramque fluit devexo pondere cervix.*

The plowman goes sadly as he unyokes the bullock grieving for his brother's death, and he leaves the plow still buried in the midst of the work. The shadows of the deep groves cannot move his spirit, nor the sweet meadows, nor the stream which seeks the plain, flowing through the rocks clearer

---

[30] Verg. *G.* 2.458–74, and 490–512; cf. A. Wallace-Hadrill, "The Golden Age and Sin in Augustan Ideology," *P&P* 95 (1982): 23.

[31] Verg. *G.* 2.510. On the corruption of the rustic ideal in the *Georgics* see D. O. Ross, *Virgil's Elements*, 125–26, and M.C.J. Putnam, "Italian Virgil and the Idea of Rome," in *Janus*, ed. L. L. Orlin, 176–79.

[32] Patterns in the structure of *Georgics* Books 1 and 3 support the parallelism: the natural violence of the storm in 1.311–34 is answered by the violence of civil wars 1.463–514; similarly in Book 3, the natural violence of sexual passion 3.242–83 is paired with the destructive violence of the plague 3.478–566. On structural patterns in the *Georgics* see R. F. Thomas, ed., *Virgil Georgics*, 2:130–31.

than silver;[33] but the bullock's flanks go slack, numbness presses his list-less eyes, and his neck sinks heavily down to the ground. Verg. G.3.517–24

After the plague, the bullocks no longer low in the shade as they did in the ideal world described in the second book of the *Georgics*; instead, their lowing echoes a lament as the herd dies.[34] Vergil endows the animals with a human empathy describing the bull's death as *fraterna morte*, "for a brother's death." Their condition, yoked together to the plow, enacts the cooperation and sense of identity essential to fraternal *pietas*. The yoke itself can symbolize their partnership: they are, in a sense, *consortes*, since they share each other's fate, both in daily labor and in death; when one dies, the other loses his spirit, his interest in life. Servius, *ad loc.*, glosses *fraterna morte iuvencum* as *consortis interitu*. The yoke-mates can also represent partnership, *societas*, on a larger scale, in the sense of the fraternal partnership among citizens. As the plague can be seen as a parallel to civil war in the first book of the *Georgics*, so the mourning of the bull for his brother yoke-mate expresses the loss inherent in civil war. Vergil's depiction of the bees in *Georgics 4* also represents an idealized social morality in potentially fraternal terms. The bees hold their property undivided and their children in common, *solae communis natos, consortia tecta urbis habent*, as if in a collective household.[35] This arrangement reflects traditional Roman patterns of family organization and social relationships in which collective virtues thrive. The term *consortia* emphasizes these traditional values, linking them to fraternal *pietas*.

When brothers took the field as soldiers, the stakes were higher because of the emotional intensity inscribed in the fraternal relationship. Poetic depictions of brothers fighting together explore the power of fraternal *pietas*, dramatizing the metaphorical fraternity of ordinary soldiers. Many brothers appear on the battlefields of Vergil's *Aeneid*. Among Turnus' allies are the twins from Tibur, Coras and Catillus, while Teuthra and his brother Tyres fight for the Trojans. More brothers die together than fight together: Clausus slays the three sons of Thrace as

[33] Electrum is actually an alloy of silver and gold; the same word is used of amber in Verg. *E.* 8.54 and *A.* 8.402 and 624, see R.A.B. Mynors, ed., *Virgil. Georgics*, 255.

[34] Verg. *G.* 2.467–74, cf. 3.554–55; for the connection of these pastoral scenes, see Thomas, *Georgics*, 1:13, 248, and on the pathos of the scene 2:138.

[35] Verg. *G.* 4.153, and see Ross, *Virgil's Elements*, 208–209; R. F. Thomas, *Lands and Peoples in Roman Poetry*, 74; J. Griffin, "The Fourth Georgic, Virgil, and Rome," *G&R* 26 (1979): 61–80; G. B. Miles, *Virgil's Georgics*, 241ff. For citizens as *consortes*, Ovid, *Pont.* 3.2.82, and Lucan 4.178 where, during a truce, soldiers on opposing sides of the civil war hail each other as *hospes*, *propinquus*, and *consors*.

well as the three sons of Idas and Ismara. Aeneas kills Maeon, Alcanor,
and Numitor, and later he kills Ligus and then refuses to spare his
brother, Lucagus, so that the brothers will not be separated in death, a
grim travesty of fraternal solidarity. Pallas kills a the twins Laris and
Thymber, who differ only in the manner of their death.[36] On the Trojan
side, Pandarus and Bitias fall to Turnus, as do Amycus and Diores and,
with one blow, three brothers from Lycia. When brothers close ranks on
the battlefield in Vergil's *Aeneid*, their formation is the same as in
Seneca's metaphor. Aeneas attacks Cydon, whose seven brothers defend
him, a *stipata cohors*, "a close guard."[37] Although all the brothers in the
Aeneid fight on the same side, the specter of fraternal discord looms over
the battlefield. The evil Allecto, who provides the impetus for the war
between Trojans and Latins, has the power to cause fraternal strife:

> *Tu potes unanimos armare in proelia fratres*
> *atque odiis versare domos, tu verbera tectis*
> *funereasque inferre faces, tibi nomina mille,*
> *mille nocendi artes.*

You can pit brothers who are soul mates against each other in battle, and stir
up families with hate; you bring scourges and funereal torches into their
houses; you come in a thousand guises with a thousand ways to hurt them.
Verg. A. 7.335–38

Allecto's evil power is quantified through an inversion of fraternal *pietas*:
she is so powerfully evil that she can make even brothers bear arms
against each other. The description of brothers as *unanimi*, emphasizing
their unity and conversely the discord caused by Allecto, again seems to
invoke the idealized equality between brothers. Although the *Aeneid*
does not deal explicitly with civil war, the war between Latins and Etruscans (as allies of the Trojans) could be interpreted as a civil war of sorts.
Despite the shadow of fratricidal war, brothers remain united in Vergil's
epic of Rome's founding, an epic which, through its focus on Aeneas,
sidesteps the fratricidal strife in the other foundation myth. Written after
the civil wars at the end of the Republic, the *Aeneid* reaffirmed traditional roles for brothers, as soldiers fighting together for the glory of
Rome, answering wartime anxieties about civil war that threatened fraternal harmony.

[36] Coras and Catillus, Verg. A. 7.670–77, and 11.465, 604; Teuthra and Tyres fight for
the Trojans, 10.401–404; Clausus' victims, 10.345–52. Aeneas and Maeon, Alcanor, and
Numitor, 10.335–341, and Ligus and Lucagus, 10.575–601. Pallas and the twins Laris and
Thymber, 10.390–93. See also P. R. Hardie, "Tales of Unity and Division in Imperial Epic,"
62.
[37] Verg. A. 10.328, for Turnus and Trojan brothers, 9.703–55, and 12.509–20.

Fraterna Comminus Arma: Brother against Brother

Where military tradition glorified fraternal *pietas*, accounts of civil war focused on breaches in the relations between brothers. In the Sullan era and later in the years leading up to Octavian's principate, brothers found themselves fighting on both sides. Whereas the sources for the Sullan wars catalogue divided families, those for the later wars emphasize familial solidarity and strategies for preserving an heir and even the family property.[38] For example, although Cicero, his brother, his son, and his nephew were all proscribed, his son managed to survive. Furthermore, as Plutarch tells it at least, fraternal *pietas* triumphed at the brothers' final parting, despite the bitter differences that had arisen between them.[39] Civil war tested *pietas* of all kinds, as accounts of heroic rescues and sacrifices during the proscriptions attest.[40] But the relationship between brothers drew special attention as a representation of the dilemmas of civil war both because fraternal *pietas* was the idealized form of male intimacy and because brothers had a traditional role as soldiers fighting for Rome. When brothers were divided by civil war, it was not only a personal relationship that was at stake, but the Roman notion of civic identity that depended on the *mos maiorum*. Thus, the image of brothers battling against each other combined the personal with the political in representing the Roman experience of civil war.

In the Roman historical tradition, the earliest example of brothers facing off on the battlefield is associated with the *Historiae* written by L. Cornelius Sisenna, praetor in 78.[41] Livy included this incident in his account of the war in 87 between L. Cornelius Cinna, consul of that year, and Cn. Pompeius Strabo, consul in 89. As it happened, a soldier and his brother were fighting on opposite sides, and one unintentionally killed the other:

> *In quo bello duo fratres, alter ex Pompei exercitu, alter ex Cinnae, ignorantes concurrerunt, et cum victor spoliaret occisum, agnito fratre ingenti lamentatione edita, rogo ei extructo, ipse se supra rogum transfodit et eodem igne consumptus est.*

---

[38] F. Hinard, "Solidarités familiales et ruptures à l'époque des guerres civiles et de la proscription," in *Parenté et stratégies familiales dans l'antiquité romaine*, ed. J. Andreau and H. Bruhns, 558–60 and 565–67 with references cited there to Hinard's prosopographical studies of the proscriptions.

[39] Plut. *Cic.* 47.1–2, cf. Shackelton Bailey, *Cicero*, 276–78.

[40] Val. Max. 6.7.2–3 and 6.8, App. *BC* 4.21–24.

[41] Sisenna *hist*. fr. 129, cf. Tac. *Hist*. 3.51 and below pp. 186–88.

In this war there were two brothers, one in Pompey's army, the other in Cinna's. Unwitttingly they engaged each other in combat, and after the victor had despoiled his victim, he recognized his brother and let loose a loud cry of grief. Then, after he built a funeral pyre for his brother, he stabbed himself over the pyre and was burned with the same fire. Livy *Epit.* 79

The soldier's intense grief conforms to other Roman laments for the loss or death of a brother, for instance in Catullus' poetry or Cicero's letters from exile.[42] But this soldier goes one better; he kills himself to avoid being separated from his brother. His suicide also makes a fitting punishment for the murder of a brother, for the destruction of the fraternal relationship in which his own identity is anchored. Suicide may also reflect the empathy underlying fraternal *pietas*. Valerius Maximus tells a similar tale about two brothers in Pompey's war against the followers of Sertorius in 77. The shared pyre, *communibus flammis*, emphasizes the common fate of the brothers. Moreover, the brother's unwillingness to accept pardon for fratricide suggests the degree of immorality associated with this deed. Nothing but sharing the same fate could begin to atone for it:

> *Licebat ignorantiae beneficio innocenti vivere, sed ut sua potius pietate quam aliena venia uteretur, comes fraternae neci non defuit.*
> Though he could have gone on living, innocent because he did not know what he had done, instead, so as to enjoy his own devotion rather than the grace of another, he did not fail to be his brother's companion in death. Val. Max. 5.5.4

The dramatic coloring of the incident corresponds to the spiritual attachment between brothers as well as the intense emotions of men in war. The lack of enmity between the brothers—the fact that the soldier kills without knowing that his brother is his enemy until it is too late—lends pathos to the story: each is doing what he perceives as his duty, fighting for his side and winning, ignorant of the cost to himself. Both anecdotes of brother killing brother occur in narratives of civil war, and it is likely that they represent a rhetorical *topos*. Variations on this theme recur throughout histories of the civil war between Caesar and Pompey in 49–48 B.C.E.. An examination of these episodes will reveal what aspects of civil war are expressed through the fraternal relationship, and how Roman

---

[42] Compare also Appian's narrative of fraternal devotion during the proscriptions of 43, *BC* 4.22. When one brother sees his brother arrested, he rushes to turn himself in and begs to be killed before his brother. The implied motive is to avoid the grief of seeing his brother die and to share his brother's death. The executioner agrees saying, "εἰκότα ἀξιοῖς . . σὺ γὰρ πρὸ τούτου γέγραψαι."

assumptions about brothers are invoked in dramatizations of civil war battles to express the painful unpredictability, and the special cruelty, of civil war.

In the opening line of Lucan's epic of the war between Pompey and Caesar, civil war is described as *bella plus quam civilia*, "more than civil war." This enigmatic phrase refers generally to the excesses of civil war and also alludes to the specific focus of this violence, kinship. This is both literally a conflict between kin—Caesar is Pompey's father-in-law—and metaphorically fraternal strife among the soldiers, as the Berne scholiast notes: *ut (pote) inter generum et socerum gesta. ubi et filii cum parentibus et fratres dimicavere cum fratribus*, "that is, wars waged between son-in-law and father-in-law, and when sons do battle with fathers and brothers with brothers."[43] The excessive quality of this war resides in its power to set kin against each other, and the ultimate, most intense expression of this kind of war, is when brothers come face to face on the battlefield. Throughout Lucan's epic, the individual soldier's experience of civil war is epitomized by the loss of a brother.[44] Brothers are also implicated in his explanation of the causes of the war.

Lucan traces the origins of this civil war back to the so-called first triumvirate, the informal power-sharing arrangement between Caesar, Pompey, and Crassus that dominated Roman politics in the 50s. The triumvirs are introduced with remarks on cosmic dissolution. The sibling rivalry between Apollo and his sister Diana[45] leads directly to a description of the triumvirate as a fraternal *consortium*. The triumvirs are co-*domini;* they share ownership of Rome just as *fratres consortes* share a patrimony:

> *dum terra fretum terramque levabit*
> *aer et longi volvent Titana labores*
> *noxque diem caelo totidem per signa sequetur,*
> *nulla fides regni sociis, omnisque potestas*
> *impatiens consortis erit.*

As long as the earth holds up sea, and air the earth, and as long as unending labors drive the sun in orbit, as long as night follows day through the same number of heavenly constellations, there will be no trust among partners in kingship: power will not endure a partner. Lucan 1.89–93

---

[43] *Comm. Bern. ad* Lucan 1.1.

[44] In a scene reminiscent of the incidents reported in Livy and Valerius Maximus, a veteran of the Sullan civil wars recalls the violence and misery in great detail, and at the center of his speech, he tells of his own personal grief when he came upon the mutilated corpse of his brother on the battlefield, Lucan 2.169–73, cf. other battle scenes, 2.151; 3.326–27, 354–55; 7.182, 463ff.

[45] Lucan 1.77–78.

The reference to *consortium* is ironic, because power does not accommodate partners any more than brotherly devotion. In searching for a historical *exemplum* to illustrate his point, Lucan says, there is no need to look far. Rome's foundation story is at hand with a built-in link between political partnership and fraternal *pietas*. The conflict between Pompey and Caesar is equated with the fratricidal strife between Romulus and Remus and their civil war perpetuates this primal fratricide.[46] The point of comparison between the twins and the triumvirs is also significant. Whereas Pompey and Caesar are fighting over a large, rich empire, Romulus and Remus came to blows over a small, poor piece of land. In neither case, Lucan says, was the prize worth the price. No gain compensates for fratricide and the violation it represents. Lucan's explanation of the failure of the triumvirate draws on the idealization of *consortium* and simultaneously undermines it. The failure of the triumvirate dooms traditional beliefs in the power of fraternal *pietas* to reconcile conflicts of interest. This pessimistic irony arises from conventional representations of civil war as a battle between brothers.

Because Pharsalus was the decisive battle in the war between Pompey and Caesar, it became a literary focal point for fraternal symbolism. The absence of brothers from Caesar's own account of the battle gains significance in comparison with the emphasis on fraternal sentiments in both Lucan's and Appian's descriptions of the battle. In all three accounts, the moment before the battle is fraught with tense anticipation. After both armies are arrayed on the field at Pharsalus, an ominous stillness descends on the men. They freeze, arrested by what they see:

> *vultus, quo noscere possent*
> *facturi quae monstra forent, videre parentes*
> *frontibus adversis fraternaque comminus arma,*
> *nec libuit mutare locum. Tamen omnia torpor*
> *pectora constrinxit, gelidusque in viscera sanguis*
> *percussa pietate coit, totaeque cohortes*
> *pila parata diu tensis tenuere lacertis.*

They see their fathers looking at them face to face and brothers bearing arms in hand-to-hand combat, so they could understand the monstrous things they were about to do. Nor was there a desire to change places. Nevertheless, paralysis clutched all their hearts; the blood gathered cold in their guts struck by *pietas*. The whole regiment for a long time held their spears poised, with their arms flexed. Lucan 7.463–69

The soldiers stand suspended, swords raised, as they realize who it is that they are about to kill, not just fellow citizens, but fathers and brothers.

---

[46] Lucan 1.93–97.

The recognition engenders horror in them and in the audience, as both stop and wait, pondering what is to come—while the thought of fratricide and parricide grows real for the soldiers. At the peak of battle, fathers and brothers face each other at the center of the battleline; in the aftermath, ghosts of the slain haunt the survivors, each his own victim, old, young, fathers and brothers.[47]

In Appian's account, as in Lucan's, the moment before battle is marked with fraternal symbolism. Both armies stand their ground, looking at each other, hesitating before the battle. When Pompey sees his men hesitating, he fears that their formations will fall into disarray, and so he gives the signal for battle; Caesar follows suit and the armies engage. The soldiers from both armies advance in silence, awed, it seems, at the prospect of the coming battle. Appian does not address the soldiers' motivations directly, but his explanation of the generals' motivations expresses the fears and doubts shared by all Romans on this battlefield. Like their troops, Pompey and Caesar hesitate, contemplating their own actions and motivations, how their ambitions brought these armies to battle and how this war between Italians was destroying ties of citizenship, friendship, and kinship between them, and also among the men in their armies. The moment before civil war is so heavy with emotion because these battles destroy the bonds among citizens, even the most intimate bonds among brothers:

> . . . ξίφη νῦν φέρουσι κατ᾽ ἀλλήλων καὶ τοὺς ὑποστρατευομένους ἐς ὁμοίας ἀθεμιστίας ἄγουσιν, ὁμοεθνεῖς τε ὄντας ἀλλήλοις καὶ πολίτας καὶ φυλέτας καὶ συγγενεῖς, ἐνίους δὲ καὶ ἀδελφούς.
>
> . . . now they were pointing swords at each other and leading armed men toward the same impious goals, men who were of the same stock and the same citizenship and tribe and kin, and even some who were brothers. Appian *BC.* 2.77

The list of the victims in this sentence comes to a climax at the end with brothers. The combination of particles, δὲ καὶ, reinforces the emphasis, setting off brothers from the other relationships in the list, and the word ἀδελφούς is placed emphatically at the end of the sentence.

Brothers are absent from Caesar's account of the battle of Pharsalus.[48] Caesar first describes the deployment of the troops and reports two pre-battle speeches to the troops. Then the trumpets sound and Caesar's

---

[47] Peak of battle, Lucan 7.550, and aftermath, 7.772–75. See M. Rambaud, "L'Apologie de Pompée par Lucain au livre viii de la *Pharsale*," *REL* 33 (1955): 269. Similarly, in the final scene of Sallust's *Catiline*, the survivors find friends and relatives among the dead, *multi . . . volventes hostilia cadavera amicum alii, pars hospitem aut cognatum reperiebant*, *BC* 61.8.

[48] Caes. *BC* 3.90–93.

army advances, charging and shouting. But they stop halfway across the field, because Pompey's troops are not making a countercharge. According to Caesar, Pompey ordered his men not to charge, but to hold their positions so that they would face the attack in a well-ordered, unbroken formation. In addition, by holding his troops back, Pompey will force Caesar's army to charge twice the distance. This strategy was designed, so Caesar hypothesizes, to give Pompey's army a better defense and to tire out Caesar's army, weakening their attack. Caesar claims that this plan is misconceived because it denies Pompey's soldiers the battle-rage that charging fires.[49] In order to frustrate Pompey's strategy, the Caesarian army stops halfway across the field, rests, then renews the charge and the troops engage. This pattern of charge, hesitation, and engagement may have reflected the actual progress of the battle and may lie behind the moment of hesitation in both Lucan's and Appian's accounts. The break in the action provided later writers with a context for reflection on the coming battle, an opportunity to explore the motives and emotions of the troops, and to draw the audience into the historical moment. Appian emphasizes the silence of the hesitation before Pharsalus. The silence is implicit in the generals' introspection and explicit in his description of the armies' advance. It is a sharp contrast to the clamorous charge that Caesar describes and a departure from both military and literary conventions of battle narratives.[50] This inversion of conventional literary features draws attention to and dramatizes the extraordinary quality of this battle. The silence in Appian's account corresponds, in a literary sense, to Caesar's silence about the soldiers' motivations: what is a literary silence in Caesar's narrative becomes a dramatic reality in Appian's.

As Caesar's, Appian's account unfolds primarily from the perspective of those in command, yet there is a significant difference in what we see in the hesitation before battle. Whereas Caesar characterized the generals in their military capacity showing how strategic considerations determined their behavior, Appian developed the thoughts and emotions that motivated the generals. In addition, instead of implicitly asserting the authority or superiority of one general, as Caesar does, Appian portrays both generals pondering the same reservations and inspired by simi-

---

[49] On the negative characterization of the Pompeians, see J. H. Collins, "Caesar as Political Propagandist," *ANRW* 1, no. 1 (1972): 922–66; E. Gabba, *Appiano e la storia delle guerre civili*, 136–40; F.-H. Mutschler, *Erzählstil und Propanganda in Caesars Kommentarien*, 214–15.

[50] In Caesar's account of the civil war, several major battles begin with a charge: Ilerda 1.43–44, Massilia 2.14, Utica 2.34. Herodotus, 6.112, credits the Athenians at Marathon with being the first to begin battle with a charge. See also F. E. Adcock, *The Roman Art of War under the Republic*, 9–11, and H. P. Judson, *Caesar's Army*, 59–62.

lar motives. The inner monologue that Appian attributes to Caesar and Pompey adds an emotional dimension lacking in Caesar's narrative. Since Appian's battle narratives tend to minimize such rhetorical elements,[51] his development of this dramatic moment is even more striking. In Appian's account, both Caesar and Pompey are men who empathize with their troops, who regret the destructive consequences of their ambitions, who have genuine emotions, even tears, when they confront their awesome responsibility for this civil war. Appian's characterization of the generals is perhaps idealizing, but it is compelling as an explanation of the causes of this battle, as an expression of the complex issues—political and emotional—that led to the battle of Pharsalus.

Caesar, however, does not exploit the emotive potential of the moment before Pharsalus. Rather, his account focuses on military strategy. This emphasis on strategy lends both detachment and authority to the account—the writer is, after all, an experienced general and one of the principals in the war. Even though Caesar is discussing the outbreak of a battle, battle-rage in fact, the approach is analytical. He explains the function of a charge in inspiring battle-rage, but does not describe the emotion itself—we have no idea whether the charge actually inspired Caesar's troops, or whether Pompey's troops were especially apathetic because of his strategy. Caesar was no stranger to the doubts, fears, and drives that motivate fighting men. In many other passages of the *Bellum Civile*, Caesar reports and comments on the mood of the troops and their motivations.[52] Before the battle of Pharsalus, he reports that the soldiers were burning with eagerness before the battle, but their emotions respond to his speech of exhortation, another sign of his expertise: *hac habita oratione, exposcentibus militibus et studio pugnae ardentibus tuba signum dedit.*[53] In addition, there is no description of emotion during the battle, and Caesar's history avoids the conventions of fraternal symbolism, perhaps because including these sentiments would interfere with the justification of his own actions. In fact, the only brothers in Caesar's *Bellum Civile* are not even Romans, they are Allobroges, who

[51] For Appian's restraint, see A. M. Gowing, *The Triumviral Narratives of Appian and Cassius Dio*, 210.

[52] See, for example, Caes. *BC* 1.20–21, 44–45, 64.7, 67.3, 71.1, 74.2; 2.12–13, 29, 31, 33; 3.6.1, 47–51, 69.2, 73, 80.7.

[53] Caes. *BC* 3.90, with J. M. Carter, ed., *Julius Caesar: The Civil War Book III*, 213–14. Of Caesar's reflection that his fourth line would secure the victory, Carter writes, "it is very unlike Caesar to interpose a reflection of this sort in the middle of the action, and also uncharacteristic of him to draw attention so unsubtly and so rhetorically to his own foresight and grasp of the situation (contrast his treatment in 92.4–5)." In other words, Caesar rarely uses an authorial interjection to voice his authority; it is instead the silent hand behind his battle narrative.

are hardly exemplary soldiers.[54] At first, they are esteemed for their valor both by Caesar and by their own troops. Then, overconfident, they begin to cheat the cavalry of its wage and to hog all the booty. When the troops complain to Caesar, he shows them indulgence, which turns out to be misplaced, since they soon desert to Pompey, turning over information that leads to the defeat of Caesar's army at Durrachium. Here is fraternal *pietas* run amok. The brothers are partners only to each other; because their fraternal feeling does not extend to their fellow soldiers, they become traitors to the common cause. In a history of civil war, the only brothers who take the battlefield reject the traditional role of brothers as defenders of Rome.

Despite the absence of brothers from Caesar's civil wars, fraternal imagery persists in other accounts of civil war and of the proscriptions enacted by the next set of triumvirs, Lepidus, Antony, and Octavian. Even before the Second Triumvirate, Antony and his brothers were known to have violent proclivities. Throughout Cicero's *Philippics*, the brothers Antonii are a threefold scourge to the city. Cicero groups M. Antonius with his brothers, calling them collectively Antonii and characterizing them all as rapacious, base villains who are united in wreaking destruction on all good Romans.[55] His arguments assume that the brothers share character traits. He distinguishes them only so far as to say that Lucius, the youngest, is the most bestial, and Gaius, the middle brother, rivals the other two in vices. The brothers have the same ambitions.[56] Like Africanus, Antony procured a province, Macedonia, for his brother Gaius; but it was an immoral and unlawful appointment, which only served to satisfy the greed and violence of the brothers. Antony, too, led military operations with his brother Lucius; but again, not to the glory of Rome but to sate their lust for blood and corrupt pleasures. Instead of earning glory, their exploits bring shame both on their family and on Rome, in contrast to the Romans, whom Cicero urges to imitate their brothers who died fighting against Antony.[57] Finally, in the proscriptions of the late 40s, Antony along with his fellow triumvirs turned violence against their own kin.

Proscriptions became part of the battlefield violence against brothers at the battle of Philippi.[58] Before the battle, in Appian's account, Cassius

[54] Caes. *BC* 3.59 ff.

[55] See, for example, Cic. *Phil.* 5.25, 7.16, 10.4–5, 13.2, 10, 26, 49, and cf. *Fam.* 2.18.2 where Cicero advises Q. Minucius Thermus not to provoke the wrath of three so nobly born brothers.

[56] Cic. *Phil.* 3.31, 10.10, and 21–22.

[57] Macedonia for Gaius, Cic. *Phil.* 3.26, 7.3, 10.9–10; operations with Lucius, *Phil.* 11.10, 13.4, 14.8–9; Cicero's exhortation to imitate brothers who died for Rome, *Phil.* 14.34–35.

[58] See App. *BC* 4.107–12 and Dio 47.6.2–3.

gave a speech to his army, setting forth the causes of the war and the crimes of the triumvirs: "they proscribed brothers, uncles and guardians before others," αὐτοὶ πρὸ τῶν ἄλλων ἀδελφοὺς καὶ θείους καὶ ἐπιτρόπους προγράψαντες.[59] Their abuse of fraternal relationships epitomized the wrongs that the liberators were fighting to avenge. Cassius' reference to the proscription of brothers should have evoked an angry response from soldiers who might have lost a brother in this war or in the earlier proscriptions, or soldiers who simply felt a fraternal bond among themselves. After the battle, specters of proscribed brothers haunted the triumvirs' triumph in Velleius Paterculus' account. Velleius laments the proscription of loyal wives, children, and slaves, and notes that no one proscribed his son, because doing so cut off hope for the future. Older and collateral male relatives were not, however, immune:

Ne quid ulli sanctum relinqueretur, velut in dotem invitamentumque sceleris Antonius L. Caesarem avunculum, Lepidus Paulum fratrem proscripserant; nec Planco gratia defuit ad impetrandum, ut frater eius Plancus Plotius proscriberetur. Eoque inter iocos militaris, qui currum Lepidi Plancique secuti erant, inter execrationem civium usurpabant hunc versum:
        De germanis, non de Gallis duo triumphant consules.

So that nothing sacred might be left for anyone, as if in a lure or invitation to crime, Antonius proscribed his mother's brother L. Caesar and Lepidus proscribed his brother Paulus; nor did Plancus lack the influence to demand that his brother, Plancus Plotius, be proscribed. For this reason, those who followed the triumphal chariot of Lepidus and Plancus kept repeating this ditty amidst the soldiers' mocking taunts and the citizens' curses:
        Two consuls triumph not over the Gauls, but over the Germans
        [or their brothers]. Vell. 2.67.3

The proscriptions culminated in the consuls' proscriptions of their own brothers, as if these acts were representative of all the abuses attendant on civil war. The untranslatable pun on *germani* has a bitter ring even though Lepidus' brother did not die in the proscriptions, because his guards let him escape: they, at least, honored his relationship with his brother more than his brother, "ἀδελφὸν αὐτοκράτορος."[60] One of the purposes of verbal abuse of triumphant generals was to remind them that they were still human, that victory did not confer deity. Triumphators were subject to the laws of the state and the *mos maiorum*. The black

[59] App. *BC* 4.95, cf. Val. Max. 6.8.5.
[60] App. *BC* 4.37. Cf. Val. Max. 6.8.5. According to Appian *BC* 4.12, Lepidus' brother Paulus was first on the proscription list, and L. Caesar was second, because these two had been among the first to vote Lepidus and Antony enemies of the people. On the various versions of the proscription of Lepidus' brother, see Gowing, *Triumviral Narratives*, 134.

humor in the pun on brothers calls attention to a transgression of these norms. Public ridicule might mitigate divine censure, but in the human world, humor played counterpoint to grief, reinforcing the validity of fraternal *pietas*. The public context of these taunts suggests that, even outside of the literary tradition, the conflicts of the civil war were experienced in terms of fraternal *pietas*.

Romulus and Remus Reconsidered

Though the legend of Romulus and Remus was told in many versions with variable details, two events are of particular importance in later political evocations of the myth: the twins' early life as leaders of a band of shepherds and the fratricide—when Romulus is building the walls of Rome, he kills his brother.[61] References to Romulus and Remus focus on these two elements of the story, which represent the two poles of fraternal symbolism, cooperation and violent conflict. Because the foundation story was at once political and fraternal, the figures of Romulus and Remus represented the traditional coherence of fraternal *pietas* and the *mos maiorum*. The names Romulus and Remus, like other terms in the Roman political vocabulary, were redefined in the process of the civil wars and the creation of the principate.[62] By retelling the history of the foundation, Romans formulated the changes and turmoil of the late Republic as a conflict between brothers. Cicero, Livy, and Dionysius of Halicarnassus each present a version of the foundation myth and there are numerous allusions to the twins in Augustan poetry. Augustan poets, with the exception of Ovid, deflect attention from the fratricide, and focus on reconciliation, as if putting the civil war aside to move forward under Augustus' peace. The literary orientation of the elegists, with their refusal to compose martial epic, seems to justify this omission. The triumviral poems of Vergil and Horace, however, reflect the pessimistic

[61] Fraternal strife was, in a sense, the twins' heritage. Their grandfather, Numitor, and his brother, Amulius, were also rivals and they fit the pattern of brothers as opposites, who can also be expected to come into conflict precisely because of their differences, Livy 1.3.10–11, cf. D.H. 1.76, 81.6, and see R. M. Ogilvie, *A Commentary on Livy, Books 1–5*, 46–48. For the Indo-European parallels for the early kings of Rome, see J. Poucet, *Les origines de Rome*, 177–78.

[62] On the redefinition of the political vocabulary, see R. Syme, "History and Language at Rome," in *Roman Papers*, ed. A. R. Birley, 3:953–61. For Romulus in particular see J. Poucet, "L'influence des facteurs politiques dans l'évolutions de la geste de Romulus," in *Sodalitas*, 1:1–10; Ross, *Backgrounds*, 13 at n. 1; R. Schilling, "Romulus l'élu e Rémus le réprouvé," in *Rites, Cultes, Dieux de Rome*, 111–16; H. Wagenvoort, "The Crime of Fratricide," in *Studies in Roman Literature, Culture and Religion*, 169; D. C. Earl, *The Political Thought of Sallust*, 106–108; J. C. Classen, "Romulus in der römischen Republik," *Philologus* 106 (1962): 173–204.

view of fraternal *pietas* and of the fratricide, which is perhaps most clearly represented in Cicero's *De Officiis*. Where Romulus and Remus were involved, fratricide expressed not just battlefield trauma but a more pervasive sense of loss, a loss of social cohesion and civic identity rooted in shared moral assumptions. The civil wars of the late Republic charged the foundation myth with contemporary significance as Romans identified themselves with the brother-citizens who founded their city. This late Republican perspective is cast into relief by comparison with earlier attitudes toward Romulus and Remus.

The foundation story developed into its familiar form during the middle Republic, in part as a response to and as an expression of contemporary political events. As the plebeians fought for equal political rights with the patricians, they exploited the story of twin founders to express their political ideology. For example, the statue of the Capitoline Wolf, erected in 296 B.C.E. (either with the twin infants or to accompany already existing statues of the twins), may have commemorated power-sharing between plebeians and patricians.[63] The early life of Romulus and Remus, when they jointly led a band of shepherds, can be seen as corresponding to the duality of the consulship when a plebeian consul shared power with his patrician colleague in a tacit metaphor of fraternity.[64] Even far from Italy, the Romans were associated with the figures of Romulus and Remus: on the island of Chios the twins were named in a religious celebration, documented in an inscription of the early second century.[65] One provincial festival is not decisive evidence, yet the joint commemoration of the brothers in a celebration honoring Rome is sug-

[63] "The establishment of explicit power-sharing between patricians and plebeians in the fourth century BC provides the necessary condition for the creation of the story of the twins. . . . The Ogulnian monument is our earliest evidence for the existence of the Remus story. I suggest that the story and monument alike were created to celebrate that 'new equality'" (Wiseman, *Remus*, 107, cf. 72–76, and see Livy 10.23.10–11.). T. J. Cornell suggests that the elimination of one brother may symbolize the creation of political unity out of two originally separate political communities, namely the synoecism of the early Palatine and Quirinal settlements ("Aeneas and the Twins," *PCPS* 2d ser., 21 [1975]: 31). These groups have also been associated with *collegia* or *sodalitates*: for a discussion of the evidence from the *lapis Satricanus* inscription, see J. Bremmer, "The Suodales of Poplios Valesios," *ZPE* 47 (1982): 133–47. Livy's sources for the rustic life of the twins may have been Cassius Hemina, see Cassius Hemina fr. 11 *hist*. See also T. J. Luce, *Livy*, 174 at n. 80; D. Konstan, "Narrative and Ideology in Livy: Book 1," 210; Poucet, *Les origines*, 280–84; R. Girard, *La violence et le sacré*, 96, 371; T. J. Cornell, *The Beginnings of Rome*, 60–63.

[64] Livy's account of Romulus and Remus' life before the founding of Rome reflects some of these themes (1.4.8–1.6.4). On the characterization of the twins, see Schilling, "Romulus l'Élu," 104–105, 106–107.

[65] The name of Romulus is missing from the inscription because of a break in the stone; it has been restored alongside Remus' name, which does appear on the stone, see P. S. Derow, W. G. Forrest, "An Inscription from Chios," *ABSA* 77 (1982): 79–82.

gestive. If the brothers' partnership symbolized Roman political identity, then the fratricide is a troublesome episode in their story. Neither the statue of the wolf nor the accompanying inscription refer to the fratricide, but Remus' death is a regular part of literary accounts, beginning with Ennius' *Annales*. Wiseman reconciles the two apparently inconsistent elements by associating the Romulus and Remus story with events of 296 B.C.E. when Rome was in danger of losing the battle for control of central Italy to a coalition of Samnites, Etruscans, and Gauls. Remus' death was connected with a human sacrifice offered for Rome's victory and commemorated in the temple to Victory on the Palatine, which was dedicated in 294. Because the temple was built into defensive walls, the story that Remus was killed when Rome's first walls were being built becomes "a legendary analogue to the horrifying necessities of 296 BC."[66] As the crisis faded into memory, the story of Remus' death was converted into an exemplary tale, explaining the fratricide as a necessary sacrifice for the safety of Rome and an expression of Romulus' patriotism. This seems to be the moral of the story as Ennius told it in his epic of Roman history, the oldest surviving literary evidence.

Four fragments, six lines, of Ennius' version of the Romulus and Remus legend remain to suggest an outline of the story. The first fragment is part of a longer passage that describes how the twins settled the dispute about the new city's name—should it be Roma or Remora?—by taking auspices. At the end of the passage, after Romulus had observed the favorable sign of twelve birds, he proceeded to secure the foundations of his city and his power.[67] In the second fragment, one of the twins, presumably Romulus, expressed a preference or a prayer for the security of walls rather than security won by force: *Iuppiter ut muro fretus magis quamde manu sim*, "Jupiter, let me rely on this wall more than force." The third fragment suggests that this prayer went unanswered: *Ast hic quem nunc tam torviter increpuisti?* "Is this the man whom you threatened just now so sternly?" While we cannot be certain who speaks this third fragment, the outcome of the story makes Romulus the likely speaker of the fourth:

> *Nec pol homo quisquam faciet impune animatus*
> *Hoc nec tu: nam mi calido dabis sanguine poenas.*

There will certainly be no one living who will do this with impunity, not even you, since you will now pay me back with your living blood. Enn. *Ann.* 1.94–95

[66] Wiseman, *Remus*, 125, cf. 117–25.

[67] Enn. *Ann.* 1.72–91 frags. 47–50 Skutsch. Ennius' version directs attention to Romulus, linking him with the contemporary political community, see S. M. Goldberg, *Epic in Republican Rome*, 105–108.

Romulus makes an example of his brother to deter others who might challenge the safety of Rome's walls and the sovereignty of its rulers. The repetition *nec pol . . . hoc nec tu* emphasizes Romulus' refusal to make any exception, not even for his brother; the wall was too important to the stability of the city. This view may constitute a healthy corrective to fraternal collusion in politics, exemplified by the Scipiones in Ennius' era, and later by the Gracchi, or worse yet the kind of behavior that Cicero condemns in M. Antonius and his brothers. Such concerns seem to have been outweighed in the late Republic by other anxieties, caused by political uncertainty. Despite the potential for brothers to tyrannize Rome, Romans in the late Republic found fraternal discord more troubling than the possibility that brothers might get too much political mileage out of fraternal *pietas*. Arguably, Cicero's outrage at the Antonii coheres with such a reactionary idealization of brothers. The wicked exploitation of fraternal *pietas* is a corollary to fratricide: both undermine traditional values, both attend tyranny, both end in immoral violence. Our interpretation of Ennian fragments is, however, inevitably influenced by later Roman readings that attribute the threat to Remus and the retribution to Romulus.

Especially toward the end of the Republic, leading generals presented themselves as new founders of the city, identifying themselves with Romulus in their public image-making.[68] Romulus and Remus, as founders of the city, represented the archetypal Roman citizen.[69] They served as both a standard against which to judge the present and a source of inspiration for the future.[70] References to Romulus could evoke the pure morality of an idealized past, as for example in Catullus' hymn to

[68] Sulla is *scaevos iste Romulus* "that wicked Romulus," Sal. *Hist.* 1.55.5. Plutarch, *Pomp* 25.4, records that one of Pompey's opponents threatened that if he kept acting like Romulus, he would suffer the same fate. Even Cicero is styled *Romule Arpinas* in [Sal.] *Cic.* 7. Both Julius Caesar and Augustus were associated with Romulus: Caesar, Catullus 29.5 and 9; Augustus, Verg. *A.* 6.777–95, 809–12. On the figure of Romulus in general and the identification of Caesar with Romulus see K. Scott, "The Identification of Augustus with Romulus-Quirinus," *TAPA* 56 (1925): 96–97; Classen, "Romulus," 192–203; W. Burkert, "Caesar und Romulus-Quirinus," *Historia* 11 (1962): esp. 368–71; S. Weinstock, *Divus Julius*, 175–77, 180–99; Z. Yavetz, *Julius Caesar and His Public Image*, 40, 42–43, 182; M. Gelzer, *Caesar, Politician and Statesman*, trans. P. Needham, 318 at n. 4; Earl, *Sallust*, 106–108; A. Wallace-Hadrill, "The Golden Age and Sin," 26–27; Syme, *Sallust*, 237.

[69] Romulus and Remus are ideals in virtue and physical prowess as well; see, for example, Cic. *Rep.* 2.4 (cf. *Rab. Perd.* 13 for Romulus, Numa, and Tarquin as model lawgivers). See also Polyb. 6.5.7, with F. W. Walbank, *A Historical Commentary on Polybius*, 1:652, and Livy 1.4.8–9, with Ogilvie, *Commentary on Livy*, 50–51.

[70] T. J. Cornell, "The Value of the Literary Tradition Concerning Archaic Rome," in *Social Struggles in Archaic Rome*, ed. K. A. Raaflaub, 82–83. A. G. Pontone, "Fratricide as the Founding Myth of Rome," collects the literary sources for the fratricide from the Republic and the early Empire, with a focus on the historians.

Diana, Poem 35, or patriotic tradition, as in Livy's report that the Romans compared Aulus Cornelius Cossus to Romulus as he marched with the *spolia opima* to the temple of Jupiter Feretrius in 437 B.C.E..[71] By the late Republic, identification with Romulus was a double-edged sword, on the one hand invoking tradition and an idealized past,[72] on the other recalling the fratricidal strife between Rome's first citizens.

The earliest explicit evidence for the vilification of Romulus is found in Cicero's *De Officiis*, where Romulus' murder of his brother illustrates the dilemma of apparent advantage. Cicero argues that what is truly right, *honestum*, never conflicts with what is advantageous, *utile*.[73] This argument relies on an identification of self-interest with the common good, an identification which, in the *De Officiis*, is the core of our humanity and is rooted in kinship. This notion of humanity is expressed through an analogy to the body and as a partnership through the term *consortio*.[74] The moral imperatives of this partnership make it wrong to harm other people in the pursuit of one's own interest, and it makes no difference whether they are kin or strangers, citizens or brothers. After setting up this system, Cicero examines potentially confusing incidents drawn mostly from Roman history and social situations. The examples begin at the beginning with Romulus and L. Junius Brutus, who expelled the kings from Rome and founded the Republic.[75] In these first examples, the question of advantage involves a conflict between personal and political duty. When in the early days of the Republic Rome's leading men resolved to remove all traces of Tarquins' rule from the city, Brutus was faced with a dilemma because his partner in expelling the Tarquins and establishing the Republic, L. Collatinus, was also related to the Tarquins. Brutus decided to allow the expulsion of Collatinus. Cicero deems Brutus' decision *utile*, advantageous, because it was based in concern for Rome. It was also *honestum*, morally right, so right, in fact, that even Collatinus himself was obliged to agree. The case of Brutus sets forth a moral hierarchy: duty to Rome should precede personal obligations. The second example, Romulus, problematizes patriotic duty by admitting the possibility that patriotism is not always the true advantage or morally right, but that it can be a pretense for some other apparent and immoral advantage. Romulus was motivated to kill his brother not out of moral compunction but by expediency alone. The fratricide undid both *pietas* and the human partnership that grounds morality:

[71] Livy 4.20.2–3.

[72] For example, Cicero's treatment of Romulus in the *De Re Publica* 2, with Zetzel, "Looking Backward," 24–25.

[73] Cic. *Off.* 3.19–20, cf. 1.54–56, 3.20–26.

[74] Cic. *Off.* 3.26, cf. 27–28.

[75] Cic. *Off.* 3.40–42.

(41) At in eo rege, qui urbem condidit, non item: species enim utilitatis animum pepulit eius; cui cum visum esset utilius solum quam cum altero regnare, fratrem interemit. Omisit hic et pietatem et humanitatem, ut id quod utile videbatur neque erat adsequi posset, et tamen muri causam opposuit, speciem honestatis nec probabilem nec sane idoneam. Peccavit igitur, pace vel Quirini vel Romuli dixerim. (42) Nec tamen nostrae nobis utilitates omittendae sunt aliisque tradendae, cum his ipsi egeamus, sed suae cuique utilitati, quod sine alterius iniuria fiat, serviendum est.

But in the case of that king, the one who founded the city, it is not the same. For the appearance of advantage so drove his thinking that he killed his brother, since it seemed to him more advantageous to rule alone than with someone else. He disregarded both *pietas* and *humanitas* so that he could achieve what seemed advantageous but really was not, and yet he raised the issue of the wall as a reason, a pretense of moral probity that was neither likely nor appropriate. Therefore he did wrong, whether I speak of him as Quirinus or as Romulus. (42) Still we should not sacrifice our own interests and yield them to others when we are ourselves are in need of them, but each must take care of his own advantage as far as he can without harm to another. Cic. *Off.* 3.41–42

The opening phrase signals the change in perspective. Even without the adversative particle *at*, the substitution of *is rex* for *Romulus* suggests a less than flattering notoriety (*is* almost has the force of *iste*).[76] Because the fratricide was immoral, it could not have been expedient, and expedience is an insubstantial pretext for self-interest, *visum esset utilius solum quam cum altero regnare*, and security no substitute for morality, *speciem honestatis nec* . . . . Cicero's judgment pulls the rug out from under the traditional justifications for the fratricide. Duty to the state could be attributed to Romulus, but his motives remain corrupt and the fratricide immoral. The fratricide symbolizes the cost of founding the city and also the cost of the security that followed the civil wars. From a late Republican perspective, the fratricide was a problem for Rome's legendary founder-king, because the civil wars were seen as a reiteration of the

[76] Although *rex* is not always a negative term in Cicero—sometimes *rex* is contrasted with the evil *tyrannus*—in this passage in particular, *rex* seems to have connotations of *tyrannus*. On the concept of the tyrant at Rome, see J. Béranger, "Tyrannus." The passage may reflect Cicero's response to the civil wars of 49–48 and may be intended as a commentary on the behavior of one particular founder, Julius Caesar. The sentence, *peccant igitur, pace vel Quirini vel Romulo dixerim*, may be a play on Caesarian propaganda, which associated Caesar with Romulus, see H. J. Krämer, "Die Sage von Romulus und Remus in der lateinischen Literatur," in *Synusia*, ed. H. Flashar and K. Gaiser, 359–60. Cf. also Cic. *Off.* 1.26: *nulla sancta societas, nec fides regni est*, which Lucan, 1.89–93, seems to echo; for the possibility Cicero refers to Caesar, see P. Jal, *La guerre civile*, 403 at n. 10. Compare the idealizing treatment of Romulus in Cicero's *De Re Publica*, with M. Fox, *Roman Historical Myths*, 5, 14–20.

immoral utilitarianism that Cicero condemns in Romulus.[77] Romulus' failure is the failure of the civil wars, the failure of Romans to sustain the *mos maiorum* and to treat each other as citizens and brothers.[78] Civil strife in the late Republic destabilized traditional political morality and led Romans to reevaluate other sources of moral sanction, namely kinship and its ethical basis in *pietas*. In evaluations of Romulus, the traditional opposition between public duty and personal devotion collapsed when it appeared that Remus' death served neither Rome nor fraternal *pietas*. All Romans shared the consequences of Romulus' failure, and their shared suffering is vividly depicted at the end of Horace's seventh *Epode*, where Remus' blood flows over them all, even the innocent.[79]

Where the literature of the triumviral period explored the implications of fratricide, Augustan writers tended to avoid what had become a volatile literary motif. Even after the violence of the civil wars had begun to ebb, a certain sensitivity to the foundation myth and its implications remained. According to Dio, Octavian had wanted the title "Romulus,"[80] but he took the name Augustus instead. Although Ennius could justify fratricide in the interests of Rome, Cicero (and doubtless others) had already contemplated less consoling interpretations and Livy's treatment reflects these shifting views. Tradition and revision are woven into Livy's treatment of the fratricide which includes two versions of the event:

> *Inde cum altercatione congressi certamine irarum ad caedem vertuntur; ibi in turba ictus Remus cecidit. Volgatior fama est ludibrio fratris Remum novos transiluisse muros; inde ab irato Romulo, cum verbis quoque increpitans adiecisset, "Sic deinde, quicumque alius transiliet moenia mea," interfectum.*

> Then a crowd gathered hurling abuse and in the angry dispute they turned to murder; there in the mob Remus was struck down. The more popular story has it that Remus jumped over the new city walls in mockery of his brother and then he was killed by an angry Romulus, who threatened and

---

[77] Schilling, "Romulus l'Élu," 107–14; Wagenvoort, "Crime of Fratricide," 176–79.

[78] Cicero, *Planc.* 93–94, conveys the traditional cooperation that allowed the Roman nobility to overcome their rivalries, cf. Cic. *Fam.* 1.9.21, *Balb.* 61. There was, however, a fine line between cooperative flexibility and treachery. Consider Livy's formulation of the *necessitas* that compels citizens to give in to self-interest at the expense of the common good, 3.65.11. See also Hopkins, *Death and Renewal*, 81: "Repeated civil wars were at once a symptom of extreme political individualism and a mechanism for disrupting old social ties between kinsmen and friends, and for destroying traditional values and obligations; the civil wars and political discord provided the excuse and the social space for individuals to pursue their own advantage." Cf. C. Wirszubski, *Libertas as a Political Ideal at Rome*, 39; Jal, *La guerre civile*, 391–93; Griffin, "Fourth Georgic."

[79] For this interpretation of Epodes 7, 9, and 16, see R. A. Gurval, *Actium and Augustus*, 137–65, esp. 147–52.

[80] Dio 53.16.7.

added these words, "Whoever else jumps over my walls again will perish thus." Livy 1.7.2

In both versions, Livy focuses on anger as a motive, in a shift from political justification to personal morality, which could make Romulus a sympathetic figure: haven't we all succumbed to anger and regretted it later?[81] In the first version, Remus' death seems strangely impersonal because the killer is not named; even the grammatical construction—an intransitive verb with passive participle—deflects blame. Similarly, in the second version, the verb is passive, *interfectum*, and comes at the end of the sentence, separated from its subject, *Remum*, by a subordinate clause and by the quotation ascribed to Romulus. The structure of the sentence holds the reader in suspense:[82] did Romulus only threaten or did he . . .? Livy's characterization of the second version as *volgatior fama*, "the more popular story," tends to undermine its credibility and thus to further deflect blame from the founder. Although the characterization of Remus as a provocateur was available in the annalistic tradition,[83] it is absent from Livy's treatment except for the restrained *ludibrio*, further downplaying the theme of fraternal conflict. It seems noteworthy that Remus just disappears from Livy's narrative, almost as suddenly and with as little trace as Romulus when he disappears in a thunderstorm. But, whereas Romulus' continued presence is assured by the report of his apotheosis and in the name of the city, Remus is not mentioned again. As for fratricide, it might seem, the less said the better. Such reticence may represent one Roman response to the fratricidal civil wars which were thought to devolve from these inauspicious beginnings.[84]

The narrative structure of Livy's treatment also suggests the awkwardness of having to tell the story of the fratricide. The degree of compression is both characteristic of Livy's presentation of the early history of Rome and significant for the figure of Romulus. Although Livy did have an enormous amount of material to cover and thus needed to be selective about what events he presented at length, his account of the fratricide is quite short. Compare, for example, the version in Dionysius of Halicarnassus, which elaborates the motives of not only the twins but also of

---

[81] Krämer, "Die Sage von Romulus und Remus," 357–58.

[82] Ogilvie, *Commentary on Livy*, 55, describes it as "dramatic."

[83] Represented, for example, in D.H. 1.87.4. Dionysius, however, also seems to have played down the theme of rivalry, see Fox, *Roman Historical Myths*, 56–58. This characterization of Remus is also reflected in Ovid's account of the fratricide, *Fasti* 2.142, 4.841–44, 5.471, and see Schilling, "Romulus l'Élu," 109–14. For the symbolism of walls with fraternal discord in this passage, see Konstan, "Narrative and Ideology," 198–210.

[84] Romulus' apotheosis, Livy 1.16.1–2, 5–8, cf. 1.7.3, with Ogilvie, *Commentary on Livy*, 54. On the date of Livy's composition see Syme, "History and Language," 956–58 and "Livy and Augustus," *HSCP* 64 (1959): 27–87.

their father and uncle, Numitor and Aemulius, dwelling on the fraternal conflict in both generations. In addition, Dionysius discusses more variant accounts and at greater length than Livy.[85] Livy omits many of the mitigating factors added to the story in the annalistic tradition to explain the death of Remus, for instance the involvement of Celer (Romulus' bodyguard) and Romulus' grief.[86] The degree of compression may reflect a wish to touch lightly on a delicate issue, since to omit the story altogether could be interpreted as an even greater condemnation of the founder, and might even have reflected on Augustus' project of refounding the city. In addition, the account of the foundation seems to be paired with the following event, the encounter between Hercules and Cacus.[87] The juxtaposition of these two stories suggests that they should be considered together; parallels in the two stories may be significant. Both begin in a pastoral setting. Hercules, like Romulus, is a herdsman and a hero. In killing Cacus, Hercules eliminates a monster who threatens the early Roman community. In this sense, Hercules is an agent of civilization and a protector of the Roman state. Romulus, too, is a protector and a civilizer.[88] The act of founding a city promotes civilization and the death of Remus is justified on the basis of civic security. Was Remus a monster? If not, what happens to Romulus' justification?[89]

Augustan poets, with the exception of Ovid, return to the association of Romulus and Remus with an idealized past: their allusions to the foundation story emphasize reconciliation by picturing the brothers together. Even Vergil's *Georgics*, which belongs to the triumviral period, only hints at the contradictions in the foundation story. In the final lines of *Georgics* Book 2, after the vision of the Golden Age and the corrupt present, the

---

[85] Variants in dating D.H. 1.74–76, in the family history of Romulus and Remus and the names of Romulus' brother D.H. 1.72–73, in the pastoral background and the roles of Amulius, Numitor and Faustulus 1.80, 84, in the death of Remus 1.87; on other founders 1.89; recapitulation 2.3. Dionysius, by his own account, draws largely on Fabius Pictor, D.H. 1.79.4.

[86] The name commonly attributed to this scapegoat, Celer, seems an attempt to excuse the deed: he acted too quickly for his own good; speed was his only crime. For the Celer story, see Valerius Antias fr.2 *hist.* = D.H. 2.13.2, cf. D.H. 1.87.4; Diod. 8.6.3; Festus p.48L; Ovid, *Fasti* 4.837–38, 5.469–70; Plut. *Rom.* 10.2; Serv. *A.* 11.603.

[87] Bruce Frier directed my attention to this parallelism. On the association between Romulus and Hercules in Augustan propaganda, see Syme, *Roman Revolution*, 472. For a post-modern twist, see M. Serres, *Rome*, trans. F. McCarren.

[88] L. Alfonsi, "La figura di Romolo all'inizio delle Storie di Livio," in *Livius*, ed. E. Lefèvre and E. Olshausen.

[89] Livy's reexamination of traditional interpretations may be a response to the lawlessness of the triumviral years, when traditional institutions were being redefined. For a discussion of the constitutional changes, see F. Millar, "Triumvirate and Principate," *JRS* 63 (1973): 50–67.

poet describes Rome's past, the time when Rome grew strong through the rugged lifestyle of the old Sabines and Remus and his brother:

> *hanc olim veteres vitam coluere Sabini,*
> *hanc Remus et frater; sic fortis Etruria crevit*
> *scilicet et rerum facta est pulcherrima Roma,*
> *septemque una sibi muro circumdedit arces.*
> *ante etiam sceptrum Dictaei regis et ante*
> *impia quam caesis gens est epulata iuvencis,*
> *aureus hanc vitam in terris Saturnus agebat;*
> *necdum etiam audierant inflari classica, necdum*
> *impositos duris crepitare incudibus ensis.*

Long ago the old Sabines lived this life, as did Remus and his brother. Thus Etruria grew mighty, Rome became glorious in its deeds and as one city girded its seven citadels with a wall. Before even the scepter of the Dictaean king [Jupiter], before the impious [Bronze] race of men feasted on slaughtered bulls, golden Saturn lived on earth, and people had not yet heard the war trumpets sound nor the clashing of swords laid on unyielding anvils. Verg. G. 2.533–40

This description conjures an idealized world which contrasts with the swords and war trumpets that were all too easily connected with contemporary civil wars. Building a city wall led to fratricide in the foundation story, yet the grammar of Vergil's passage carefully avoids laying blame. When Rome builds her own walls, *circumdedit*, there is no cause for the fratricide, no trouble in the fraternal relationship. Similarly, the name "Remus" without "Romulus" but with "*frater*" points to the time when both brothers and their fraternal *pietas* were alive. As if in contradiction, the seven citadels suggest another city with seven gates, Thebes, that was destroyed by fraternal discord. The image of walls activates a memory of fratricide constructing the reader's experience of early Rome as a transition from fraternal harmony to divisive rivalry and fratricide.[90] The mention of only Remus focuses on the relationship that was paradigmatic of civil strife thus drawing together other relationships, political or social,

---

[90] "It was only for a brief moment that Remus and his brother could have led this visionary life together. The idyll came to an end when at the very instant of Rome's foundation Romulus killed his confrère: ambition (and one man's yearning for autocratic rule?) triumphing over any feelings of kinship. . . . [there is an implied allusion] toward that instant of violence which, to the Augustan poets, was the mythic source and prototype of the century of civil wars . . . Virgil shows the actual historical and intellectual framework in which this myth of civil strife collides with another archetypal schema which haunted the Roman imagination—the dream of a past heritage of peace, simplicity and bounty associated once upon a time on Italian soil" (Putnam, "Italian Virgil," 178, cf. Putnam, *Virgil's Poem of the Earth*, 151–55).

that the Romans felt as fraternal. The contradictions in this image of Rome's past problematize past and present alike,[91] questioning the possibility of fraternal *pietas* in any age.

In his epic of Rome's foundation, Vergil reaches further back in time, beyond Romulus and Remus' story to Aeneas and Rome's Trojan origins. Vergil's treatment of Romulus and Remus in the *Aeneid* focuses on reintegration and reconciliation. Jupiter's prophecy in the first book of the *Aeneid* traces Roman kinship from Aeneas through Ascanius and Romulus to Caesar.[92] Romulus appears glorious in the tawny coat of his wolf-nurse building Rome's fortifications and carrying on the traditions of his father Mars.[93] In the brief account of the foundation, Remus is unnamed, implicit only in Ilia's *gemina proles*. Jupiter predicts a later, peaceful era in which the gates of war are closed, Furor is contained, and Remus gives laws with his brother Quirinus, accompanied by Fides and Vesta. Romulus is associated with Rome's martial traditions, whereas Quirinus takes his place when Remus appears in a reunion representing the new or renewed society under Augustus. Only the image of Furor, chained but still thrashing, troubles this image of lawful peace and fraternal concord.

Although the refusal to compose martial epic characterizes the Roman elegists, Romulus and Remus do appear in the works of Tibullus, Propertius, and Ovid. Usually the twins are treated with careful lightness. Tibullus, 2.5, includes a reference to the fratricide in a hymn to Apollo celebrating peace. The poem moves from the god's vatic prowess through a Sibyl's prophecy to visions of contemporary peace. The Sibyl gives her prophecy in the distant past amidst Rome's archaic landscape, a setting located historically through a reference to the foundation myth. It was the time when,

---

[91] In his dicussion of the rustic world, Vergil collapses the contrast between ideal and reality: "[t]he result is to put the present (*hanc vitam* thrice repeated, 532, 533, 538) at a double remove from a Hesiodic-Aratean golden age, and as well to underscore the irony in the lines on the Italian past by means of the inescapable observation that it too is post-Saturnian, that the old Sabines, Romulus and Remus, Etruria and Rome are descendants of that *impia gens* which first fed upon their slaughtered bullocks, who heard the war trumpets and who forged swords" (D. O. Ross, *Virgil's Elements*, 128). See also Thomas, *Virgil Georgics*, 1:262. References to Remus in Latin poetry are collected by M. B. Poliakoff, "Remus in Latin Poetry," *APAA* (1987): 135.

[92] Verg. A. 1.257–96. Anchises' prophecy in Book 6 also treats Romulus as the successor to Aeneas, 6.761–79.

[93] Compare the recollection of Romulus' role in creating the Roman community as remembered in Evander's tour of the site of Rome: Romulus is described as harsh, *acer*, suggesting his martial heritage, 8.342. Similarly, the scene on Aeneas' shield focuses on the mother and child image of the wolf and twin sons of Mars, 8.630–34, with Gurval, *Actium*, 218–19.

Romulus aeternae nondum formaverat urbis
moenia, consorti non habitanda Remo

Romulus had not yet built the walls of the eternal city where his brother
Remus was not to live in partnership. Tibullus 2.5.23–24

The term *consors* recalls the expectation that brothers would share their
inheritance,[94] while the lack of partnership looks ahead to the fratricide.
The wall is similarly ambiguous: it may be connected with the ritual sacrifice to secure the walls or it can also symbolize the dispute that fraternal
pietas could not reconcile.[95] Later in the poem, the Sibyl corrects an
implied connection between Rome and fratricide when she greets Rome's
other founder as Cupid's brother: *Impiger Aenea, volitantis frater
Amoris, / Troica qui profugis sacra vehis ratibus,* "Eager Aeneas, capri-
cious Cupid's brother, sailing on refugee ships with the household gods of
Troy."[96] One founder may have failed in fraternal *pietas*, but the other,
Aeneas, is brother to the ancestor of the successful Julian gens. Rather
than emphasizing crime or suffering, the allusion to Remus' murder may
increase by contrast "the sense of peace, harmony, and innocence in the
following verses."[97]

In Propertius' elegies, Romulus and Remus are usually associated with
Rome's heroic past,[98] and only two passages address aspects of the foundation story that might stir unhappy memories. In Poem 2.6, Romulus is
the *criminis auctor* of the rape of the Sabines, an unflattering epithet but
with no necessary reference to fratricide. If we read 3.9.50, *caeso moenia
firma Remo,* with Wiseman as an allusion to the ritual human sacrifice to
secure the city walls,[99] this passage, too, need not involve the founders as
brothers. Two passages do, however, draw attention to the fraternal relationship between Romulus and Remus. In the opening of his fourth

[94] "Mention of *moenia* elicits the subsequent phrase, recalling that Romulus killed his
twin brother Remus for leaping over the wall. . . . *consorti*: brother and co-heir but, ironically, not a sharer in Romulus' lot" (M.C.J. Putnam, *Tibullus*, ad loc.).

[95] Plutarch, scolds brothers who are unable to share their land without building boundary walls, moats, and fortifications (*Aem.* 5.9–10), and compares these quarrelsome
brothers with the Aelii Tuberones, who lived in a *consortium*-like household and exemplified traditional Roman morality, see above Chapter 1 pp. 000–00.

[96] Tib. 2.5.39–40.

[97] P. Murgatroyd, ed., *Tibullus Elegies II*, 183–84. Murgatroyd also finds the separation
of the names Romulus and Remus suggestive.

[98] As leader of the rape of the Sabine women, he is *criminis auctor*, Prop. 2.6.19; living
together with Remus 4.1.9–10 and with the Tities, Ramnes and Luceres, 4.1.32, and as
defender of Rome 4.4.27–28 and as military leader 4.4.79, in connection with Jupiter
4.10.5, 14. Cf. Remus as a theme appropriate to epic, 2.1.23, and the death of Remus as a
guarantee or security, 3.9.50. The military heroism of Romulus and Remus can be seen as
part of a thematic contrast in Propertius Book 4 between the uncivilized world of early
Rome and the sophisticated present, see M. Fox, *Roman Historical Myths*, 176–77.

[99] Wiseman, *Remus*, 125.

Book, the poet includes the twins in a description of early Rome, locating them at home together before Remus' death:

> Hoc quodcumque vides, hospes, qua maxima Roma est,
>   ante Phrygem Aenean collis et herba fuit;
> Qua gradibus domus ista Remi se sustulit, olim
>   unus erat fratrum maxima regna focus.

Whatever you see here, visitor, where greatest Rome now is, was a grassy hill before Phrygian Aeneas . . . the place where that well-known house of Remus rose up at the stairs [i.e. at the top of the *Scala Caci*], long ago this great empire was just a single fraternal hearth. Propertius 4.1.1–2, 9–10

The image of brothers around the hearth invokes traditional family life, which might reassure Romans that these peaceful traditions would outlast the legacy of fratricide.[100] Again, in the fourth Book, in an account of the battle of Actium, Propertius has Apollo cite Romulus as an historical example in his speech to Augustus assuring him success in the coming battle:

> quam nisi defendes, murorum Romulus augur
>   ire Palatinas non bene vidit avis

If you don't defend your [homeland], Romulus as augur for his walls did not see clearly the birds flying over the Palatine. Propertius 4.6.43–44

The god's advice predicates Augustus' success on the legitimacy of Romulus' power in early Rome, establishing a line of succession between the new founder and the old. The conditional clause suggests just the shadow of a doubt about the legitimacy of either rule.[101]

If Propertius hints at anxiety about the fratricide, Ovid's treatment of the foundation story in the *Fasti* renews the problematic theme of fraternal *pietas*. Building on Stephen Hind's analysis of Romulus in the *Fasti*,[102] my discussion focuses on several details which, by invoking fraternal *pietas,* heighten the ambiguity surrounding Romulus in the *Fasti*. First, in Ovid's account of the origins of the Lupercalia, Romulus resents his brother's achievements.[103] The festival arises from a pastoral incident. When robbers attack Romulus and his brother as they exercise with their fellow shepherds, the twins lead the defense. They set out in opposite directions, each leading a separate band of followers, Remus the

---

[100] Mention of Remus' death later in the poem, 4.1.50–54, could be interpreted as undermining this peaceful image, or alternatively, "as an apparent disaster leadiing to something good" (Fox, *Roman Historical Myths*, 151–52).

[101] For the ambiguity of these lines, see Gurval, *Actium*, 267–68, cf. 249–78, and works cited there.

[102] S. Hinds, "*Arma* in Ovid's *Fasti*: Part 1" and "*Arma* in Ovid's *Fasti*: Part 2," *Arethusa* 25 (1992): 81–154.

[103] Ovid, *Fasti* 2.371–78.

Fabii, Romulus the Quintilii.[104] Remus' group wards off the robbers and recovers the stolen goods. Because the Fabii are one of the most famous historical examples of fraternal solidarity, their support of Remus emphasizes the tension between the twins by setting up an implicit comparison between fraternal *pietas* and resentful rivalry. This rivalry reappears in Ovid's presentation of the foundation story, which was linked with the celebration of the Parilia, the anniversary of Rome's founding: *ambigitur, moenia ponat uter,* "there was a difference of opinion between the two over which one would lay the foundations."[105] Ovid presents the version of the fratricide in which Romulus' henchman Celer kills Remus, shifting the blame from Romulus and eliding the fratricide. Yet his description of Romulus' reaction is suspicious. Though Romulus held back his tears at the news of his brother's death, he wept at his brother's burial, revealing the devotion that his earlier reticence had concealed:

> *dat tamen exsequias; nec iam suspendere fletum*
> *sustinet, et pietas dissimulata patet.*
> *osculaque applicuit posito suprema feretro*
> *atque ait "invito frater adempte, vale!"*

Yet he performed the burial rites and he was no longer strong enough to hold back his tears, and his devotion concealed before was now apparent. He give his brother a final kiss when the bier was lowered and he said, "farewell, brother taken from me when I didn't want to lose you." Ovid, *Fasti* 4.849–52

At best it seems like special pleading to call it concealed *pietas* when Romulus has said, after he heard of his brother's death, *sicque meos muros transeat hostis,* "and so dies an enemy who crosses my walls."[106] This threat echoes Livy's *sic deinde, quicumque alius transiliet moenia mea,* "whoever else jumps over my walls again will perish thus," and generates ambiguity similar to that in the historian's version. In Ovid, Romulus' stoic refusal to mourn his brother's death may be as much a sign of callous ambition as of traditional Roman toughness.[107] The mention of *pietas* draws attention to Romulus' failure to show appropriate devotion to his brother, implying a contradiction between traditional values, fraternal *pietas* and *duritia*. The verbal echo of Catullus' epitaph for his brother undermines Romulus' sincerity because Ovid rings a change on the Catullan refrain, omitting the adverb *indigne*, "wrong-

---

[104] On this episode, see B. Harries, "Ovid and the Fabii: *Fasti* 2.193–474," *CQ* 41 (1991): 150–67.

[105] Ovid, *Fasti* 4.812, cf. 810–62.

[106] Ovid, *Fasti* 4.848 with Hinds, "*Arma* in Ovid's *Fasti*," esp. 125–27.

[107] This personal insensitivy seems counterpart to Romulus' barbaric approach to government in Ovid, *Fasti* 2.133–44 as analyzed by Fox, *Roman Historical Myths*, 217–19.

fully," but adding the adjective *invito*, "unwilling," which seems an unnecessary qualification for honest fraternal grief. Finally, when Remus' ghost rises and addresses the twins adoptive parents, Faustulus and Acca, he too excuses his brother.

> *Noluit hoc frater, pietas aequalis in illo est:*
> *quod potuit, lacrimas in mea fata dedit,*
>
> My brother didn't want this, there was equal *pietas* in him. He did what he could, he shed tears for my fate. Ovid, *Fasti* 5.471–72

Again, explanation only raises doubts. Why does Remus need to assert the equal devotion between him and his brother? Were tears all that Romulus could have done? Ovid's Romulus is the sad outcome of civil wars, a man incapable of empathy even with a brother, unable to do more than weep for his brother.

The foundation story and Romulus' murder of Remus reflects the impact of civil war on relations between fellow citizens and soldiers. The twin brothers were an especially suitable way to figure fraternal *pietas*. The representation of opposing ideas in pairs of brothers was familiar from literature and Greek culture,[108] and the physical similarity between twins embodies the emotional identification between brothers or alter-egos. Since twins look exactly alike, when they do not act alike, it is even more striking. Rivalry between Romulus and Remus symbolized the violence against the self implicit in fratricide,[109] and expressed the self-

---

[108] The focus on the immorality of the fratricide may also be an undercurrent in Greek, anti-Roman, accounts of the founding; it was certainly an aspect of later Christian interpretations, see Wagenvoort, "Crime of Fratricide," 172–75. Scholars have puzzled over why Rome's foundation story involves twins. J. N. Bremmer and N. M. Horsfall, "Romulus, Remus and the Foundation of Rome," in *Roman Myth and Mythography*, 25–48, esp. 35, discuss several explanations for the phenomenon of twins, none of which is entirely satisfactory. See also T. J. Cornell, "Aeneas and the Twins." There is a comparable Italic myth, the foundation of Tibur by twin brothers, Coras and Catillus, Verg. *A.* 7.672 ff., Serv. *A.* 7.670, or in an alternate version, Tibur is founded by three brothers, Coras, Catillus, and the eponymous Tiburtus, Cato *hist.* fr. 56, Hor. *Carm.* 1.18.2, Pliny, *NH* 16.237. Romulus and Remus can also be compared to the Castores, another pair of twins in which one is dominant, see R. Schilling, "Les 'Castores' Romains à la lumière des traditions indo-européenes," in *Rites, Cultes, Dieux de Rome*, 338–53.

[109] Rivalry between twins represents an intense case of what R. Girard defines as mimetic desire, the ultimate cause of human violence. "Desire is usually thought to be focused on the desirable object whose value is inherent; in reality, however, the value of the desired object is a result of the fact that someone else desires it. Thus desire is learned, by imitating the other, and soon becomes not primarily a desire for the object, but a desire to be like the other. Not knowing this, the imitator assumes that he does well to value the object of desire only to discover that the closer he comes to its acquisition, the greater becomes the hostility of and rejection by the one imitated. This creates what Girard calls the 'double bind' in the relationship. The one imitated has said, in effect, 'Be like me: value the object.' But when the imitator reaches out to take it, rivalry occurs, and the one imitated says, 'Do not be like me.

destructive violence of a war in which citizens failed to recognize each other as brothers.[110] It is thus fitting, then, that at least one institution revived by Augustus to promote unity, the Arval Brethren, expressly evoked both the foundation story and fraternal sentiment. The Augustan Arvales were drawn from a cross-section of the Italian aristocracy,[111] as if this religious brotherhood could somehow restore the fraternal bond of citizenship that civil war had damaged. The original Arvales were the sons of Acca Larentia, Romulus' nurse, and Romulus himself.[112] Romulus and the sons of Acca Larentia become brothers through membership in the Arvales; theirs was a fraternity based not on biological kinship but in social, religious, and political identity, like the relationship among citizens. Augustus' renovation of the shrine of the Lupercal, the site where the twins were suckled by the wolf,[113] may be connected with the fraternal symbolism of the Arvales. Remus was absent from the civic fraternity of Romulus and his descendants, as if the natural relationship between brothers could somehow be set aside if not erased. Romulus appeared with Aeneas in Augustus' forum,[114] emphasizing kinship between generations, from father to son over many generations, as a paradigm for the new imperial order. Collateral relations, most poignantly represented by brothers, are displaced with Remus and give way to new forms of civic fraternity that at once imitate and challenge the real thing. Romulus and his brother represented both idealized fraternity and its willful destruction. Allusions to Romulus or Remus in triumviral poetry implicate Romans, past and present, in the fratricide, undermining the simplicity of an idealized past, expressing the dilemma of civil war, and carrying traditional fraternal *pietas* into the future.

It's mine.' Veneration and rejection, mimesis and difference, are therefore experienced together in tension. The disclosure of rivalry then transforms the image of the model into that of one's 'monstrous double.' It is this problem that is the motivator and frustrator of human interaction" (B. Mack, "Introduction: Religion and Ritual," in *Violent Origins*, ed. R. G. Hamerton-Kelly, 8–9). Cf. Hardie, "Tales of Unity," 57–59.

[110] Compare the across-the-trenches truce between Caesar's and Pompey's troops, described by Lucan, 4.178ff., cf. Jal, *Guerre civile*, 322–52, and see above pp. 152–53.

[111] J. Scheid, *Les Frères Arvales*, 343–51.

[112] Pliny, *NH* 18.6, Gellius *NA* 7.7.8. Gellius names Masurius Sabinus, the early first-century jurist, as his source, and modern scholars also trace Pliny's account to him, see R. Syme, *Some Arval Brethren*, 103–108, and F. Münzer, *Beiträge zur Quellenkritik der Naturgeschichte des Plinius*, 349. Varro's reference to the Arvales, *LL* 5.85, is the only notice in Republican literature.

[113] *Anc.* 19.

[114] P. Zanker, *The Power of Images in the Age of Augustus*, 203–207.

FIVE

AT THE PALACE

*Celeberrimos auctores habeo tantam victoribus adversus fas
nefasque inreverentiam fuisse ut gregarius eques occisum a
se proxima acie fratrem professus praemium a ducibus
petierit.*
I have the most well-known evidence that there was among
the victors so great a disregard for right and wrong that a
rank-and-file cavalry man declared that his brother had been
slain by him in the latest battle and sought a reward from
his leaders.
(Tac. *Hist.* 3.51)

THIS ANECDOTE about a brother's seeking a reward for fratricide, which Tacitus includes in his account of the civil strife of
69–70 c.e., indicates a continuity in the symbolism of civil war
between Republic and Empire. Despite the changes in political and social
life that Empire brought, expectations of fraternal *pietas* remain constant. My earlier chapters assume this continuity as they rely on both
Republican and early Imperial literature. In discussing brothers' public
careers, however, I have focused on Republican politics. Similarly, my
analysis of the Romulus and Remus mythology reflects reactions to late
Republican politics and the civil wars that Augustus ended with the con-
solidation of his principate. In this new political order, the fraternal relationship retained its traditional shape and Roman expectations of fraternal *pietas* remained constant. Yet the transition from Republic to Empire
created new political contexts and representations of fraternal *pietas*. Because the figures of Romulus and Remus were problematized in the literature of the civil wars, Augustus and the Julio-Claudian emperors sought
new mythological paradigms for the fraternal harmony that had long
represented Roman civic unity. Castor and Pollux (the Dioscuri) replace
the founders as a paradigm of brotherly partnership. The emperor became a new audience for fraternal image-making, and the existence of an
imperial court generated a dynastic politics and rivalry for succession
among brothers in the emperor's family.

   This chapter offers a sketch of the development of fraternal symbolism
in the early Imperial era, charting both continuities and divergences between Republican and Imperial ideas about brothers. This sketch focuses

on fraternal dynamics within the Imperial family and on two mythological paradigms of fraternity, Castor and Pollux and the Theban brothers, Polynices and Eteocles. Tacitus' *Annales* and Suetonius' biographies of the emperors offer complementary perspectives on brothers in the Julio-Claudian family and Roman attitudes toward them. Statius' epic, the *Thebaid*, embodies a new mythological reflection of traditional Roman notions about fraternal *pietas* and rivalry. Observers of the imperial family were, it seems, more interested in power struggles between brothers than harmonious fraternal *pietas*, though the depictions of fraternal rivalry in the writings of Tacitus and Statius, for example, draw on traditional Roman notions about brothers and exploit the emotive power of these long-standing cultural and moral norms.

. . . . .

The very presence of an emperor changed the dynamics of fraternal *pietas* in Roman politics, as is evident in Ovid's celebration of C. Pomponius Graecinus and his brother and their shared glory in achieving successive consulships:

> quaeque est in vobis pietas, alterna feretis
> gaudia, tu fratris fascibus, ille tuis . . .
> multiplicat tamen hunc gravitas auctoris honorem,
> et maiestatem res data dantis habet.

The devotion you two share will bring you reciprocal rejoicing, you in your brother's consulship, he in yours . . .

The authority of the man who bestows this office increases its honor and the duty of the office obtains the grandeur of the giver. Ovid, *E.P.* 4.9.61–62 and 67–68

As in the Republican era, brothers cooperated in their public careers, but now their political success was oriented around the *princeps*. It may be no surprise that brothers of freedmen closely affiliated with the emperor attained high office,[1] and that such proximity to power entailed risks. Political trials provided a venue for negotiating this precarious relationship with power and, as in Republican politics, both prosecution and defense exploited appeals to fraternal *pietas*. M. Scribonius Libo Drusus appeared at his treason trial leaning on his brother's arm. Prosecuted at the end of Tiberius' reign, P. Vitellius and Pomponius Secundus found

---

[1] Not only Sejanus' adoptive brothers, the sons of the jurist Q. Aelius Tubero, but even his natural brother, L. Seius Tubero, all served as consul (L. Seius Tubero, cos. suff. 18 C.E. and, by adoption, Q. Aelius Tubero cos. 11 B.C.E. and Sex. Aelius Catus cos. 4 C.E.), see F. Adams, "The Consular Brothers of Sejanus," *AJP* 76 (1955): 70–76. Pallas' brother, Antonius Felix, was governor of Judea, Tac. *Ann.* 12.54.

their only protection in their brothers' devotion.[2] After Gaius' ascension, Pomponius' brother attempted both to win the new emperor's favor and at the same time to avenge his brother by prosecuting those who had put him on trial. The political vicissitudes of Iunii Silani offer a full picture of the dangers as well as the potential for fraternal success in imperial politics.

The Iunii Silani were great-great-grandsons of Augustus and they were prominent during Claudius' reign.[3] Their kinship with the former emperor proved both profitable and dangerous. All three achieved a variety of public distinctions, and all three fell victim to the younger Agrippina's ambitions, as Tacitus tells the story. Marcus was consul in 46, his younger brother Decius (surnamed Torquatus) in 53; the youngest, Lucius, praetor in 48, died before he rose to the consulship. Despite his early death, Lucius seems to have been the most successful. In 41, Claudius betrothed his younger daughter Octavia to him, and Silanus presided over the *Feriae Latinae* with Cn. Pompeius Magnus in the same year. Two years later, Lucius participated in Claudius' expedition to Britain, and at the subsequent triumphal celebrations, the emperor conferred on him the triumphal regalia. In the year after Lucius' praetorship, Agrippina contrived his death to facilitate a dynastic marriage with Octavia for her own son, the future emperor Nero.[4] Marcus was the next brother to attract Agrippina's attention. During his proconsulship in Asia in 54, she had him poisoned, fearing that he might avenge his brother's death or that he

---

[2] Vitellius and Secundus, Tac. *Ann.* 5.8, cf. 6.18, and Scribonius, Tac. *Ann.* 2.29.

[3] They are M. Iunius Silanus, *PWRE s.v.* Iunius 176, D. Iunius Silanus Torquatus, *PWRE s.v.* Iunius 182, L. Iunius Silanus, *PWRE s.v.* Iunius 180. On their kinship with Augustus, Pliny, *NH* 7.58. An earlier generation of brothers, M. and D. Iunius Silanus, was active under Augustus and Tiberius. In 8 C.E., D. Silanus was sent into exile on a charge of adultery with the emperor's granddaughter Julia. The sentence of exile, Tacitus tells us, was a concession to the friendship between the emperor and Silanus; other adulterers could expect death. If this sex scandal was a cover for political conspiracy, as Syme has argued (*History in Ovid*, 205–14), we might have expected Silanus' brother to be implicated. Yet his brother, Marcus, an influential orator, interceded on his behalf with Tiberius and the Senate after Augustus' death, Tac. *Ann.* 3.24. Marcus' influence with Tiberius may have something to do with what Tacitus calls *adulatio* of the emperor, *Ann.* 3.57. Although Tiberius allowed Decimus to return from exile, he prohibited him from future public honors, in a show of respect for Augustus' wishes. As if to confirm the rehabilitation of the family, in 33 Marcus' daughter Claudia was married to Germanicus' son Gaius, the future emperor, Tac. *Ann.* 6.20. The brothers' continuing proximity to the royal family is attested in an anecdote about Germanicus' son Drusus. In 31, some young man was passing himself off in Greece and the Islands as Drusus, but when he was apprehended, he claimed instead to be the son of M. Silanus, Tac. *Ann.* 5.10. See R. Syme, "The Junii Silani," in *The Augustan Aristocracy*, 188–99.

[4] Lucius' death, Tac. *Ann.* 12.3, 4, 8, and Suet. *Cl.* 29.1; accompanying Claudius, Dio 60.21.5, 60.25.8, and Suet. *Cl.* 24.3; betrothed to Octavia, Dio 60.5.7, and Suet. *Cl.* 27.2; presiding at the *Feriae Latinae*, Dio 60.5.8.

might, relying on his kinship with Augustus, challenge her son's ascension to the throne.[5] The third brother, Decius, almost survived Nero's reign. In 64, motivated by the same fears as Agrippina, Nero compelled him to open his veins.[6]

The proximity of the Silani not only to current emperors but also to Augustus' blood line marked them as potential rivals for imperial power. Tacitus' presentation of these brothers focuses on their illustrious family background, illustrating at once the demise of the Republican aristocracy and the problem of succession among the Julio-Claudians. Both themes are advanced through the vilification of Agrippina, who personifies a vengeful ambition. Agrippina was related to Augustus and more closely than the Silani.[7] Thus, her hostility to these brothers operated within a familial context, which highlighted the arbitrariness of distinguishing the "royal family" from other aristocratic lineages. The fears attributed to Agrippina focus on fraternal cooperation, creating an implied contrast between Republican and Imperial politics.[8] In the Republican era, fraternal *pietas* exerted influence both in making careers and in reining in excessive ambition. An emperor could stand alone—Agrippina acts out this solitary ambition in Tacitus' account—and collusion among brothers (his own or others') could be perceived as a threat. The brothers represent traditional Republican political ideals, which appeared as challenges to the relatively new imperial regime. Agrippina's hostility toward the Iunii expresses the imperial response to this challenge. In fact, the degree of her hostility may reflect the success of the Iunii Silani in sustaining their family's reputation and in moving toward the center of power. Tacitus' presentation implicitly privileges fraternal and Republican ethics by suggest-

[5] Marcus poisoned by Agrippina, Tac. *Ann.* 13.1.

[6] Decius' suicide, Tac. *Ann.* 15.35, and his consulship, Tac. *Ann.* 12.58. Suspicion fell on the next generation as well: Decius' nephew, L. Iunius Silanus Torquatus (probably the son of Marcus; *PWRE s.v.* Iunius 183), was implicated with C. Cassius Longinus in an attempted rebellion. Tacitus casts doubt on his complicity, describing him as terrified by his uncle's death, *Ann.* 16.8–9. Lucius was exiled and then killed while defending himself against the commander of the praetorian guard, who had been sent to kill him.

[7] The Iunii Silani were the grandsons of Cornelia, who was the daughter of Scribonia by her first husband, P. Cornelius Scipio. Cornelia was thus half-sister to Julia, the daughter of Augustus and Scribonia. The two Agrippinas descend from Julia, the younger in the same generation as the three Iunii Silani. Thus, the brothers are as closely related to Augustus as their nemesis, the younger Agrippina, but she descends directly from Augustus while they are related on their mother's side to Augustus' first wife. Agrippina is further insinuated into the Julio-Claudian clan through marriage to Claudius, who was descended from Livia, Augustus' second wife. Reckoning by birth alone, Agrippina and her son have a double link to Augustus whereas the Iunii have half a link.

[8] But for Agrippina's vigilance, these might not have been empty fears: both Vitellius and Vespasian were supported by politically active brothers before and during their brief reigns, Suet. *Vit.* 2, 5, 13.2, 15.2, 18, and *Vesp.* 1.3, 2.2, 4.3.

ing that Agrippina's behavior is excessive and ineffective. Her persistent attacks on these brothers is capped by the ridiculous (Tacitus implies) renaming of the month of June, as if changing the name would eradicate the memory of these noble brothers: *testificante Cornelio Orfito, qui id censuerat, ideo Iunium mensem transmissum, quid duo iam Torquati ob scelera interfecti infaustum nomen Iunium fecissent.* "Cornelius Orfitus, who proposed the change, averred that the month of June was changed because two Torquati who were killed for their crimes had made the name Iunius unlucky."[9] In the story of the Junii Silani, fraternal *pietas* represents traditional Roman politics as against the unsavory behavior of the royals. Within the imperial family, however, the treatment of brothers involved a more complex reinterpretation of Republican symbolism and morality.

In the highly charged context of Julio-Claudian succession, fraternal rivalry and devotion were most tellingly deployed among the brothers who were heirs to power. A bid for power could generate rivalry between brothers in the imperial family, but in courting public opinion, emperors and their heirs sought to project an image of fraternal cooperation. Official imagery promoted traditional values through a public mythology of fraternal *pietas* represented by Castor and Pollux. Because Romulus and Remus reminded Romans of civil strife, references to the founder in imperial literature are few and far between; Ovid's portrait may have been the final blow. Yet imperial brothers could project an appearance of *pietas* through association with Castor and Pollux.[10] Already in the Republic, Castor and Pollux were invoked to represent political partnership.[11] Imperial invocations of the Dioscuri exploit the ambiguity in their twinship: on the one hand they are identical and equal, on the other Castor is empowered with immortality, which his brother shared only through his favor. Augustus marked his grandsons' public image with allusions to the Dioscuri. As *principes iuventutis*, the princes led the procession in the *transvectio equitum*, the annual ritual celebrating the Roman victory at Lake Regillus, which Castor and Pollux attended.[12] Augustus' renovation of the temple of Castor and Pollux may have been

[9] Tac. *Ann.* 16.12.

[10] For imperial invocations of Castor and Pollux, see B. Poulsen, "The Dioscuri and Ruler Ideology," *Symbolae Osloenses* 66 (1991): 119–46. See also R. Schilling, "Les 'Castores' Romains à la lumière des traditions indo-européenes," 338–53. Cf. Martial's epigram about the Domitii, discussed above Chapter 1.

[11] Suetonius, *Jul.* 10.1, reports that Julius Caesar and his consular colleague Bibulus were called Castor and Pollux. This pair, however, reflects the potential inequality between the twins, because Caesar was associated with Castor, who is the dominant twin in the Roman tradition.

[12] Livy 2.20.12–13, D. H. 6.13.4. On Gaius and Lucius as well as Tiberius and Drusus, see B. Poulsen, "The Dioscuri and Ruler Ideology," 122–27.

initially connected with his grandsons, though after their death the project was attached to another pair of brothers, Tiberius and Drusus. In 6 C.E., the new heir apparent, Tiberius, dedicated the temple in his own name and in the name of his brother, Drusus, who had died fifteen years earlier during their military service in Germany.[13] The temple dedication may have promoted the memory of an earlier show of fraternal *pietas*: when Drusus died in Germany, Tiberius walked in front of his brother's body as it was carried all the way to Rome.[14] For Tiberius, his brother's death removed the possibility of rivalry and offered a traditional context for his expressions of fraternal *pietas*. Identification of imperial heirs with Castor and Pollux mitigates the tension between fraternal *pietas* and imperial power. Since only one brother could succeed, imperial brothers could not enjoy complete partnership in their political careers as Republican brothers or even the Silani did. The prominence of Castor corresponds to the primacy of the brother who would become emperor, while the shared immortality of the Dioscuri offsets the inequality. And this inequality could be problematic.

Suetonius records tensions between Tiberius and Drusus,[15] and, according to Tacitus, after Augustus died, Romans expected rivalry between the younger Drusus and Germanicus: *adulescentibus qui rem publicam interim premant quandoque distrahant*, "the youths who first would oppress the state and then in time tear it apart."[16] When Augustus adopted Tiberius, he compelled him to adopt his brother's son, Germanicus. Before the adoption, Germanicus and Drusus, Tiberius' son by birth, were already *fratres*, cousins, and Germanicus had a natural brother, the future emperor Claudius. Augustus' rejection of Claudius shaped fraternal rivalries among the heirs to the throne. Now that Drusus and Germanicus were in the position of brothers, they were treated as such in imperial publicity and in the historical tradition. Tacitus' description of these brothers, their actions and motives, suggests that either he or his sources were preoccupied with the potential for fraternal rivalry.[17] There is also a new awareness of tensions between

---

[13] Suet. *Tib.* 20, Val. Max. 5.5.3, cf. Ovid, *Fasti* 1.705–708; *Fasti Praenestini, Inscr. It.* XIII.2.117. For Augustus' adoption of Tiberius, Suet. *Tib.* 15.

[14] Suet. *Tib.* 7.

[15] Tiberius made public a letter in which Drusus argued for persuading Augustus to restore the Republic, Suet. *Tib.* 50. Such a letter might well damage Drusus' reputation and his chances for political success in a climate controlled by the *princeps*.

[16] Tac. *Ann.* 1.4, and for Tiberius' adoption of Germanicus, Suet. *Tib.* 15.2.

[17] Drusus offered a show of fraternal devotion, presiding over gladiatorial games given in his own and his brother Germanicus' name, Tac. *Ann.* 1.76, as Germanicus and his natural brother Claudius had also done, Suet. *Cl.* 2. When Tacitus mentions that Drusus showed too much pleasure in bloodshed at these games, he may imply that this public display of fraternal *pietas* masked antagonistic ambitions.

adopted brothers, which may result from the circumstances of imperial succession. In the mostly open pluralism of Republican politics, brothers could afford to treat natural and adoptive brothers equally. When opportunity was limited under the Empire, the degree of kinship with the emperor generated friction not only among distantly related challengers like the Silani, but also between *fratres* and adopted heirs.

The rivalry between Germanicus and Drusus seems to be have been constructed by those around them, including their father. When Germanicus was about to complete the settlement of Germany, Tiberius called him back, asking him to give his brother Drusus a chance to win military glory. According to Tacitus, Germanicus interpreted Tiberius' appeal to fraternal *pietas* as a pretense for advancing his own son and for ill-will toward himself, although the author later claims that Tiberius did not favor Drusus until after Germanicus' death.[18] If Germanicus suspected that the emperor was trying to foster rivalry between his sons, others at the palace shared this suspicion and eagerly took sides. Tiberius' decision to send Cn. Piso to Syria during Germanicus' campaign in Armenia could be interpreted as evidence the emperor was biased in his treatment of his sons. According to Tacitus, Piso saw an ulterior motive in the emperor's sending him to Syria: *nec dubium habebat se delectum qui Syriae imponeretur ad spes Germanici coercendas*, "he had no doubt that he was chosen to be in charge of Syria in the hopes of controlling Germanicus."[19] Piso, like other observers of the imperial court, seems to cloak his own ambition by raising suspicions of fraternal rivalry. Palace satellites were invested in the fraternal relationship between Drusus and Germanicus, perhaps in part because their own fates depended on alliance with the brother who would ultimately succeed to imperial power. Instead of expecting fraternal *pietas* to motivate the brothers to cooperate, Tacitus and the Romans he depicts here seem preoccupied with the inequality that empire imposed.

Despite the tense atmosphere, Drusus and Germanicus themselves expressed brotherly devotion in their actions. On his way to Armenia, Germanicus visited Drusus in Dalmatia. After Germanicus' death, when his body was being transported back to Rome, Drusus went with Germanicus' natural brother (Claudius) and his children to meet the body at Terracina. Like a *consors frater*, Drusus took responsibility for his brother's sons, fulfilling his brother's deathbed request that he care for his sons like a father. Drusus grieved for his brother, though Piso rather expected him to rejoice because it removed his rival for power.[20] Again,

---

[18] Tac. *Ann.* 3.56, cf. *Ann.* 2.26.

[19] Tac. *Ann.* 2.43.

[20] Drusus' grief, Tac. *Ann.* 3.8; his care for Germanicus' sons, Tac. *Ann.* 4.4 and 8; their visit in Dalmatia, Tac. *Ann.* 2.53. See also B. Levick, *Tiberius the Politician*, 50, 148–49.

Piso's interpretation of the brothers' behavior reveals a fascination with fraternal politics. Tacitus' presentation of Germanicus' funeral reflects this fascination. Germanicus' funeral hardly honored him properly by comparison with his father's, a change that connotes decline to the historian.[21] Moreover, when Drusus died, his uncle Augustus traveled in winter weather all the way to Ticinium to meet his body whereas Germanicus' brother made a journey of only one day. In an earlier generation, as Cicero argued in the *Pro Rabirio Perduellionis Reo*, an uncle's devotion would not have exceeded a brother's.

Drusus and Germanicus disappear from the scene before they fulfill the Romans' dire expectations of rivalry,[22] but the theme persists in Suetonius' biographies of Titus and Domitian. Domitian was ever plotting against Titus:

> *fratrem insidiari sibi non desinentem, sed paene ex professo sollicitantem exercitus, meditantem fugam, neque occidere neque seponere ac ne in minore quidem honore habere sustinuit, sed, ut a primo imperii die, consortem successoremque testari perseveravit, nonnumquam secreto precibus et lacrimis orans, ut tandem mutuo erga se animo vellet esse.*

Titus was not cruel enough either to kill or to exile his brother or even to hold him in less esteem, even though Domitian never stopped plotting against him, although almost openly he incited the army to revolt and was always thinking about deserting. Instead, Titus, as from the very first day of his reign, always continued to maintain that his brother was his partner and heir; yet sometimes he privately begged him,with tears and entreaties, to be willing to return his affection in the same spirit. Suet. *Tit.* 9

Titus and Domitian act like typical Roman brothers, quarreling over their paternal inheritance—one brother an angry instigator, the other fostering cooperation. Their situation, as Suetonius paints it, would fit as

---

[21] Germanicus' funeral, Tac. *Ann.* 3.2 and 5.

[22] In the next generation of Julio-Claudians, Tiberius shifts his attention to Germanicus' three sons, Nero, Drusus, and Caligula. He designates another pair of imperial heirs, Nero and Drusus, by celebrating their accension to the Senate, while ignoring Caligula for the most part, Suet. *Tib.* 54 and *Cal.* 10. Again, the process of succession sets up a pair of brothers for rivalry. Despite this early show of favor, Tiberius ulitmately lets Nero and Drusus starve to death, clearing the slate of fraternal rivalry, Suet. *Tib.* 54.

Their brother, however, does not forget them, and once he becomes emperor Caligula honors his brothers as best he can. He burns the records of their prosecution and attacks those senators who betrayed them; then he enshrines their ashes along with their mother's in the Mausoleum of Augustus, Suet. *Cal.* 15, 30. His *pietas* was, however, limited to his own siblings: he had his cousin, Tiberius Gemellus, Drusus' son, killed, Suet. *Cal.* 23. Suetonius tells us that, before he became emperor, Caligula had even attempted to murder Tiberius to avenge his mother and brothers, Suet. *Cal.* 12. Caligula's public show of fraternal *pietas* counters the expectations of fraternal rivalry that pervaded Tiberius' reign and attests to continuing interest in the relations between brothers in the imperial household.

well into Seneca's *Controversiae* as into one of Cicero's letters about his friends or acquaintances. This pair of brothers could not reconcile their differences, even though one of them appealed to fraternal *pietas* invoking both affection, *mutuo erga se animo*, and familial roles, *consortem successoremque*, to bring his brother around. But Titus and Domitian were not any old brothers, and their dispute was about more than the family farm: the emperor and his brother were divided by imperial power.

It was with this tension between Titus and Domitian as a backdrop that Statius composed an epic about fraternal rivalry. Although the *Thebaid* focuses on fraternal rivalry, it treads carefully, distancing fraternal themes from Roman and especially Imperial contexts.[23] In dedicating the *Thebaid* to Domitian, Statius avoids mention of the emperor's own brother. He describes Domitian as his father's successor,[24] even though his brother, Titus, succeeded Vespasian and ruled immediately before Domitian. The choice of a Theban rather than a Roman myth of fraternal strife may also be significant in this respect. Vergil avoided the Romulus and Remus mythology, choosing the Greek story of Aeneas, and Augustan imagery inaugurated Castor and Pollux as new paradigms of fraternity. With rather less scruple, Lucan boldly assumes continuity between the founding brothers and Pompey and Caesar—but neither of them was emperor. If Lucan's war was *plusquam civile*, the conflict in Statius' *Thebaid* is openly fraternal: the first word is *fraternas*. But Statius sets his exploration of fraternal rivalry in the Greek cycle of Theban myth, sidestepping direct contact with Roman paradigms. Only in imagery and verbal detail does the poet draw attention to fraternal symbolism. Intertextual allusions to images of fraternal *pietas* and rivalry in earlier Latin literature, most notably Vergil and Lucan, locate the Theban brothers within Roman traditions of fraternal *pietas*.

[23] Statius' choice of Theban brothers distances his epic from contemporary political issues, yet Theban mythology was familiar enough to the Roman audience for Petronius, 80.3, to conjure and deflate it with a quick reference to Thebes, see J. Henderson, "Form Remade/Statius' *Thebaid*," in *Roman Epic*, ed. A. J. Boyle, 165, and above Chapter 2, pp. 86–87. Two of the brothers in the *Satyricon*—Encolpius and Ascyltus—are rivals for the affection of the third, Giton. When their rivalry threatens to turn violent, Giton fears that he will witness a confrontation like the war between the Theban brothers. They manage to avoid violence, when Ascyltus decamps with Giton, leaving Encolpius to mourn his now lost companions. Encolpius describes himself as Ascyltus' "dearest comrade in arms," *carissimum sibi commilitionem*, implicitly invoking the fraternal empathy among soldiers and continuing the theme of epic conflict. The allusion to Thebes with its epic resonance seems not so much to ennoble these brothers as to undermine the seriousness of their conflict: these aren't, after all, real brothers or even real soldiers, like those who fought at Thebes, or those who fight for Rome.

[24] Stat. *Theb.* 1.17–24, esp. 23–24.

Statius' tale of fraternal strife begins, appropriately, when the brothers divide their paternal inheritance, the kingdom of Thebes, ruling in alternate years, but this arrangement did not work out so well as the peaceful alternation between Castor and Pollux.[25] Each brother is styled an heir during the year he was in exile, waiting his turn to rule, and for a while *pietas* did prevent open hostility.[26] In a flashback to the time when the lots were first drawn, Statius dramatizes the scene, singling out one Theban to speak for the whole crowd. The brother returning from exile reminds him of Cadmus, Thebes' founder, and he fears that these brothers will revive the internecine wars that followed Cadmus' sowing of the dragon's teeth. Letting each brother rule alone, he is certain, will only aggravate their ambition and endanger Thebes: *cernis, ut erectum torva sub fronte minetur / saevior adsurgens dempto consorte potestas,* "you see how power, lurking in his fierce eyes, threatens to burst forth, it rises fiercer when his partner is gone."[27] This speech reasserts the idealized Roman view of fraternal *pietas* and its power to reconcile competing interests. The overall movement of the *Thebaid*, however, undermines this traditional ideal and coheres with earlier poetic reflections on political partnerships. Lucan, for example, in his remarks on Caesar and Pompey, asserts that shared power is dangerously unstable—only sole rule is secure—and Romulus and Remus serve as a historical example.[28] Both Lucan and Statius pose the problem of power sharing in terms of the brothers' inheritance, and both express pessimism about the efficacy of fraternal *pietas* in situations where ambition and power are irresistibly great.

In rhetorical *Controversiae*, fathers were frequently implicated in their sons' disputes about inheritance, and it is no different in this mythological family. Oedipus curses his sons and conjures Tissiphone to bring them to blows: *i media in fratres, generis consortia ferro / dissiliant,* "go between the brothers, let them shatter their family partnership with the sword."[29] Statius' resurrection of the evil spirit Tissiphone frames the morality of this fraternal rivalry. In the *Aeneid*, Tissiphone presides over

[25] Polynices and Eteocles, however, do not share as rich a prize as immortality. Statius draws attention to the relative poverty of Thebes at the time of the war between Eteocles and Polynices: *pugna est de paupere regno,* "it was a fight for a poor kingdom," Stat. *Theb.* 1.151, cf. 144–55. Although there is no explicit reference to the Roman past in the *Thebaid*, Statius' epic does fashion the dilemma of power-sharing in fraternal terms, much as the literature of the civil war eras did. In Lucan's *Bellum Civile*, when the triumvirs are compared to Romulus and Remus, the poet focuses on the size of the prize: the triumvirs are fighting over a rich prize, but only a small plot is at stake for the founder and his brother.

[26] Stat. *Theb.* 1.138–43.

[27] Stat. *Theb.* 1.186–87, cf. 1.177–85.

[28] Lucan 1.89–97.

[29] Stat. *Theb.* 1.84–85.

that region of the underworld where the impious suffer eternal labors. Among her charges are those who hate their brothers, strike their parents, and cheat their clients: *hic, quibus invisi fratres, dum vita manebat, / pulsatusve parens et fraus innexa clienti.*[30] Like the bad sons in Seneca's *Controversiae*, Eteocles and Polynices hate each other and greedily seize their patrimony, debasing both filial and fraternal *pietas*.

Tissiphone's effect on Polynices and Eteocles is swift and sure. Hurling one of her venomous locks, she implants rage in the brothers, which makes them intolerant of partnership, *secundi / ambitus inpatiens . . . sociisque comes discordia regnis*, much like the triumvirs in Lucan's description of the causes of civil war.[31] The divisive effect of Tissiphone's missile expands into a simile. The brothers' divergent ambitions correspond to the willfulness of unbroken bullocks, forced to bend to the plow for the first time. The animals rebel, pulling in different directions, and challenge the farmer's control by loosening their reins, struggling to break free from the imposed partnership. The work of the bullocks is equated with armed service, *in . . . armos*, a proleptic description of the result of the brothers' failed partnership.[32] This simile resonates with the vignette from Vergil's *Georgics*, where the bullock's fraternal grief for his dead partner expresses the pain of civil war, as discussed above in Chapter 4. In the *Georgics*, the farmer weeps for the dead animal and, leaving the plow in the unfinished furrow, he unyokes the bullocks. The surviving bullock will no longer take pleasure in the shady pastures because of his loss; he lowers his head in grief, abandoning his accustomed work with the plow. In Vergil's poem, the fraternal grief of the bullock mirrors the human experience of loss. Both bullocks and humans are capable of partnership and of empathy. In the *Thebaid*, neither the farmer nor the equipment controls the bullocks: the crooked furrow is proof. The bullocks, like the brothers, struggle, defeating their partnership.[33] There is no hint of sympathy between them. Here, partnership represents an unacceptable limit on ambition and fraternal cooperation is unachievable.

The recurring image of a yoked pair of bullocks captures the natural poignancy of fraternal strife in the *Thebaid*.[34] Statius twice describes

[30] Verg. *A.* 6.608–609; her presence is also felt in the heat of battle ravaging both sides while the Olympian gods take pity on the mortals, Venus on one side, Juno on the other, *A.* 10.755–861.

[31] Stat. *Theb.* 1.128–30, cf. Lucan 1.89–93.

[32] Stat. *Theb.* 1.131–38, cf. Verg. *G.* 3.517–24.

[33] In this simile, the bullocks are described as *torva*, Stat. *Theb.* 1.131, just as the brothers were in the flashback in Book 1 to the original casting of lots by Polynices and Eteocles, 1.186. The verbal parallel links the simile with the brothers' rivalry for power.

[34] The bullock imagery is part of a larger pattern of allusions to fraternal *pietas*. Castor and Pollux appear among the heroes Hypsipyle saw on the Argo, Stat. *Theb.* 5.437–40, and in the funeral games for her son, Jason's sons, Thoas and Euneos, compete with admirable

Polynices with a bullock simile. First, when Polynices longs for Thebes, Statius compares him to a bull exiled from his beloved pastures by a rival. But he is grieving for his possessions, not for his brother, and his grief swells to anger, goading him to spar with an oak tree, fortifying him against his rival.[35] Then, when Eteocles slays Tydeus in battle, Polynices mourns for him inconsolably, as if he were a brother. His friends lead him away like a bull who has lost his yoke-mate, in a simile recalling the fraternal grief of Vergil's image:

> ducitur amisso qualis consorte laborum
> deserit inceptum media inter iugera sulcum
> taurus iners colloque iugum deforme remisso
> parte trahit, partem lacrimans sustentat arator.

He was led away like a bull who, when the partner of his labors is lost, leaves the furrow unfinished in the middle of the fields: listless he drags his side of the ruined yoke with bent neck, the farmer weeping holds up the other side. Stat. *Theb.* 9.82–85

Polynices laments, praising Tydeus as "another, better brother who is taken away from me," *alius ac melior mihi frater ademptus.*[36] Statius quotes and revises Catullus' lament for his brother, *heu miser indigne frater adempte mihi.* Instead of emphasizing the cruelty of fate, *indigne*, Polynices praises his friend by comparing him to his real brother: Tydeus was a better brother to Polynices than was Eteocles. While calling a friend a brother was a traditional way to express the intimacy of friendship, when Polynices calls Tydeus a brother, he calls attention to the problematic nature of fraternal relations among brothers in the *Thebaid*. The other brother, *alius frater*, brings to mind his real brother, and the comparison implicitly denigrates the fraternal *pietas* between the real brothers, and since we know that Tydeus is already a fratricide himself, there seem to be no good candidates for the post of brother.

Despite the appearance on the battlefield of a personified goddess of *Pietas*, who tries to stop them before they meet on the battlefield,[37] Poly-

---

equality, 6.340ff. From the walls of Thebes, Antigone reviews Polynices' army in a conventional teichoscopia. She assumes that Lapithaon and Alatreus are brothers because they are so similar (they turn out to be father and son), and wishes that her own brothers had such harmony: *utinam haec concordia nostris*, 7.291–304. And the trope of brother unwittingly killing brother on the battlefield recurs, 8.448–52.

[35] Stat. *Theb.* 2.323–30, cf. 4.396–404 where the Sphinx foresees the battle as a confrontation between two bulls. The image recurs just before the brothers meet on the battlefield: Eteocles' hate and anger are likened to rival bulls, 11.249–56.

[36] Stat. *Theb.* 9.53.

[37] Stat. *Theb.* 11.457–81. *Pietas* appears as a sister or mother grieving to see *fraterna bella* and invokes *princeps Natura* as her mother, suggesting the natural origins of fraternal *pietas*.

nices and Eteocles die in a double fratricide. After the battle, Eteocles' soldiers cremate his body, then after nightfall, Polynices' wife and sister meet over his corpse on the battlefield. The women, intent on giving him a proper burial, find one pyre still smoldering and lay his body upon it. The silent pyre responds only after Polynices' corpse is laid upon it:

> neque adhuc, quae busta, repertum,
> sed placidus quemcumque rogant mitisque supremi
> admittat cineris consortem et misceat umbras
> ecce iterum fratres: primos ut contigit artus
> ignis edax, tremuere rogi et novus advena busto
> pellitur; exundant diviso vertice flammae
> alternosque apices abrupta luce coruscant.

Not yet was it discovered whose pyre it was, but they [the women] asked whomever it was to accept kindly and gently a partner to his ashes and to unite their shades. Behold, brothers again: when the devouring flame first touched Polynices' limbs the ashes quivered and the newly arrived corpse was hurled from the pyre; flames with forked peaks poured forth gleaming, their light split in double points. Stat. *Theb.* 12.426–32

The women draw back in fear, and Antigone, explaining the pyre's violent reaction, concludes that the war did not resolve the brothers' rivalry: *vivunt odia inproba, vivunt.* / *nil actum bello; miseri, sic, dum arma movetis* / *vicit nempe Creon*, "impious hate lives, they live; nothing has been accomplished in the war; so, while you pitiful ones bear arms, certainly Creon has won."[38] The double flame reenacts the brothers' rivalry. Even death cannot compose these brothers with fraternal *pietas*. Just as devoted brothers are united in death—when one dies, the other loses part of himself—hostile brothers still fight each other as they did when they were alive. After Antigone speaks, the natural world reacts: earthquakes confirm the tenacity of this fraternal conflict. Whereas earlier poems of civil war emphasize the survival of fraternal *pietas* in the face of war and cruel fate, Statius' epic dramatizes the persistent tensions between brothers.

If Statius' reading of Theban mythology is any guide, Romans in the first century C.E. felt the same tug of fraternal *pietas*, recognized the same norms in brothers' behavior, as their Republican predecessors. Long after the Republican civil wars, brothers were still killing brothers on Roman battlefields. A soldier in the war between Vespasian and Vitellius killed his brother in battle, in the passage cited at the beginning of this chapter.

[38] Stat. *Theb.* 12.441–42; the earthquakes, 12.447–55. An earlier scene describing the death of two brothers together as a partnership in death, *consortia leti*, 3.166, creates a contrast to the self-destructive partnership between the Theban heros. One pair of brothers are united forever in death, the other two are divided, not only in spirit but in burial.

Tacitus compares this incident to a similar one in Sisenna's account of the civil war between Strabo and Cinna.[39] In each instance, brother killed brother unintentionally, but the inadvertent murderers react differently. The Republican soldier kills himself when he finds that he has killed his brother, whereas the Flavian soldier seeks a reward from his commanding officers. For this soldier, ambition outweighs all other considerations, even fraternal *pietas*. His commanding officers, while they do not reward him, fail to condemn the fratricide. The reasoning that Tacitus attributes to the officers, *nec aut ius hominum . . aut ratio belli*, "neither human rights . . . nor the logic of war," is a sterile reproach, lacking grief and moral outrage. Their reticence, the historian suggests, may even be interpreted by the soldier as praise. Tacitus comments on the discrepancy between old and new values, using emotive moral terms to heighten the contrast. He observes that Romans used to feel glory and regret more keenly, *tanto acrior apud maiores, sicut virtutibus gloria, ita flagitiis paenitentia fuit*. The comparison points to a perceived decline in morality: not only the rank-and-file soldiers have become amoral, but their leaders also are unable or unwilling to impose a moral standard. Neither external authority nor innate *pietas* regulates the behavior of the brother in the Flavian army. Just as Romulus' murder of Remus represented the moral chaos of the Republican civil wars, this fratricide expresses a broader failure in Imperial society. Citizens in the Republic might identify their own moral dilemmas with that of the founder; under the Empire, they became willing fratricides themselves.

Tacitus' criticism of Flavian society is rooted in the traditional symbolism of fraternal *pietas*. His sentiments are not far from Cicero's when he condemns Oppianicus or praises Caecilius. The family patterns associated with *consortium* bridged the transition between Republic and Empire, creating a continuity in brothers' roles in the family. When brothers fulfilled Roman expectations or gave the impression of being good brothers, they earned praise. Sometimes Romans adapted traditional expectations of brothers to meet the challenges they faced in military service, inheritance, politics, and civil war. A pretense of fraternal *pietas* could gloss over otherwise unacceptable conduct and explain away selfish or novel ambitions. At other times, brothers were judged harshly for neglecting traditional norms. Romans writing at the time of the Republican civil wars contrasted their present with an idealized past through images of fraternal *pietas*. Early Imperial literature operates within a rhetoric of pessimism that answers the nostalgia of the Republic. Polynices and Eteocles, who fight on after death in Statius' *Thebaid*, are not so different from Romulus and Remus, though the founders and their

---

[39] Tac. *Hist.* 3.51, and Val. Max. 5.5.4.

world have faded into the past. Castor and Pollux, another traditional pair of brothers, represent in Imperial imagery the compromise that empire imposed: a miraculous beam of light in the night sky saves Castor and Pollux from unwitting fratricide on a battlefield in Valerius Flaccus' *Argonautica*.[40] Yet Romulus and Remus, and their failed fraternal *pietas*, still evoke most strongly the Roman experience of brotherhood in its complex and fragile reality.

[40] Val. Flac. *Arg.* 3.186–89, and see Hardie, "Tales of Unity," 60–61.

CONCLUSION

FRATRICIDE evokes a strong moral and emotional response in many cultures from the biblical Cain and Abel to poetry from the American Civil War.[1] The Romans' responses to the Romulus and Remus story arise within their experience of the fraternal relationship, their ideas about how brothers should act and feel toward one another. At the outset of my research on brothers, I hoped to explore the cultural and social contexts that gave meaning to the story of Romulus' murder of his brother at the founding of Rome. Of course, this Roman fratricide can be understood at least in part through cross-cultural beliefs about fraternity; our shared assumptions about brothers connect us to the Romans and give us a stake in interpreting their cultural symbols. As striking as the continuities can be between modern and ancient responses to fratricide, the differences are also important because they lead us to fuller understanding of Roman literature and society. Romulus and Remus are two of the best-known Roman brothers, but an appreciation of what their story meant to the Romans requires investigation into the historical events, social practices, and cultural expectations that surrounded Roman stories about both real and mythological brothers. This study of Roman brothers has attempted to re-create the contexts and practices that shaped not just literary representations of brothers but also the everyday reality of being a brother in ancient Rome.

The family was the most immediate context in which Roman ideas about brothers arose. For the Romans the relationship between brothers was essentially a natural phenomenon created by their common birth or natural (what we would call biological) kinship. Although they could not have known, as we do, that siblings share the most similar genetic makeup, Romans recognized an especially close bond between brothers, which made them seem nearly identical, alter egos, even if they were not twins. Because kinship was thought to arise from nature rather than from civic status, Romans acknowledged fraternal relationships not just in elite families or among citizens but even among slaves. This natural kinship was thought to create an unbreakable bond between brothers, a

---

[1] For example, K. B. Sherwood, "Albert Sidney Johnston," H. Melville, "Memorial on the Slain at Chickamauga," and B. Taylor, "Gettysburg Ode," all in *The Columbia Book of Civil War Poetry, from Whitman to Walcott,* ed. R. Marius, 279–82, 391–92, 402–10, 438. See also H. McCarthy, "The Bonnie Blue Flag," in *Confederate War Poems,* ed. W. B. Jones, 17–18. And compare also "The Tale of the Two Brothers," in *The Literature of Ancient Egypt,* ed. W. K. Simpson, 92–107. See also R. J. Quinones, *The Changes of Cain.*

sense of devotion that Romans knew as *pietas*, the blend of affection and duty that characterized familial relationships. Fraternal *pietas* was distinguished from other familial devotion because brothers were considered to have the closest relationship. Brothers may also have been given special status since not everyone had a brother: because of the mortality rates and demographic shape of Roman society, only about half of Roman men would have had a brother. If a Roman did have a brother, his brother would be his partner in family life, from childhood education through their adult years. Mythological pairs of twin brothers, like Romulus and Remus or Castor and Pollux, embodied this inherent fraternal identity, and their stories dramatized both the strengths and weakness of fraternal *pietas*. Fraternal *pietas* also affected the workings of brothers' family life.

At home, brothers shared responsibilities for managing the family property and caring for other close relatives. The process of inheritance cast brothers' roles into relief because the transfer of property from one generation to the next was an occasion for brothers to question, change, or simply articulate their rights and duties toward one another and the rest of the family. Brothers' roles in the family can be investigated through several legal institutions relating to inheritance, including intestate succession, partible inheritance, wills, guardianship, partnership, and *consortium*, an archaic form of succession that established a partnership among the family heirs who jointly owned the property inherited from their father. While sisters could also participate in *consortium*, Romans identified brothers with *consortes*, and fraternal *pietas* represented the reconciliation of conflict through shared interests that had been institutionalized in *consortium*. Although *consortium* originally arose through intestate succession, even as writing wills became more common during the Republican era, the legal rules and the traditions of intestate succession continued to influence Roman inheritance practice. Romans usually divided their property equally among all their children (that is, they practiced partible inheritance), whether they wrote a will or the estate was passed down by intestate succession according to the traditional rules encoded in the *Twelve Tables*. Because the practice of partible inheritance could fragment a family's wealth, brothers had a better chance of sustaining financial success if they worked together, sometimes keeping their paternal estate undivided, as if in *consortium*, other times preserving the cooperation of *consortium* while owning property individually and exercising economic autonomy. Although the high mortality rates of Roman society limited the fragmentation caused by partible inheritance, brothers' cooperation was an essential component in a family's stability and well-being.

After *consortium* was no longer a common legal practice, it came to represent the idealized relationship between brothers and the social norms that defined fraternal *pietas*. Brothers and fathers alike invoked fraternal *pietas* to encourage each other to live up to the ideal of fraternal cooperation and to resolve conflict within the family. Fraternal *pietas* also had a broader significance in Roman social relations. Because Romans recognized kinship as a natural phenomenon and brothers as the closest kin, the fraternal relationship represented an idealized form of intimacy between men. When Cicero wanted to express the depth of his affection for Atticus, he wrote that he loved him like a brother. The relationship between brothers, with its familial partnership, could also be considered analogous to the relationship between spouses or domestic partners, and thus lovers might also call each other *frater* as a sign of their lasting love. When Romans compared friends and lovers to brothers they transferred to these other relationships both the inherent similarity of fraternal kinship and the equality between brothers that was promoted in inheritance practices. Because certain types of intimacy between men, in particular taking a passive sexual role, were considered disgraceful, the fraternal relationship offered a socially acceptable and even praiseworthy way to express men's devotion. While the innate equality between brothers masked the inequality associated with sexual passivity, brothers' devotion could express what Romans thought was best in relationships between men. In the context of Roman political rhetoric, which stigmatized male homoeroticism, fraternal devotion was an alternative paradigm for intimacy among men. Fraternal *pietas*, because it was rooted in natural kinship, also symbolized a lasting devotion in contrast to the various and changeable relationships that Romans knew as *amicitia*.

The importance of Roman ideas about brothers extended beyond private relationships to the public arena of the Roman forum. Success in Roman politics depended in part on creating networks of relatives, friends, and clients, and a brother was an especially valuable supporter because brothers shared each other's successes and failures in public life. The lives of Cicero and his brother, Quintus, aptly illustrate both the crossover between public and private life and the ways that brothers could work the political system to their advantage. A brother's support could tip the balance in a campaign for elected office, and it was not uncommon for brothers to be elected in successive years. A successful man like Scipio Africanus or Cicero could help his brother's career, even when the brother was not considered as talented. In political trials and debates, appeals to fraternal *pietas* were a powerful political tool, and brothers like Gaius Gracchus and Scipio Asiagenus played on Roman sympathy with brotherly sentiments. Romans recognized that brothers had an advantage in politics that could either help or harm the community as a whole. Brothers might cooperate in the forum and on the battlefield, using their fraternal relationship to serve both their own ambitions and Rome's. On the other hand, if brothers exploited the Romans' sympathy for fraternal *pietas* solely for their own benefit, their behavior was seen as a threat to the traditional balance of power that Rome's system of annual magistrates sustained. Romans invoked law and the *mos maiorum* to mark out limits on fraternal *pietas* in matters of state. Cicero's arguments for Sulla and his ambivalence about the Gracchi reflect the potential tension between fraternal devotion and the concerns of the larger political community.

Although brothers mostly from elite families pursued public careers, the rhetoric of fraternal *pietas* reached a broad audience for several reasons. The political symbolism of fraternal *pietas* was powerful for the Romans because their ideas about brothers transcended social class. Brothers from elite families who pursued public careers might readily identify their own experience of politics with the larger social concerns that were expressed in fraternal symbolism. Because the Romans believed that all humans, regardless of social class, shared in the natural kinship between brothers, anyone in the audience of a political speech could identify with fraternal sentiments that brothers might invoke. The relationship among fellow citizens and soldiers was felt to be fraternal in a metaphorical way. Romans who served together in the army considered themselves brothers of a sort, sharing a mess as brothers share a home, united by the shared risks of battle. Roman citizens might also think of themselves as descendants of a common ancestor, grandsons of Romulus, as Catullus put it, and thus also metaphorically brothers. Brothers provided a model for intimacy in various relationships between men— members of *sodalicia* or *collegia*, friends, and even lovers whose close relationship perhaps is most similar to that of brothers. The relationship between brothers represented for the Romans a nearly universal standard for the kind of affection and duty that ought to exist between men. Because Romans believed in a natural basis for fraternity, all Romans could share the experience of fraternal *pietas* that made fratricide such a potent metaphor for civil war.

The image of brothers took on a broad symbolism for the Romans as they grappled with the changes of civil war and the dynastic struggles of empire. In the literature of the late Republic, stories of brother killing brother on the battlefield epitomized the Roman experience of the destruction of social relationships in civil war. Romulus and Remus, and the story of the foundation of the city, became a focal point for anxieties about power and Roman political identity. Just the mention of Remus' name, as in Horace's *Epode* 7, could conjure the sense of tragic fate, guilt, and loss that pervades the literature of the triumviral years, from Cicero's *De Officiis* to Vergil's *Georgics*. Because retellings of the foundation story were indelibly marked by the Roman experience of civil war, the twins Castor and Pollux became the preferred symbols of fraternal *pietas* in Augustan political image-making and in early imperial literature such as Statius' Thebaid. Instead of resolving conflict with fratricide, Castor and Pollux perpetuate fraternal cooperation by sharing one portion of immortality. What better myth to mitigate the unequal reconciliation between brothers who were rivals for imperial power, when one brother would become a soon-to-be-deified emperor while the other could not hope for either power or immortality?

At Rome, as in many societies, family relationships affected social practices and historical events. Brothers had a particularly important place in ancient Roman society both on account of Roman ideas about their natural kinship and because brothers played important roles in sustaining the family. The relationship between brothers symbolized personal devotion as well as the fraternal feelings that united citizens and fellow soldiers. Although we may recognize familiar family problems or political issues in Roman depictions of brothers, we share even more in the broader symbolism of fraternal *pietas* that developed at Rome. We still think of brotherhood as a partnership among equals who share a special status and devotion that separate them from other men. Such metaphorical fraternity, like real kinship, can be inclusive and exclusive; it can promote both unity and dissension.[2] As the Romans already knew, fraternal relationships encompassed both the permanency of kinship and the changeable rivalries that led brothers to renegotiate and recreate the idea of brotherhood as they lived it.

[2] Consider the recent debate about renaming the International Brotherhood of Teamsters to include "sisters" with the gender-neutral Teamsters International Union; see P. T. Kilborn, "Cause for Sibling Rivalry at Teamsters," *New York Times*, 17 July 1996, Midwest Edition, A10.

BIBLIOGRAPHY

Adams, F. "The Consular Brothers of Sejanus." *AJP* 76 (1955): 70–76.

Adcock, F. E. *The Roman Art of War under the Republic.* Cambridge, Mass.: Harvard University Press, 1940.

Alfonsi, L. "La figura di Romolo all'inizio delle storie di Livio." In *Livius. Werk und Rezeption*, ed. E. Lefèvre and E. Olshausen. Munich: C. H. Beck, 1982.

Anderson, M. "The Sentiments Approach." In *Approaches to the History of the Western Family 1500–1914*. London: Macmillan, 1980.

Andreau, J. "Activité financière et les liens de parenté en Italie romaine." In *Parenté et stratégies familiales dans l'antiquité romaine, Actes de la table ronde des 2–4 octobre 1986*, ed. J. Andreau and H. Bruhns. Collection de l'École Française de Rome. Vol. 129. Rome: École française de Rome, 1990.

Arrangio-Ruiz, V. "Frammenti di Gaio." *PSI* 1182 (1935): 1–52.

——— and A. Guarino, eds. *Brevarium Iuris Romani.* 7th ed. Milan: A. Giuffre, 1989.

Asheri, D. "Laws of Inheritance, Distribution of Land and Political Constitutions in Ancient Greece." *Historia* 12 (1963): 1–21.

Astin, A. E. *Scipio Aemilianus.* Oxford: Clarendon Press, 1967.

Badian, E. "Tiberius Gracchus and the Beginning of the Roman Revolution." *ANRW* 1, no. 1 (1972): 668–731.

Bailey, C., ed. *Titi Lucreti Cari De Rerum Natura Libri Sex.* 3 vols. Oxford: Clarendon Press, 1947.

Balme, D. M. *Aristotle De Partibus Animalium I and De Generatione Animalium I (with passages from II.1–3).* Oxford: Clarendon Press, 1972.

Balsdon, J.P.V.D. *Romans and Aliens.* Chapel Hill, N.C.: University of North Carolina Press, 1979.

———. "L. Cornelius Scipio: A Salvage Operation." *Historia* 21 (1972): 224–34.

Benveniste, E. *Le vocabulaire des institutions indo-européennes.* 2 vols. Paris: Éditions de Minuit, 1969.

Béranger, J. "Les jugements de Cicéron sur les Gracques." *ANRW* 1, no. 1 (1972): 732–73.

———. "Tyrannus." *REL* 13 (1935): 85–94.

Berkner, L. K., and F. F. Mendels. "Inheritance Systems, Family Structure, and Demographic Patterns in Western Europe, 1700–1900." In *Historical Studies of Changing Fertility*, ed. C. Tilly. Princeton, N.J.: Princeton University Press, 1978.

Bertman, S. ed. *The Conflict of the Generations in Ancient Greece and Rome.* Amsterdam: G. R. Grüner, 1976.

Betzig, L. "Roman Polygyny." *Ethnology and Sociobiology* 13 (1992): 309–49.

Blass, F. *Ausführliche Grammatik der griechischen Sprache*, ed. R. Kühner. 2 vols. Hanover: Hahn, 1890–1904.

Blayney, J. "Theories of Conception in the Ancient Roman World." In *The Fam-*

ily in Ancient Rome: New Perspectives, ed. B. Rawson. Ithaca, N.Y.: Cornell University Press, 1986.

Bömer, F. P. *Ovidius Naso Metamorphosen*. 7 vols. Heidelberg: C. Winter, 1969–86.

Boswell, J. *Same-Sex Unions in Premodern Europe*. New York: Villard Books, 1994.

Bourdieu, P. *Outline of a Theory of Practice*, trans. R. Nice. Cambridge: Cambridge University Press, 1977.

Bowman, A. K. *Egypt after the Pharaohs 332 BC–AD 642*. Berkeley, Calif.: University of California Press, 1986.

Boyer, G. "Le droit successorial romain dans les oeuvres de Polybe." *RIDA* 4 (1950): 169–86.

Bradley, K. R. *Discovering the Roman Family*. New York: Oxford University Press, 1991.

Bramble, J. C. "Structure and Ambiguity in Catullus LXIV." *PCPS* 16 (1970): 22–41.

Bremmer, J. N. "The Suodales of Poplios Valesios." *ZPE* 47 (1982): 133–47.

———, and N. M. Horsfall. "Romulus, Remus and the Foundation of Rome." In *Roman Myth and Mythography*. London: University of London, Institute of Classical Studies, Bulletin Supplement, 1987.

Bretone, M. " 'Consortium' e 'communio.' " *Labeo* 6 (1960): 163–215.

Brettell, C. B. "Kinship and Contract: Property Transmission and Family Relations in Northwestern Portugal." *Comparative Studies in Society and History* 33 (1991): 443–65.

Brink, C. O. *Horace on Poetry*. 3 vols. Cambridge: Cambridge University Press, 1963–82.

Brink, C. O., and F. W. Walbank. "The Construction of the Sixth Book of Polybius." *CQ* 48 (1954): 97–122.

Briscoe, J. *A Commentary on Livy Books XXXIV–XXXVII*. Oxford: Clarendon Press, 1981.

Broughton, T.R.S. *The Magistrates of the Roman Republic*. 3 vols. New York: American Philological Association, 1951–86.

Bruhns, H. "Parenté et alliances politiques à la fin de la république romaine." In *Parenté et stratégies familiales dans l'antiquité romaine, Actes de la table ronde des 2–4 octobre 1986*, ed. J. Andreau and H. Bruhns. Collection de l'École Française de Rome. Vol. 129. Rome: École française de Rome, 1990.

Brunt, P. A. "Cicero's *Officium* in the Civil War." *JRS* 76 (1986): 12–32.

———. "*Amicitia* in the Late Roman Republic." Rev. ed. in *The Fall of the Roman Republic*. Oxford: Clarendon Press, 1988. First published in *PCPS* 11 (1965): 1–20.

Büchner, C., ed. *Fragmenta Poetarum Latinorum Epicorum et Lyricorum*. Rev. ed. Leipzig: Teubner, 1982.

Büchner, K. *Sallust*. Rev. ed. Heidelberg: Winter, 1982.

Buck, C. D. *Comparative Grammar of Greek and Latin*. Chicago: University of Chicago Press, 1933.

Burkert, W. "Caesar und Romulus-Quirinus." *Historia* 11 (1962): 356–76.

Carawan, E. M. "Cato's Speech against L. Flamininus." *CJ* 85 (1990): 316–29.

Carcopino, J. *Daily Life in Ancient Rome: The People and the City at the Height of the Empire*, ed. H. T. Rowell, trans. E. O. Lorimer. New Haven: Yale University Press, 1940.

Cardauns, B., ed. *M. Terentius Varro Antiquitates Rerum Divinarum*. 2 vols. Mainz: Akademie der Wissenschaften und der Literatur, 1976.

Carter, J. M., ed. *Julius Caesar: The Civil War Book III*. Warminster: Aris & Phillips, 1993.

Champlin, E. *Final Judgments: Duty and Emotion in Roman Wills, 200 B.C.– A.D. 250*. Berkeley, Calif.: University of California Press, 1991.

———. "*Creditur Vulgo Testamenta Hominum Speculum Esse Morum*: Why the Romans Made Wills." *CP* 84 (1989): 198–215.

Chanman, W. J., and A. Boskoff, eds. *Sociology and History: Theory and Research*. New York: Free Press of Glencoe, 1964.

Clark, A. C., ed. *Q. Asconii Pediani Orationum Ciceronis Quinque Ennarratio*. Oxford: Clarendon Press, 1907.

Classen, C. J. "Zur Herkunft der Sage von Romulus und Remus." *Historia* 12 (1963): 445–56.

———. "Romulus in der römischen Republik." *Philologus* 106 (1962): 173– 204.

Cohen, D. *Law, Sexuality and Society: The Enforcement of Morals in Classical Athens*. Cambridge: Cambridge University Press, 1991.

Collart, J., ed. and trans. *Varro. De Lingua Latina Livre V*. Paris: Les Belles Lettres, 1954.

Collinder, B. "The Name Germani." *Arkiv för Nordisk Filologi* 59 (1944): 19– 39.

Collins, J. H. "Caesar as Political Propagandist." *ANRW* 1, no. 1 (1972): 922– 66.

Cool, L. E. "Continuity and Crisis: Inheritance and Family Structure on Corsica." *Journal of Social History* 21 (1987): 741–46.

Cooper, A. B. "The Family Farm in Greece." *CJ* 73 (1977–78): 162–75.

Cooper, J. M. "Aristotle on Friendship." In *Essays on Aristotle's Ethics*, ed. A. O. Rorty. Berkeley, Calif.: University of California Press, 1980.

Cooper, J. P. "Patterns of Inheritance and Settlement by Great Landowners from the Fifteenth to the Eighteenth Centuries." In *Family and Inheritance: Rural Society in Western Europe, 1200–1800*, ed. J. Goody, J. Thirsk, and E. P. Thompson. Cambridge: Cambridge University Press, 1976.

Corbier, M. "Les comportements familiaux de l'aristocratie romaine (IIe siècle av. J.-C.-IIIe siècle ap. J.-C.)." In *Parenté et stratégies familiales dans l'antiquité romaine, Actes de la table ronde des 2–4 octobre 1986*, ed. J. Andreau and H. Bruhns. Collection de l'École Française de Rome. Vol. 129. Rome: École française de Rome, 1990.

Cornell, T. J. *The Beginnings of Rome: Italy and Rome from the Bronze Age to the Punic Wars (c. 1000–264 BC)*. London: Routledge, 1995.

———. "The Value of the Literary Tradition Concerning Archaic Rome." In *Social Struggles in Archaic Rome*, ed. K. A. Raaflaub. Berkeley, Calif.: University of California Press, 1986.

———. "The Historical Tradition of Early Rome." In *Past Perspectives: Studies in Greek and Roman Historical Writing*, ed. I. S. Moxon, J. D. Smart, and A. J. Woodman. New York: Cambridge University Press, 1986.

———. "Aeneas and the Twins: The Development of the Roman Foundation Legend." *PCPS* 2d ser., 21 (1975): 1–32.

Courtney, E. *The Fragmentary Latin Poets.* Oxford: Clarendon Press, 1993.

———. *The Poems of Petronius.* Atlanta, Ga.: Scholars Press, 1991.

———. "Fragmenta Poetarum Latinarum." *BICS* 31 (1984): 131–36.

———. *A Commentary on the Satires of Juvenal.* London: Athlone Press, 1980.

———. "The Prosecution of Scaurus in 54 BC." *Philologus* 105 (1961): 151–56.

Cox, C. A. "Sibling Relationships in Classical Athens: Brother-Sister Ties." *Journal of Family History* 13 (1988): 377–95.

Crook, J. A. "Intestacy in Roman Society." *PCPS* 19 (1973): 38–44.

———. *Law and Life of Rome, 90 B.C.–A.D. 212.* Ithaca, N.Y.: Cornell University Press, 1967.

———. "Patria Potestas." *CQ* 2d ser., 17 (1967): 113–22.

Dalla, D. *Ubi venus mutatur: omossessualità e diritto nel mondo Romano.* Milan: A. Guiffrè, 1987.

D'Arms, J. H. *Commerce and Social Standing in Ancient Rome.* Cambridge, Mass.: Harvard University Press, 1981.

Daube, D. "The Preponderance of Intestacy at Rome." *Tulane Law Review* 39 (1965): 187ff.

David, J.-M. "L'action oratoire de C. Gracchus. L'image d'un modèle." In *Demokratia et aristokratia à propos de Caius Gracchus*, ed. C. Nicolet. Paris: Université de Paris I, 1983.

———. "Solidarités Familiales et Stratégies Judiciares." In *Parenté et stratégies familiales dans l'antiquité romaine, Actes de la table ronde des 2–4 octobre 1986*, ed. J. Andreau and H. Bruhns. Collection de l'École Française de Rome. Vol. 129. Rome: École française de Rome, 1990.

De Dominicis, M. "Il 'ius sepulchri' nel Diritto Successorio Romano." *RIDA* 13 (1966): 177–204.

Derow, P. S., and W. G. Forrest. "An Inscription from Chios." *ABSA* 77 (1982): 79–82.

Diósdi, G. *Ownership in Ancient and Preclassical Roman Law.* Budapest: Akademiai Kiado, 1970.

Dixon, S. *The Roman Family.* Baltimore, Md.: The Johns Hopkins University Press, 1992.

———. *The Roman Mother.* Norman, Okla.: Oklahoma University Press, 1988.

———. "Family Finances: Terentia and Tullia." In *The Family in Ancient Rome: New Perspectives*, ed. B. Rawson. Ithaca, N.Y.: Cornell University Press, 1986.

Dondin-Payre, M. "La stratégie symbolique de la parenté sous la Républicque et l'Empire romains." In *Parenté et stratégies familiales dans l'antiquité romaine, Actes de la table ronde des 2–4 octobre 1986*, ed. J. Andreau and H. Bruhns. Collection de l'École Française de Rome. Vol. 129. Rome: École française de Rome, 1990.

Dougan, T. W., and R. M. Henry, eds. *M. Tulli Ciceronis Tusculanarum Disputationum Libri Quinque.* Cambridge: Cambridge University Press, 1905.

Douglas, A. E., ed. *M. Tulli Ciceronis Brutus.* Oxford: Clarendon Press, 1966.

Dover, K. J., ed. *Aristophanes. Clouds.* Oxford: Clarendon Press, 1968.

Dumézil, G. *Archaic Roman Religion*, trans. P. Krapp. Chicago: University of Chicago Press, 1970.

Earl, D. C. *The Moral and Political Tradition of Rome.* London: Thames and Hudson, 1967.

———. *The Political Thought of Sallust.* Cambridge: Cambridge University Press, 1961.

Edgerton, R. B. *Rules, Exceptions, and Social Order.* Berkeley, Calif.: University of California Press, 1985.

Edson, C. "Perseus and Demetrius." *HSCP* 46 (1935): 191–202.

Ellickson, R. C. *Order without Law: How Neighbors Settle Disputes.* Cambridge, Mass.: Harvard University Press, 1991.

Epstein, D. *Personal Enmity in Roman Politics 218–43 BC.* London: Croom Helm, 1987.

Ernout, A., and A. Meillet. *Dictionnaire étymologique de la langue latine.* 4th ed. Paris: C. Klincksieck, 1959–60.

Evans, H. B. *Publica Carmina: Ovid's Books from Exile.* Lincoln, Nebr.: University of Nebraska Press, 1983.

Fantham, E. "*Hautontimorumenos* and *Adelphoe*: A Study of Fatherhood in Terence and Menander." *Latomus* 30 (1971): 970–98.

Fayer, C. *Aspetti di vita quotidiana nella Roma antica dalle origini all'età monarchica.* Studia archaeologia 22. Rome: L'Erma, 1982.

Ferrary, J.-L. *Philhellénisme et imperialism. Aspects idéologiques de la conquête romaine du monde hellénistique, de la seconde guerre de macédoine à la guerre contra Mithridate.* Rome: École française de Rome, 1988.

Flambard, J.-M. "Collegia Compitalicia: phénomène associatif, cadres territoriaux et cadres civiques dans le monde romain à l'époque républicaine." *Ktema* 6 (1981): 143–66.

———. "Clodius, les collèges, la plèbe et les esclaves. Recherches sur la politique populaire au milieu du Ier siècle." *MEFRA* 89 (1977): 115–56.

Flobert, P. *M. Terenti Varronis La Langue Latine Livre VI.* Paris: Les Belles Lettres, 1985.

Fordyce, C. J. *Catullus: A Commentary.* Oxford: Clarendon Press, 1978.

Forsyth, P. Y. "The Irony of Catullus 100." *CW* 70 (1977): 313–17.

Foucault, M. *Les mots et les choses: une archéologie des sciences humaines.* Paris: Gallimard, 1966.

Fox, M. *Roman Historical Myths: The Regal Period in Augustan Literature.* Oxford: Clarendon Press, 1996.

Fraccaro, P. *Opuscula.* 3 vols. Pavia: Presso la Rivista "Athenaeum," 1956–57.

Frank, M. "The Rhetorical Use of Family Terms in Seneca's *Oedipus* and *Phoenissae*." *Phoenix* 49 (1995): 121–29.

Frank, T. "Cicero and the Poetae Novae." *AJP* 40 (1919): 396.

Frederiksen, M. "Caesar, Cicero and the Problem of Debt." *JRS* 56 (1966): 128–41.

Frier, B. W. *The Rise of the Roman Jurists: Studies in Cicero's "pro Caecina."* Princeton, N.J.: Princeton University Press, 1985.

Funaioli, G., ed. *Grammaticae Romanae Fragmenta.* Leipzig: Teubner, 1907.

Fussell, P. *The Great War and Modern Memory.* New York: Oxford University Press, 1975.

Gabba, E. "Per un'interpretazione politica de *de Officiis* di Cicerone." *Atti della Accademia Nazionale dei Lincei* 34 (1979): 117–41.

———. *Appiano e la storia delle guerre civili.* 1st ed. Florence: La Nuova Italia, 1956.

Garnsey, P., and R. Saller. *The Roman Empire: Economy, Society, and Culture.* London: Duckworth, 1987.

Gaudemet, J. *Les communautés familiales.* Paris: M. Rivière, 1963.

———. *Étude sur le regime juridique de l'indivision en droit romain.* Paris: Librarie du Recueil Sirey, 1934.

Geertz, C. "Thick Description: Toward an Interpretive Theory of Culture." In *The Interpretation of Cultures.* New York: Basic Books, 1973.

Geiger, J. "Plutarch's Parallel Lives: The Choice of Heroes." *Hermes* 109 (1981): 90–94.

Gelzer, M. *Caesar, Politician and Statesman*, trans. P. Needham. Oxford: Blackwell, 1968.

———. *Die Nobilität der römischen Republik.* 2d ed. Stuttgart: Teubner, 1983. First published Leipzig, 1912.

Getty, R. J., ed. *M. Annaei Lucani De Bello Civili liber 1.* Cambridge: Cambridge University Press, 1940.

Girard, R. *La violence et le sacré.* Paris: B. Grasset, 1972.

Goldberg, S. M. *Epic in Republican Rome.* Oxford: Oxford University Press, 1995.

———. *Understanding Terence.* Princeton, N.J.: Princeton University Press, 1986.

Goody, J. R., ed. *The Character of Kinship.* Cambridge: Cambridge University Press, 1973.

———. "The Evolution of the Family." In *Household and Family in Past Time*, ed. P. Laslett, with R. Wall. Cambridge: Cambridge University Press, 1972.

Gowing, A. M. *The Triumviral Narratives of Appian and Cassius Dio.* Ann Arbor, Mich.: University of Michigan Press, 1992.

Gratwick, A. S., ed. *The Brothers*, by Terence. Warminster, Wiltshire, England: Aris & Phillips, 1987.

Griffin, J. "The Fourth Georgic, Virgil, and Rome." *G&R* 26 (1979): 61–80.

Griffin, M. "Philosophy, Politics and Politicians at Rome." In *Philosophia Togata: Essays on Philosophy and Roman Society*, ed. M. Griffin and J. Barnes. Oxford: Clarendon Press, 1989.

Gruen, E. S. *Studies in Greek Culture and Roman Policy.* Berkeley, Calif.: University of California Press, 1990.

———. *The Hellenistic World and the Coming of Rome.* Berkeley, Calif.: University of California Press, 1984.

———. *The Last Generation of the Roman Republic.* Berkeley, Calif.: University of California Press, 1974.

———. "The Last Years of Philip V." *GRBS* 15 (1974): 221–46.

———. "Pompey, the Roman Aristocracy and the Conference of Luca." *Historia* 18 (1969): 71–108.

————. *Roman Politics and the Criminal Courts 149–78 B.C.* Cambridge, Mass.: Harvard University Press, 1968.

Guarino, A. "*Societas consensu contracta.*" *Atti dell'Accademia di scienze morali e politiche di Napoli* 3 (1972): 261–359.

Gurval, R. A. *Actium and Augustus: The Politics and Emotions of Civil War.* Ann Arbor, Mich.: University of Michigan Press, 1995.

Hallett, J. *Fathers and Daughters in Roman Society: Women and the Elite Family.* Princeton, N.J.: Princeton University Press, 1984.

Halperin, D. "Heroes and Their Pals." In *One Hundred Years of Homosexuality: And other Essays on Greek Love.* New York: Routledge, 1990.

Hansen, K. V. " 'Our Eyes Behold Each Other': Masculinity and Intimate Friendship in Antebellum New England." In *Men's Friendship*, ed. P. M. Nardi. Newbury Park, Calif.: Sage Publications, 1992.

Hardie, P. R. "Tales of Unity and Division in Imperial Latin Epic." In *Literary Responses to Civil Discord*, ed. J. H. Molyneux. Nottingham: University of Nottingham Press, 1993.

————. *Virgil's Aeneid: Cosmos and Imperium.* Oxford: Clarendon Press, 1986.

Harevan, T. K. "The Family as Process: The Historical Study of the Family Cycle." *Journal of Social History* 7 (1973–74): 322–29.

Harmon, D. P. "The Family Festivals of Rome." *ANRW* 16, no. 2 (1978): 1593–1603.

Harries, B. "Ovid and the Fabii: *Fasti* 2.193–474." *CQ* 41 (1991): 150–67.

Harrison, A.R.W. *The Law of Athens.* 2 vols. Oxford: Clarendon Press, 1968–71.

Harvey, R. A. *A Commentary on Persius.* Leiden: Brill, 1981.

Hatzfeld, J. *Les trafiquants italiens dans l'orient hellenique.* Paris: E. de Boccard, 1919.

————. "Les Italiens résidant à Délos mentionnés dans les inscriptions de l'ile." *BCH* 36 (1912): 1–218.

Hauthal, F. *Acronis et Porphyrionis Commentarii in Q. Horatium Flaccum.* 2 vols. Berlin: J. Springer, 1864.

Hellegouarc'h, J. *Le vocabulaire latin des relations et des partis politiques sous la République.* Paris: Les Belles Lettres, 1963.

Henderson, J. "Form Remade/Statius' *Thebaid.*" In *Roman Epic*, ed. A. J. Boyle. London: Routledge, 1993.

Herlihy, D. *Medieval Households.* Cambridge, Mass.: Harvard University Press, 1985.

Hillard, T. W. "The Claudii Pulchri 76–48 B.C.: Studies in Their Political Cohesion." Ph.D. Diss. Macquarie University, 1976.

Hinard, F. "Solidarités familiales et ruptures à l'époque des guerres civiles et de la proscription." In *Parenté et stratégies familiales dans l'antiquité romaine*, *Actes de la table ronde des 2–4 octobre 1986*, ed. J. Andreau and H. Bruhns. Collection de l'École Française de Rome, Vol. 129. Rome: École française de Rome, 1990.

Hinds, S. "*Arma* in Ovid's *Fasti*: Part 1: Genre and Mannerism" and "*Arma* in Ovid's *Fasti*: Part 2: Genre, Romulean Rome and Augustan Ideology." *Arethusa* 25 (1992): 81–154.

Hobson, D. W. "House and Household in Roman Egypt." *YCS* 28 (1985): 211–29.

Hodkinson, S. "Land Tenure and Inheritance in Classical Sparta." *CQ* 36 (1986): 378–406.

Holden, H. A., ed. *M. Tulli Ciceronis De Officiis Libri Tres*. 7th ed. Cambridge: Cambridge University Press, 1891.

Hopkins, K. *Death and Renewal*. Sociological Studies in Roman History, Vol. 2. Cambridge: Cambridge University Press, 1983.

———. "Brother-Sister Marriage in Roman Egypt." *CSSH* 22 (1980): 303–54.

Housman, A. E., ed. *M. Annaei Lucani Belli Civilis Libri Decem*. Oxford: Basil Blackwell, 1926.

How, W. W., ed. *Cicero: Select Letters*. 2 vols. Oxford: Clarendon Press, 1925.

Howell, P., ed. *A Commentary on Book One of the Epigrams of Martial*. London: Athlone Press, 1980.

Hughes, D. "Domestic Ideals and Social Behavior: Evidence from Medieval Genoa." In *The Family in History*, ed. C. E. Rosenberg. Philadelphia, Pa.: University of Pennsylvania Press, 1975.

Humphreys, S. "Family Quarrels." *JHS* 109 (1989): 182–85.

———. "Kinship Patterns in the Athenian Courts." *GRBS* 27 (1986): 57–91.

———. *The Family, Women and Death*. London: Routledge, 1983.

Jal, P., *La guerre civile à Rome étude littéraire et morale*. Paris: Presses Universitaires de France, 1963.

Johnston, D. "Prohibitions and Perpetuities: Family Settlements in Roman Law." *ZRG* 102 (1985): 220–90.

Jones, C. P. *Plutarch and Rome*. Oxford: Clarendon Press, 1971.

Jones, W. B., ed. *Confederate War Poems*. Nashville: Bill Coats, Ltd., 1959.

Judson, H. P. *Caesar's Army: A Study of the Military Art of the Romans in the Last Days of the Republic*. New York: Biblo and Tannen, 1888.

Kajanto, E. *God and Fate in Livy*. Turku: Turun Yliopiston Kustantama, 1957.

Kaser, M. "Neue Literatur zur 'Societas.'" *SDHI* 41 (1975): 278–338.

———. *Das römische Privatrecht*. 2 vols. 2d ed. Munich: C. H. Beck, 1971.

Kauer, R., and W. M. Lindsay, eds. *P. Terenti Afri Comoediae*. Oxford: Clarendon Press, 1926.

Keesing, R. M. *Kin Groups and Social Structure*. New York: Holt, Rinehart and Winston, 1975.

Kehoe, D. "Private and Imperial Management of Roman Estates in North Africa." *Law and History Review* 2, no. 2 (1984): 241–63.

Keil, H. *Grammatici Latini*. 8 vols. Leipzig: Teubner, 1855–70.

Kenney, E. J., ed. *Lucretius: De Rerum Natura. Book 3*. Cambridge: Cambridge University Press, 1971.

Kent, F. W. *Household and Lineage in Renaissance Florence*. Princeton, N.J.: Princeton University Press, 1977.

Kilborn, P. T. "Cause for Sibling Rivalry at Teamsters." *New York Times*, 17 July 1996, Midwest Edition, A10.

Kilpatrick, R. S. *The Poetry of Friendship: Horace, Epistles 1*. Edmonton, Alb.: The University of Alberta Press, 1986.

Kirschenbaum, A. *Sons, Slaves and Freedmen in Roman Commerce*. Jerusalem: The Magnes Press, The Hebrew University, 1987.

Kneissl, P., and V. Losemann, eds. *Alte Geschichte und Wissenschaftsgeschichte: Festschrift für Karl Christ zum 65. Geburtstag*. Darmstadt: Wissenschaftliche Buchgesellschaft, 1988.

Koerte, A., and A. Thierfelder, eds. *Menandri quae supersunt*. 2 vols. Leipzig: Teubner, 1959.

Konstan, D. "Narrative and Ideology in Livy: Book 1." *Cl. Ant.* 5 (1986): 198–215.

Krämer, H. J. "Die Sage von Romulus und Remus in der lateinischen Literatur." In *Synusia. Festgabe für Wolfgang Schadewaldt zum 15 Marz 1965*, ed. H. Flashar and K. Gaiser. [Pfullingen]: Neske, 1965.

Krause, J.-U. *Witwen und Waisen im Römischen Reich III. Rechtliche und soziale Stellung von Waisen*. Stuttgart: Franz Steiner, 1995.

Krenkel, W., ed. *Lucilius Satiren*. 2 vols. Leiden: Brill, 1970.

Kretschmer, P. "Die griechische Benennung des Bruders." *Glotta* 2 (1910): 201–13.

Kuehn, T. *Law, Family & Women*. Chicago: University of Chicago Press, 1991.

Kunkel, W. "Ein unbeachtetes Zeugnis über das römische *consortium*." *Annales. Faculté de Droit d'Istanbul [Istanbul, Université, Hukuk Facultesi]* 4 (1954): 56–78.

Kurfess, A. *Appendix Sallustiana*. 2 vols. Lepizig: Teubner, 1970.

Lacey, W. K. "Patria Potestas." In *The Family in Ancient Rome: New Perspectives*, ed. B. Rawson. Ithaca, N.Y.: Cornell University Press, 1986.

———. "Clodius and Cicero: A Question of *Dignitas*." *Antichthon* 8 (1974): 75–92.

———. *The Family in Classical Greece*. Ithaca, N.Y.: Cornell University Press, 1968.

Lacombe, P. *La famille dans la société romaine: étude de moralité comparé*. Paris: Lecrosnier et Babe, 1889.

Lamar, M. " 'Choosing' Partible Inheritance: Chilean Merchant Families, 1795–1825." *Journal of Social History* 28 (1994): 125–45.

Lane Fox, R. "Inheritance in the Greek World." In *Crux: Essays in Greek History presented to G.E.M. de Ste. Croix on his 75th Birthday*, ed. P. A. Cartledge and F. D. Harvey. London: Duckworth, 1985.

Lange, W. *Die Germaniades Tacitus*, comm. R. Much. Heidelberg: Winter, 1967.

La Penna, A. *Sallustio e la rivoluzione romana*. Milan: Feltrinelli, 1968.

Lavely, W., and R. Bin Wong. "Family Division and Mobility in North China." *Comparative Studies in Society and History* 34 (1992): 439–63.

Lazzarini, S. *Sepulcra familiaria: Un' indagine epigrafico-giuridica*. Padua: CEDAM, 1991.

Leach, E. W. "*Meam Quom Formam Noscito*: Language and Characterization in the *Menaechmi*." *Arethusa* 2 (1969): 30–45.

Leacock, E. B. Introduction to *The Origin of the Family, Private Property and the State, in the light of the researches of Lewis H. Morgan*, by F. Engels. New York: International Publishers, 1972.

Le Play, P.G.F. *L'organisation de la famille selon le vrai modèle signalé par l'histoire de toutes les races et de tous les temps*. Paris Tequi: Bibliothécaire de l'oeuvre Saint-Michel, 1871.

Levi-Strauss, C. "The Family." In *Man, Culture and Society*, ed. H. L. Shapiro. New York: Oxford University Press, 1956.

Levick, B. *Tiberius the Politician*. London: Thames and Hudson, 1976.

Lewis, N. *Life in Egypt under Roman Rule*. Oxford: Clarendon Press, 1983.

Lilja, S. *Homosexuality in Republican and Augustan Rome*. Commentationes Humanarum Literarum 74. Helsinki, Finland: Societas Scientiarum Fennica, 1983.

Lindskog, C., and K. Ziegler. *Plutarch: Vitae Parallelae*. 4 vols. Liepzig: Teubner, 1914–80.

Lintott, A. W. *Violence in Republican Rome*. Oxford: Clarendon Press, 1968.

Lloyd, G.E.R. *Science, Folklore and Ideology: Studies in the Life Sciences in Ancient Greece*. Cambridge: Cambridge University Press, 1983.

Long, G., ed. *M. Tulli Ciceronis Orationes*. 4 vols. 2d ed. London: Whittaker, 1855–62.

Luce, T. J. *Livy: The Composition of His History*. Princeton, N.J.: Princeton University Press, 1977.

Luck, G., ed. *P. Ovidius Naso Tristia*. 2 vols. Heidelberg: Winter, 1977.

Mack, B. "Introduction: Religion and Ritual." In *Violent Origins: Walter Burkert, Rene Girard & Jonathan Z. Smith on Ritual Killing and Cultural Formation*, ed. R. G. Hamerton-Kelly. Stanford, Calif.: Stanford University Press, 1987.

MacMullen, R. "The Legion as a Society." *Historia* 33 (1984): 440–56.

Makowski, J. F. "Nisus and Euryalus: A Platonic Relationship." *CJ* 85 (1989): 1–15.

Malcovati, E., ed. *Oratorum Romanorum Fragmenta Liberae Rei Publicae*. 2d ed. Turin: G. B. Paravia, 1955.

Manson, M. "La *Pietas* et le sentiment de l'enfance à Rome d'après les monnaies." *Revue belge de numismatique et de sigillographie* 121 (1975): 21–80.

Marius, R., ed. *The Columbia Book of Civil War Poetry, from Whitman to Walcott*. New York: Columbia University Press, 1994.

Marshall, B. A. *A Historical Commentary on Asconius*. Columbia, Mo.: The University of Missouri Press, 1985.

Martin, R. H. *Terence Adelphoe*. Cambridge: Cambridge University Press, 1976.

Mauss, M. *The Gift: Forms and Functions of Exchange in Archaic Societies*, trans. I. Cunnison. Glencoe, Ill.: Free Press, 1954.

McDermott, W. C. "Q. Cicero." *Historia* 20 (1971): 702–717.

Meiggs, R., and D. Lewis, eds. *A Selection of Greek Historical Inscriptions*. Oxford: Clarendon Press, 1969.

Mencacci, F. *I fratelli amici: la reppresentatzione dei gemelli nella cultura romana*. Venice: Marsilio, 1996.

Meyer, E. A. "Explaining the Epigraphic Habit in the Roman Empire: The Evidence of Epitaphs." *JRS* 80 (1990): 74–96.

Michel, A. "Fonction et structure de la famille. La famille agnatique ou *consortium*." *Cahiers internationale de sociologie* 29 (1960): 113–35.

Miles, G. B. *Virgil's Georgics: A New Interpretation.* Berkeley, Calif.: University of California Press, 1980.

Millar, F. "Politics, Persuasion and the People Before the Social War (150–90 B.C.)." *JRS* 76 (1986): 1–11.

———. "The Political Character of the Classical Roman Republic, 200–151 B.C." *JRS* 74 (1984): 1–19.

———. "Triumvirate and Principate." *JRS* 63 (1973): 50–67.

Mitchell, T. N. "Cicero and the *Senatus Consultum Ultimum.*" *Historia* 20 (1971): 47–61.

Moore, T. J. *Artistry and Ideology: Livy's Vocabulary of Virtue.* Frankfurt am Main: Athenaum, 1989.

Moxon, I. S., J. D. Smart, and A. J. Woodman, eds. *Past Perspectives: Studies in Greek and Roman Historical Writing.* Cambridge: Cambridge University Press, 1986.

Müller, C.F.W., ed. *M. Tullius Cicero Cato Major de Senectute Laelius de Amicitia Paradoxa.* Leipzig: Teubner, 1876.

Münzer, F. *Beiträge zur Quellenkritik der Naturgeschichte des Plinius.* Berlin: Weidmann, 1897.

Murgatroyd, P., ed. *Tibullus Elegies II.* Oxford: Clarendon Press, 1994.

Murray, R. J. "Cicero and the Gracchi." *TAPA* 97 (1966): 291–98.

Mutschler, F.-H. *Erzählstil und Propanganda in Caesars Kommentarien.* Heidelberg: Winter, 1975.

Mynors, R.A.B., ed. *Virgil: Georgics.* Oxford: Oxford University Press, 1990.

Nagle, B. R. *The Poetics of Exile: Program and Polemic in the* Tristia *and* Epistulae ex Ponto *of Ovid.* Collection Latomus Vol. 170. Brussels: Latomus, 1980.

Nardi, P. M. " 'Seamless Souls': An Introduction to Men's Friendships." In *Men's Friendship.* Newbury Park, Calif.: Sage Publications, 1992.

Nauck, A., ed. *Tragicorum Graecorum Fragmenta.* Leipzig: Teubner, 1856, with supplement, ed. B. Snell. Hildesheim: G. Olms, 1964.

Nicolet, C., ed. *Demokratia et aristokratia. À propos de Caius Gracchus: mots grecs et réalités romaines.* Paris: Université de Paris I, 1983.

Nisbet, R. A. "Kinship and Political Power in First Century Rome." In *Sociology and History: Theory and Research,* ed. W. J. Cahnman and J. Boskoff. New York: Free Press of Glencoe, 1964.

Nisbet, R.G.M. "Horace's *Epodes* and History." In *Poetry and Politics in the Age of Augustus,* ed. T. Woodman and D. West. Cambridge: Cambridge University Press, 1984.

Nisbet, R.G.M., and M. Hubbard. *A Commentary on Horace: Odes Book II.* Oxford: Clarendon Press, 1978.

Ogilvie, R. M. *A Commentary on Livy, Books 1–5.* Oxford: Clarendon Press, 1965.

Orr, D. G. "Roman Domestic Religion." *ANRW* 16, no. 2 (1978): 1557–91.

Otis, B. *Virgil: A Study in Civilized Poetry.* Oxford: Clarendon Press, 1964.

Paribeni, R. *La famiglia Romana.* 4th ed. Bologna: Cappelli, 1948.

Parkin, T. G. *Demography and Roman Society.* Baltimore, Md.: The Johns Hopkins University Press, 1992.

Paul, G. M. *A Historical Commentary on Sallust's Bellum Iugurthinum.* ARCA:

Classical and Medieval Texts, Papers and Monographs 13. Liverpool: F. Cairns, 1984.

Paulus, C. *Die Idee der postmortalen Persönlichkeit im römischen Testamentsrecht: zur gesellschaftlichen und rechtlichen Bedeutung einzelner Testamentsklauseln*. Schriften zur Rechtsgeschichte 55. Berlin: Duncker und Humblot, 1991.

Pavlock, B. "Epic and Tragedy in Vergil's Nisus and Euryalus Episode." *TAPA* 115 (1985): 207–24.

Pease, A. S., ed. *Cicero de Divinatione Libri Duo*. Darmstadt: Wissenschaftliche Buchgesellschaft, 1963. Originally published as *University of Illinois Studies in Language and Literature* 6 (1920): 161–500 and 8 (1923): 153–474.

Pelling, C.B.R. "Plutarch and Roman Politics." In *Past Perspectives: Studies in Greek and Roman Historical Writing*, ed. I. S. Moxon, J. D. Smart, and A. J. Woodman. Cambridge: Cambridge University Press, 1986.

Peter, H., ed. *Historicorum Romanorum Reliquiae*. 2d. ed. 2 vols. Stuttgart: Teubner, 1914–16.

———. *Die Quellen Plutarchs in den Biographieen der Römer*. Halle: Buchhandlung des Waisenhauses, 1865.

Pitt-Rivers, J. "The Kith and the Kin." In *The Character of Kinship*, ed. J. R. Goody. Cambridge: Cambridge University Press, 1973.

Plakans, A. *Kinship in the Past: An Anthropology of European Family Life 1500–1900*. Oxford: Blackwell, 1984.

Pleket, H. W. "Agriculture in Comparative Perspective." In *De Agricultura: In Memoriam Pieter Willem De Neeve (1945–1990)*. Amsterdam: J. C. Gieben, 1993.

Plescia, J. "*Patria Potestas* and the Roman Revolution." In *The Conflict of the Generations in Ancient Greece and Rome*, ed. S. Bertman. Amsterdam: G. R. Grüner, 1976.

Poliakoff, M. B. "Remus in Latin Poetry." *APAA* (1987): 135.

Pontone, A. G. "Fratricide as the Founding Myth of Rome: The Historiographical Perspective." Ph.D. diss., New York University, 1986.

Poucet, J. *Les origines de Rome: tradition et histoire*. Brussells: Facultés universitaires Saint-Louis, 1985.

———. "L'influence des facteurs politiques dans l'evolutions de la geste de Romulus." In *Sodalitas. Scritti in onore di Antonio Guarino*, ed. V. Giuffre. 10 vols. Naples: Jovene, 1984–85.

Poulsen, B. "The Dioscuri and Ruler Ideology." *Symbolae Osloenses* 66 (1991): 119–46.

Poultney, J. W. *The Bronze Tables of Iguvium*. American Philological Society Monographs no. 18. Baltimore, Md.: American Philological Association, 1959.

Powell, J.G.F. "Two Notes on Catullus." *CQ* 40 (1990): 199–206.

———. *Cicero Cato Maior de Senectute*. Cambridge: Cambridge University Press, 1988.

Prato, C., ed. *Gli Epigrammi attribuiti a L. Anneo Seneca*. Rome: Edizioni dell'Ateneo, 1964.

Putnam, M.C.J. *Virgil's Poem of the Earth: Studies in the Georgics*. Princeton, N.J.: Princeton University Press, 1979.

———. "Italian Virgil and the Idea of Rome." In *Janus: Essays in Ancient and Modern Studies*, ed. L. L. Orlin. Ann Arbor, Mich.: Center for Coordination of Ancient and Modern Studies, 1975.

———. *Tibullus: A Commentary*. Norman, Okla.: The University of Oklahoma Press, 1973.

Quinn, K., ed. *Catullus, The Poems*. 2d ed. New York: St. Martin's Press, 1973.

Quinones, R. J. *The Changes of Cain: Violence and the Lost Brother in Cain and Abel Literature*. Princeton, N.J.: Princeton University Press, 1991.

Raaflaub, K. A., ed. *Social Struggles in Archaic Rome. New Perspectives on the Conflict of the Orders*. Berkeley, Calif.: The University of California Press, 1986.

Rambaud, M. "L'Apologie de Pompée par Lucain au livre viii de la *Pharsale*." *REL* 33 (1955): 258–96.

Rawson, B., ed. *The Family in Ancient Rome: New Perspectives*. Ithaca, N.Y.: Cornell University Press, 1986.

Rawson, E. *Intellectual Life in the Late Roman Republic*. Baltimore, Md.: The Johns Hopkins University Press, 1985.

———. "The Ciceronean Aristocracy and Its Properties." In *Studies in Roman Property*, ed. M. I. Finley. Cambridge: Cambridge University Press, 1976.

———. "The Eastern Clientelae of Clodius and the Claudii." *Historia* 22 (1973): 219–39.

———. *The Spartan Tradition in European Thought*. Oxford: Clarendon Press, 1969.

Reith, O. *Die Kunst Menanders in den Adelphen des Terenz*. Hildesheim: G. Olms, 1964.

Renier, E. *Étude sur l'histoire de la querela inofficiosi en droit romain*. Liège: H. Valliant-Carmanne, 1942.

Richardson, K. *Daggers in the Forum: The Revolutionary Lives and Violent Deaths of the Gracchus Brothers*. London: Cassell, 1976.

Richardson, T. W. "Homosexuality in the *Satyricon*." *C&M* 35 (1984): 105–27.

Richlin, A. "Not Before Homosexuality: The Materiality of the *Cinaedus* and the Roman Law Against Love Between Men." *Journal of the History of Sexuality* 3 (1993): 523–73.

Riganti, E., ed. *P. Terenti Varronis De Lingua Latina Libro VI*. Bologna: Patron, 1978.

Rorty, A. O., ed. *Essays on Aristotle's Ethics*. Berkeley, Calif.: University of California Press, 1980.

Rosenberg, C. E. *The Family in History*. Philadelphia, Pa.: University of Pennsylvania Press, 1975.

Ross, D. O. *Virgil's Elements: Physics and Poetry in the Georgics*. Princeton, N.J.: Princeton University Press, 1987.

———. *Backgrounds to Augustan Poetry: Gallus, Elegy and Rome*. Cambridge: Cambridge University Press, 1975.

———. *Style and Tradition in Catullus*. Cambridge, Mass.: Harvard University Press, 1970.

Rundell, W.M.F. "Cicero and Clodius: The Question of Credibility." *Historia* 28 (1979): 301–28.

Ryan, F. X. "The Praetorship and Consular Candidacy of L. Rupilius." *CQ* 45 (1995): 263–65.

Saller, R. P. *Patriarchy, Property and Death in the Roman Family.* Cambridge Studies in Population, Economy and Society in Past Time 25. Cambridge: Cambridge University Press, 1994.

———. "Roman Kinship: Structure and Sentiment." Forthcoming in *The Roman Family in Italy: Status, Sentiment, Space*, ed. P. Weaver. Oxford: Oxford University Press, 1996.

———. "Roman Heirship Strategies: In Principle and in Practice." In *The Family in Italy from Antiquity to the Present*, ed. D. I. Kertzer and R. P. Saller. New Haven, Conn.: Yale University Press, 1991.

———. "*Pietas*, Obligation and Authority in the Roman Family." In *Alte Geschichte und Wissenschaftsgeschichte: Festschrift für Karl Christ zum 65 Geburtstag*, ed. P. Kneissl and V. Losemann. Darmstadt: Wissenschaftliche Buchgesellschaft, 1988.

———. "Family and household." In *The Roman Empire*, ed. P. Garnsey and R. Saller. London: Duckworth, 1987.

———. "*Patria Potestas* and the Stereotype of the Roman Family." *Continuity and Change* 1 (1986): 7–22.

———. "*Familia, Domus* and the Roman Conception of the Family." *Phoenix* 38 (1984): 336–55.

Saller, R. P., and B. D. Shaw. "Tombstones and Roman Family Relations in the Principate: Civilians, Soldiers and Slaves." *JRS* 74 (1984): 124–56.

Salmon, E. T. "Cicero, *Romanus an Italicus anceps*." In *Cicero and Virgil: Studies in Honour of Harold Hunt*, ed. J.R.C. Martyn. Amsterdam: A. M. Hakkert, 1972.

Scardigli, B. *Die Römerbiographien Plutarchs.* Munich: Beck, 1979.

Scheid, J. *Les Frères Arvales: Recrutiement et origine sociale sous les empereurs Julio-Claudiens.* Paris: Presses Universitaires de France, 1975.

Scheidel, W. "Finances, Figures and Fiction." *CQ* 46 (1996): 222–38.

Schilling, R. "Romulus l'élu e Rémus le réprouvé." In *Rites, Cultes, Dieux de Rome.* Paris: Klincksieck, 1979.

———. "Les 'Castores' Romains à la lumière des traditions indo-européenes." In *Rites, Cultes, Dieux de Rome.* Paris: Klincksieck, 1979. First published in *REL* 38 (1961): 182–99.

Scott, K. "The Identification of Augustus with Romulus-Quirinus." *TAPA* 56 (1925): 82–105.

Scullard, H. H. *Roman Politics, 220–150 B.C.* 2d ed. Oxford: Clarendon Press, 1973.

———. *Scipio Africanus, Soldier and Politician.* Ithaca, N.Y.: Cornell University Press, 1970.

Seager, R., ed. *The Crisis of the Roman Republic: Studies in Political and Social History.* Cambridge: Heffer, 1969.

———. "Clodius, Pompeius and the Exile of Cicero." *Latomus* 24 (1965): 519–31.

Sedgwick, E. K. *Between Men: English Literature and Male Homosocial Desire.* New York: Columbia University Press, 1985.

Serres, M. *Rome: The Book of Foundations*, trans. F. McCarren. Stanford, Calif.: Stanford University Press, 1991.

Shackleton Bailey, D. R. *Cicero Back from Exile: Six Speeches upon His Return.* Atlanta, Ga.: Scholars Press, 1991.

———. *Cicero Philippics*. Chapel Hill, N.C.: University of North Carolina Press, 1986.

———. *Cicero Epistulae ad Quintum fratrem et M. Brutum*. Cambridge: Cambridge University Press, 1980.

———. *Cicero Select Letters*. Cambridge: Cambridge University Press, 1980.

———. *Cicero Epistulae ad Familiares*. 2 vols. Cambridge: Cambridge University Press, 1977.

———. *Cicero: A Political Biography*. New York: Charles Scribner's Sons, 1972.

———. *Cicero's Letters to Atticus*. 7 vols. Cambridge: Cambridge University Press, 1965–70.

Shatzman, I. *Senatorial Wealth and Roman Politics*. Collection Latomus Vol. 142. Brussels: Latomus, 1975.

Shaw, B. D. "A Groom of One's Own." *The New Republic*. Issues 4,148 and 4,149. July 18 & 25, 1994.

Sherwin-White, A. N. *The Letters of Pliny: A Historical and Social Commentary*. Oxford: Clarendon Press, 1966.

Sieder, R., and M. Mitterauer, eds. *The European Family: Patriarchy to Partnership from the Middle Ages to the Present*, trans. K. Oosterveen and M. Horzinger. Chicago: University of Chicago Press, 1982.

Simpson, W. K., ed. *The Literature of Ancient Egypt: An Anthology of Stories, Instructions, and Poetry*, trans. R. O. Faulkner, E. F. Wente, Jr., and W. K. Simpson. New Haven, Conn.: Yale University Press, 1972.

Skinner, M. B. "Rhamnusia Virgo." *Cl. Ant* 3 (1984): 134–41.

Skutsch, O., ed. *The Annals of Quintus Ennius*. Oxford: Clarendon Press, 1985.

Slater, N. *Reading Petronius*. Baltimore, Md.: The Johns Hopkins University Press, 1990.

Smith, H. "Family and Class: The Household Economy of Languedoc Wine Growers, 1830–1870." *Journal of Family History* 9 (1984): 64–87.

Solodow, J. B. "Livy and the Story of Horatius, 1.24–26." *TAPA* 109 (1979): 251–68.

Sommerstein, A. H., ed. and trans. *Aristophanes: Clouds*. Warminster, Wiltshire, England: Aris & Phillips, 1982.

Stärk, E. *Die Menaechmi des Plautus und kein griechisches Original*. Altertumswissenshaftliche Reihe, Vol. 1. Tübingen: Gunter Narr Verlag, 1989.

Stangl, T., ed. *Ciceronis Orationum Scholiastae*. 2 vols. Vienna: F. Tempsky; Leipzig: G. Freytag, 1912.

Stockton, D. *The Gracchi*. Oxford: Clarendon Press, 1979.

———. *Cicero: A Political Biography*. London: Oxford University Press, 1971.

Stone, L. *The Family, Sex and Marriage in England 1500–1800*. London: Weidenfeld & Nicolson, 1977.

Strauss, B. S. *Fathers and Sons in Athens: Ideology and Society in the Era of the Peloponnesian War*. London: Routledge, 1993.

Sussman, L. A. "Sons and Fathers in the Major Declamations Ascribed to Quintilian." *Rhetorica* 13 (1995): 179–92.

Syme, R. "The Junii Silani." In *The Augustan Aristocracy*. Oxford: Clarendon Press, 1986.

———. *Some Arval Brethren*. Oxford : Clarendon Press, 1980.

———. *History in Ovid*. Oxford: Clarendon Press, 1978.

———. "History and Language at Rome." In *Roman Papers*, Vol. 3, ed. A. R. Birley. Oxford: Clarendon Press, 1984. Originally published in *Diogenes 85* (1974): 1–11.

———. "People in Pliny." *JRS* 58 (1968): 135–51.

———. *Sallust*. Berkeley, Calif.: University of California Press, 1964.

———. "Livy and Augustus." *HSCP* 64 (1959): 27–87.

———. *Tacitus*. 2 vols. Oxford: Clarendon Press, 1958.

———. *The Roman Revolution*. Oxford: Oxford University Press, 1939.

———. "The Allegiance of Labienus." In *Roman Papers*, Vol. 1, ed. E. Badian, et al. Oxford: Clarendon Press, 1979. Originally published in *JRS* 28 (1938): 113–25.

Talamanca, M. *Istituzioni di diritto Romano*. Milan: A. Guiffrè, 1990.

Tatum, W. J. "The Poverty of the Claudii Pulchri: Varro, *De Re Rustica* 3.16.1–2." *CQ* 42 (1992): 190–200.

———. "Cicero and the *Bona Dea* Scandal." *CP* 85 (1990): 202–208.

———. "Cicero's Opposition to the *Lex Clodia de Collegiis*." *CQ* 40 (1990): 187–96.

Taylor, L. R. "Forerunners of the Gracchi." *JRS* 52(1962): 19–27.

———. *Party Politics in the Age of Caesar*. Berkeley, Calif.: University of California Press, 1949.

Tellegen, J. W. *The Roman Law of Succession in the Letters of Pliny the Younger*. Zutphen, Holland: Terra, 1982.

———. "Was There a *Consortium* in Pliny's Letter VIII.18?" *RIDA* 3d ser., 23 (1980): 295–312.

Thomas, Y. "Parricidium I. Le père, la famille et la cité." *MEFRA* 93 (1981): 643–715.

Thompson, D. J. *Memphis under the Ptolemies*. Princeton, N.J.: Princeton University Press, 1988.

Thomas, R. F., ed. *Virgil Georgics*. 2 vols. Cambridge: Cambridge University Press, 1988.

———. *Lands and Peoples in Roman Poetry: The Ethnographical Tradition*. Cambridge: Cambridge Philological Society Supplement 7, Cambridge, 1982.

Tifou, E. *Essai sur la pensée morale de Salluste à la lumière de ses prologues*. Paris: Klincksieck, 1973.

Tondo, S. "Ancora sul consorzio domestico nella Roma antica." *SDHI* 60 (1994): 601–12.

Treggiari, S. *Roman Marriage: Iusti Coniuges from the Time of Cicero to the Time of Ulpian*. Oxford: Clarendon Press, 1991.

Tuplin, C. J. "Catullus 68." *CQ* 31 (1981): 113–39.

Tyrrell, W. B. *A Legal and Historical Commentary to Cicero's Oratio pro C. Rabirio Perduellionis Reo*. Amsterdam: A. M. Hakkert, 1978.

Vanderbroeck, P.J.J. *Popular Leadership and Collective Behavior in the Late Roman Republic (ca. 80–50 B.C.).* Dutch Monographs on Ancient History and Archaeology, Vol. 3. Amsterdam: J. C. Gieben, 1987.

Versnel, H. S. "Suodales." In *Lapis Satricanus: Archaeological, Epigraphical, Linguistic and Historical Aspects of the New Inscription from Satricanum,* ed. C. M. Stibbe, G. Colonna, C. De Simone, and H. S. Versnel. The Hague: Ministerie van Cultur, Recreatie en Maatschappelijk Werk, 1980.

Vessey, D. *Statius and the Thebaid.* Cambridge: Cambridge University Press, 1973.

Veyne, P. "The Roman Empire." In *A History of Private Life I. From Pagan Rome to Byzantium.* Cambridge, Mass.: Belknap Press, 1987.

———. "La famille et l'amour sous le haut-empire romain." *Annales ESC* 33 (1978): 35–63.

Vinson, M. P. "Parental Imagery in Catullus." *CJ* 85 (1989): 47–53.

Voci, P. *Istituzione di diritto Romano.* 4th ed. Milan: A. Guiffrè, 1994.

———. "Diritto ereditario romano I." *ANRW* 2, no. 14 (1982): 392–448.

Von Fritz, K. *The Theory of the Mixed Constitution in Antiquity: A Critical Analysis of Polybius' Ideas.* New York: Columbia University Press, 1954.

Wagenvoort, H. "The Crime of Fratricide." In *Studies in Roman Literature, Culture and Religion.* Leiden: E. K. Brill, 1956.

Walbank, F. W. *A Historical Commentary on Polybius.* 3 vols. Oxford: Clarendon Press, 1957–79.

———. *Philip V of Macedon.* Hamden, Conn.: Archon Books, 1967.

Walde, A. *Lateinisches Etymologisches Wörterbuch,* ed. J. B. Hoffmann. 3d ed. Heidelberg: C. Winter, 1965.

Wall, R., J. R. Laslett, and P. Laslett, eds. *Family Forms in Historic Europe.* Cambridge: Cambridge University Press, 1982.

Wallace-Hadrill, A. "The Golden Age and Sin in Augustan Ideology." *P&P* 95 (1982): 19–36.

Waltzing, J.-P. *Étude historique sur les corporations professionnelles chez les Romains depuis les origines jusqu'à la chute de l'empire d'occident.* Louvain: C. Peeters, 1895–1900.

Warde Fowler, W. *The Religious Experience of the Roman People.* London: Macmillan and Co., 1911.

Wardman, A. *Plutarch's Lives.* London: Elek, 1974.

Watson, A. *Society and Legal Change.* Edinburgh: Scottish Academic Press, 1977.

———. *Rome of the XII Tables.* Princeton, N.J.: Princeton University Press, 1975.

———. *The Law of Succession in the Later Roman Republic.* Oxford: Clarendon Press, 1971.

———. *The Law of Persons in the Later Roman Republic.* Oxford: Clarendon Press, 1967.

Webster, T.B.L. *Studies in Menander.* Manchester: Manchester University Press, 1960.

Weinstock, S. *Divus Julius.* Oxford: Clarendon, 1971.

Welwei, K.-W. "Gefolgschaftsverband oder Gentilaufgebot? Zum Problem eines frührömischen familiare bellum (Liv. II.48.9)." *ZRG* 110 (1993): 331–69.

West, M. L., ed. *Hesiod: Works & Days*. Oxford: Clarendon Press, 1978.

Westrup, C. W. *Introduction to Early Roman Law: Comparative Sociological Studies and The Patriarchal Joint Family*. 3 vols. Copenhagen: Levin & Munksgaard, 1934–50.

Wheaton, R. "Family and Kinship in Western Europe: The Problem of the Joint Family Household." *Journal of Interdisciplinary History* 5 (1975): 601–28.

Williams, C. A. "Greek Love at Rome." *CQ* 45 (1995): 517–39.

Winterbottom, M., ed. *The Minor Declamations Ascribed to Quintilian*. Berlin: Walter de Gruyter, 1984.

Wirszubski, C. *Libertas as a Political Ideal at Rome*. Cambridge: Cambridge University Press, 1950.

Wiseman, T. P. *Remus: A Roman Myth*. Cambridge: Cambridge University Press, 1995.

———. *Catullus and His World: A Reappraisal*. Cambridge: Cambridge University Press, 1985.

———. *Clio's Cosmetics: Three Studies in Greco-Roman Literature*. Leicester: Leicester University Press, 1979.

———. "Pulcher Clodius." *HSCP* 74 (1970): 207–21.

———. *Catullan Questions*. Leicester: Leicester University Press, 1969.

———. "The Ambitions of Quintus Cicero." *JRS* 56 (1966): 108–15.

Wolf, E. R. "Kinship, Friendship and Patron Client Relations in Complex Societies." In *The Social Anthropology of Complex Societies*, ed. M. Banton. London: Tavistock Publications, 1968.

Woodman, T., and D. West. *Poetry and Politics in the Age of Augustus*. Cambridge: Cambridge University Press, 1974.

Yavetz, Z. *Julius Caesar and His Public Image*. Ithaca, N.Y.: Cornell University Press, 1983.

Zanker, P. *The Power of Images in the Age of Augustus*, trans. A. Shapiro. Ann Arbor, Mich.: University of Michigan Press, 1988.

Zetzel, J.E.G. "Looking Backward: Past and Present in the Late Roman Republic." *Pegasus* 37 (1994): 20–32.

Zimmerman, C. C. *Family and Civilization*. New York: Harper, 1947.

de Zulueta, F. *Institutes of Gaius*. Oxford: Clarendon Press, 1946.

———. "The New Fragments of Gaius." *JRS* 24 (1934): 168–86.

———. "The New Fragments of Gaius. Part II: *Societas ercto non cito*." *JRS* 25 (1935): 19–32.

AUTHOR INDEX

AUTHOR INDEX **221**

Plato
  Laws 922C, 41 n. 90
Plautus
  Men. 232–49, 71
  Men. 246, 71
  Men. 253–65, 71
  Men. 1063–64, 71
  Men. 1113ff., 71
  Stich. 731–34, 79
Pliny the Elder
  NH 5.18, 71
  NH 6.2, 70 n. 33
  NH 7.101, 136
  NH 7.122, 91
  NH 9.1.1, 24
  NH 14.59, 70 n. 33
  NH 15.51, 70 n. 33
  NH 16.237, 172 n. 108
  NH 18.6, 173
  NH 33.142, 50 n. 124
Pliny the Younger
  Ep. 8.18, 57–59
Plutarch
  Aem. 5.4–5, 50
  Aem. 5.7, 50
  Aem. 5.9–10, 169 n. 95
  Aem. 28.7, 50
  Aem. 39.8, 124
  Agis 2.11, 134
  Cat. Ma. 17.5–6, 96 n. 15
  Cat. Ma. 24.1, 50 n. 122
  CG 1.6, 128
  CG 2, 128
  CG 3.2–3, 129
  CG 15.2–3, 131
  Cic. 8.3, 103
  Cic. 33, 109
  Cic. 47.1–2, 149
  Crassus 1.1, 52
  Crassus. 2.1, 53
  Flam. 19.1, 95
  Luc. 1.1–2, 93
  Mor. 478B, 127 n. 145
  Mor. 479 B-C, 63 n. 2
  Mor. 480B-C, 38 n. 83
  Mor. 482A-483C, 121 n. 127
  Mor. 482 D, 12 n. 1
  Mor. 482E-483C, 38 n. 83
  Mor. 484B-C, 30
  Mor. 484D-486F, 121 n. 127
  Mor. 484D-490B passim, 126 n. 144

  Mor. 486B, 59 n. 162
  Pomp. 25.4, 161 n. 68
  Rom. 10.2, 166 n. 86
  T. Flam. 18.2–19.4, 96 n. 15
  TG 2, 127
  TG 8.7, 129
  TG 2–3, 76 n. 52
  Synkrisis Agis/Cleom, 134 n. 173
Polybius
  2.47.3, 125 n. 136
  4.81.14, 125 n. 136
  6.4.3, 173 n. 134
  6.5.7, 161
  23.11.1–8, 125
  31.28.1–5, 124
  31.28.3, 70 n. 32
Pomponius Mela
  Chorog. 1.28–29, 71 n. 34
Porphyrion
  ad Hor. *Carm.* 2.2.6, 40
Propertius
  2.1.23, 169 n. 98
  2.6.19, 169 n. 98
  3.9.50, 169 n. 98
  3.15.19, 43, 76 n. 52
  4.1.1–2, 9–10, 170
  4.1.32, 169 n. 98
  4.1.50–54, 170 n. 100
  4.4.27–28, 169 n. 98
  4.4.79, 169 n. 98
  4.6.43–44, 170
  4.10.5, 169 n. 98
  4.10.14, 169 n. 98

Quint.
  Inst. 7.1.42–45, 30
  Inst. 9.3.41, 97 n. 19
  Inst. 12.1.4, 22
[Quint.]
  Decl. 320, 20 n. 23, 58 n. 155
  Decl. 321, 72–73, 78
  Decl. 328, 72 n. 39

Res Gestae Divi Augusti (Anc.)
  19, 173

Sallust
  Hist. 1.11, 100 n. 32, 134
  Hist. 1.12, 134
  Hist. 1.17, 134
  Hist. 1.55.5, 161 n. 68

SUBJECT INDEX

pietas (*Continued*)
67; and social change, 5, 10–11, 19–
21, 25–26, 28–30, 50–52, 89–90, 92,
100–101, 113–15, 125–35, 137–38,
144–47, 151, 156, 158–60, 161–64,
171–74, 177, 186–88, 192–93; symmetrical, 22–24, 29–30, 38, 58–60, 64,
70–75, 79–80, 82, 83, 107, 120–21,
130, 150, 172. See also *consortium*;
fratricide; morality; reputation
pius, 37, 121
Plotius, L. Plancus (pr. 43), 157
politics, undue influence in, 93, 99–101,
127, 141–45, 151–52, 161–64, 177.
See also canvassing; election; power-
sharing; prosecution, political; speeches
Pollux, 5, 11, 41, 59, 174, 178, 182, 188
Polynices, 182–88
Pompeius, Cn. Magnus (triumvir), 110,
150–56, 161 n. 68
Pompeius, Sex. Strabo (cos. 89), 149,
186–87
Pomponia (wife of Q. Cicero), 104
Pomponius, Q. Atticus, 77, 104–5, 108–
9, 114–16
Pomponius, C. Graecinus (cos. suff. 16
C.E.), 175
Pomponius, P. Secundus, 175–76
Popilius, C. (cos. 172), 131 n. 160
population, 18, 20 n. 23, 41–42, 79
Porcius, M. Cato (cens. 184), 50 n. 122,
96
Portugal, 25–26
possessio: bonorum contra tabulas, 33–
34, 37, 66 n. 14. See also *collatio*
power-sharing: in fatherhood, 30–41, 64–
65, 104–6; in finances, 8, 23–25, 27–
35, 44, 46–48, 92, 103–5, 183–84; in
friendship, 22–23; in the imperial family, 11, 178–81; in partnership, 20–21,
94–95, 125, 151–52, 169, 181, 183;
political, 10–11, 94–95, 98, 109–15,
117–18, 126, 133–35, 141–45, 159–
67, 175–81; among triumvirs, 151–52,
156–57, 161, 182
procreation, 41–42, 69
Proculeius, 40
property, 4, 8, 42, 46; brothers', 4, 8, 46;
division of, 30–32, 36, 43, 48, 51–53,
59, 72, 86–89, 141–42, 169 n. 95,
183; fragmentation of, 41; jointly
owned, 13, 15–16, 18–21, 23, 36, 48–

50, 54; as security for a loan, 31–32,
53–54; and status, 42; *tutela*, 45–48.
See also finances
proscriptions, 156–57
prosecution, political, 94, 97–100, 108,
120–21, 123, 129, 131–33, 175–76.
See also litigation; speeches
provinces, allotment of, 119, 156
Punic war, second, 116–18
pupillus. See *tutela*
Pylades, 68
Pythagoreans, 23

querela de inofficioso testamento, 32
Quinctius, K. 131
Quinctius, L. Flamininus (cos. 192), 96,
117–18, 125
Quinctius, T. Flamininus (cens. 189), 70,
96, 117-18, 125
Quirinus, 163, 168

reciprocity: in death, 83–85, 128, 130,
146–50, 171–72, 178–79, 186–87;
emotional, 59–60, 71–76, 79–84, 103–
6, 115, 139–40, 152–54, 171–73,
180–81; in friendship, 22–23, 67–69,
82–85, 104–6, 113–15, 117, 119,
121–22, 185; in inheritance, 14–16,
25, 30–31, 51–53, 93, 125–26, 183–
84; in partnership, 14–16, 24–25, 53–
55, 57–59, 126, 151–52; in political
repuation, 93, 99, 109–12, 118–20,
125–26, 128–31, 159–60, 168–69,
175–76, 178–81; in property, 23–25,
29–32, 49–51, 53–55, 57–59, 103–4.
See also equality; similarity
religion, family cult, 27, 29 n. 50, 69, 86–
87
Remulus, 85
Remus, 3–5, 85, 158–73, 174, 178, 187–
88; blood of, 164; death of, 137, 161–
62, 164–65, 171–72; in Chian inscription, 159; in civil war 152; and *frater*,
167; as *gemina proles*, 168; ghost of,
172
reputation for *pietas*, 50, 57–60, 76, 93–
96, 98, 107–34 passim, 138, 178–79.
See also family
rex, 163 n. 76
rhetoric, appeals to *pietas*, 5, 10, 175,
182; in inheritance, 26, 36–41, 55–56;
in rhetorical exercises, 30, 36–41, 72–

DATE DUE

MAR 2 5 1998